ROBERT REDFORD

ROBERT REDFORD

Minty Clinch

NEW ENGLISH LIBRARY

British Library Cataloguing in Publication Data

Clinch, Minty, *1942*–
    Robert Redford
    1. Cinema films. Acting. Redford, Robert, Biographies
    I. Title
    791.43'028'0924

    ISBN 0-450-42494-4

Published by New English Library,
a hardcover imprint of Hodder and Stoughton,
a division of Hodder and Stoughton Ltd,
Mill Road, Dunton Green, Sevenoaks, Kent TN13 2YE
Editorial Office: 47 Bedford Square, London WC1B 3DP

Photoset by Rowland Phototypesetting Ltd,
Bury St Edmunds, Suffolk
Printed in Great Britain by St Edmundsbury Press Ltd,
Bury St Edmunds, Suffolk

Contents

List of Illustrations   vi

1   No Hiding-Place   1

2   The Way He Was   10

3   The All-American Boy Next-Door   25

4   The Gates Of Hollywood   39

5   The Sardonic Renegade   54

6   If Only The Directors Knew Their Jobs . . .   72

7   A Highly Political Animal?   82

8   Never Say Never Again   96

9   A Doomed Romance   113

10   Home Sweet Homes   127

11   More Than Just A Pretty Face   140

12   Marking Time   156

13   Getting It Right   174

14   Business As Usual   190

15   Extraordinary People   207

16   A Kingdom In The Snow   217

Filmography   230

Bibliography   241

List of Illustrations

Redford rides the range   vii
Bob, Jamie and Amy pass through Heathrow[1]   5
Bob Redford and his elder daughter, Shauna[2]   9
Redford enjoying a laugh   22
Redford's first film: *War Hunt*   30
The family man[2]   35
Still fighting in *Situation Hopeless – But Not Serious*   40
Portrait for *Inside Daisy Clover*   42
As Bubber Reeves in *The Chase*   44
A coffee break with Jane Fonda   46
Off set, with Natalie Wood and Sydney Pollack   48
Going wild in *Barefoot in the Park*   51
Butch and Sundance hit Bolivia   58
Sundance the Sharpshooter draws again   60
Redford, Ross and Newman, headed for stardom[3]   63
Passionate about skiing: Redford in *Downhill Racer*   69
Tell Them Willie Boy Is Here with Katharine Ross   74
Time out for Big Halsy   77
Little Fauss and Big Halsy features the Redford chest   79
With Melvyn Douglas in *The Candidate*   85
Redford awaits the director's orders in *The Candidate*   88
The mountain man in *Jeremiah Johnson*   90
Jeremiah Johnson struggles against alien elements   94
The ultimate WASP in *The Way We Were*   98
With Barbra Streisand in *The Way We Were*   102
The cocky conman in *The Sting*   106
The Great Waldo Pepper at work   110
With director George Roy Hill   111
Jay Gatsby on the road   115
The domestic Gatsby   120
On the run in *Three Days of The Condor*   125
A gala occasion for Lola and Bob Redford[4]   134
Bob Woodward with his *alter ego*   142
Washington Post newsroom in *All The President's Men*   148

Richard Attenborough directs *A Bridge Too Far*   153
The delectable Jane Fonda in *The Electric Horseman*   164
In the saddle in *Brubaker*   170
Ordinary People: Redford directs Timothy Hutton   177
And Donald Sutherland   182
Baseball in *The Natural*   192
Safari-bound in *Out of Africa*   197
Passion for Denys Finch Hatton and Karen Blixen   202
Arguing the case with Debra Winger in *Legal Eagles*   205
Poised for 'Action' on *The Milagro Beanfield War*   212
With Sonia Braga, the thrill from Brazil[1]   227

Acknowledgements

All pictures by kind permission of Napthine Walsh Collections, except the
following:
1 Alpha
2 Rex Features
3 The Kobal Collection
4 The Keystone Collection

No Hiding-Place

March 19, 1988 is Milagro Day in Santa Fe: the miracle is that Robert Redford is in town. The occasion is the première of *The Milagro Beanfield War*, his second film as a director, but the man they call Ordinary Bob plans to keep a low profile, while others take their bows. By noon, the famous Santa Fe plaza is packed with the paraphernalia of carnival, New Mexican style. The crowds cheer as a parade of custom-cars, fifties chrome and fins and sparkle, noses around the square to the accompaniment of a local *oompah* band.

On the low stage, Freddy Fender, a popular Tex-Mex singer with a role in the film, performs his hits: *Before the Last Teardrop Falls* and *Wasted Days and Wasted Nights*. There is enthusiastic applause until a pale-blue 1967 Chrevolet Impala pulls up and a strawberry blond gets out. From that moment, Mr. Fender is history.

Redford climbs swiftly onto the platform and the crowd gasps. They have no eyes for his companions, Sonia Braga and Julie Carmen, the ladies of *The Milagro Beanfield War*. A thousand cameras refocus as one on the slight smiling Redford. He is in a physical mood, greeting acolytes, both male and female, with effusive hugs, and acquaintances with pump-action handshakes and a genial *'Como estas?'* As on all but the most formal occasions, he wears Levi 501s held up by a leather, silver-buckled belt. This pair is faded and worn through on the crutch.

As the custom-cars give way to the contestants in the Ugliest Pick-Up competition, Redford strips off his tan leather jacket to reveal a sea-green silk shirt and a physique honed by obsessive exercise. From ten feet away he looks no more than thirty-five; move in closer and the ravages of half a century of nervous tension can be seen in his face. The security for the fiestas is said to be tight – Redford aides provided approved drivers for the three limousines hired for his party – but the man himself seems unconcerned as members of the crowd push towards

Riding the range: Redford's favourite self-image.

him waving pencils and pieces of paper. He could, but probably wouldn't, take comfort in the certainty that anyone who harmed him would never get away alive.

'I'd kill to get his autograph,' says a middle-aged blonde bursting out of a cerise woolly. She sounds as if she means it. 'He's wearing jeans just like you and me,' says her friend approvingly. But Redford refuses these and other requests for the magic signature. 'I can't start what I can't finish,' he explains gently to a trio of pre-teen girls who have managed to wriggle through the crowds to within a yard of his chair. To assist in his role as co-judge of the ugliest pick-up, he places sinister rimless glasses over his shades and rubs salve into his lips as protection against the desert glare. Physically he is not a vain man, but then he doesn't need to be.

Later in the day, an older, smarter crowd gathers for the film's première in the down at heel little Lensic Theatre, apparently Santa Fe's only cinema. A 100-dollar ticket secures entry to one of two screenings plus admission to a Redford hour in the New Mexican Folk Museum. The famous hair glints under spotlights as the director, now wearing his favourite evening gear, a black jacket with ethnic designs on the front, and a white shirt held together at the neck by a bootlace tie, with a silver and turquoise clasp, thanks everyone who cares to take credit for the wonderful job they've done on his film.

The proceeds from this event and from the more exclusive dinner that follows – 500-dollar tickets for sixty citizens – go to New Mexican causes such as legal aid and new wells. Redford is eloquent and sounds very sincere as he lists beneficiaries and benefactors, but looks alarmed when he is presented with a lamb, symbol of a local wool trade he is trying to revive. Hastily he hands it to Sonia Braga in the hope that she has a better way with cuddly animals. She has.

The next morning finds Redford in his penthouse suite at the Eldorado Hotel, his bacon and scrambled eggs pushed away untouched. He looks exhausted – he is a chronic insomniac – but his handshake is very firm and his clear blue eyes smile bewitchingly. He is only about half an hour late, nothing by his standards. Michael Hoffman, London-based American film maker and Redford crony, has put me in the picture. 'There is Mountain time, Pacific time, Hawaiian time and Redford time, but once you get to him you feel like you're the only person who ever mattered to him in the entire world. He has extraordinary charm.'

This I now learn to be true. Face to face, Redford stands five feet ten inches tall in cowboy boots with one inch heels. I look down at him a bit which doesn't worry him at all. There is to be a retrospective of his films in Moscow shortly and he will meet Gorbachev, but that doesn't worry him either. 'Will you be nervous?' I enquire. 'No, I'll be interested. I

2

admire him so far but I'll be anxious to see how solid I think he is.' He laughs, secure in his qualifications and his right to make such snap judgments on one of the two most powerful men in the world.

The Milagro Beanfield War has received some unfavourable reviews which leads to a certain amount of barely-suppressed irritation, because Redford has to qualify criticism he won't admit to having read. Most artists like to suggest that reviews are beneath their contempt while taking every barb personally, and he is no exception. 'I'm a bit of a target after *Ordinary People*,' he tells me defensively, 'so I anticipated mixed reviews depending how people feel about me. There's too great a level of expectation, too much attention, a certain amount of cynicism. Reviews don't count that much, but sometimes they get personal and you realise the writers aren't professional.'

That brings us to the heart of the Redford enigma. He would like, or so he sometimes claims, to be a private man doing his own thing in a remote canyon in Utah. However, he has chosen one of the most high-profile occupations and proved conspicuously successful at it for over twenty years. He has always demanded, and received, high fees for his work and he manipulates Hollywood as and when it suits him. He uses his position as a charismatic actor to pursue a number of subsidiary careers, all of them dependent on his being in the limelight for their continued existence. For example, The Sundance Institute, which he founded in 1980 to promote independent American film making, requires massive funding raised largely on the Redford name. Ditto the Institute of Resource Management, a body set up in 1983 to resolve conflicts on environmental issues.

If the name is to be sufficiently prominent, then the actor has to act but the evidence suggests that Redford has always despised acting as an occupation while accepting it as a job. As a tearaway kid in Los Angeles in the fifties, he and his stepbrother, William Coomber, would go to the cinema to jeer at the leading men as they tried to grope the girl. 'Sissy' was their invariable verdict. Redford's first instinct was to be a professional sportsman, his second, a painter, and it was only when he discovered his limitations that he was persuaded to go to drama school. 'I act because it is the thing I probably do best,' he says, adding somewhat plaintively, 'I wish it was painting.'

He probably believes it but there are many who would disagree. There is no doubt that his student days, and his short stage career, were marked by exceptional recognition (there were frequent comparisons with the young Spencer Tracy); nor that he is one of the most watchable screen performers working today. However, few critics would rate him alongside Dustin Hoffman, Jack Nicholson, William Hurt and Robert de Niro, and the Oscar makers have largely ignored his bright golden presence on the screen.

Nevertheless, Redford has always had the self-confidence to believe in his right to choose. A sound commercial evaluation of his own worth has been reflected as much in the roles he has turned down as in those he has accepted. Mike Nichols, who directed him in *Barefoot in the Park* on Broadway in 1963, tried and failed to persuade him to play *The Graduate*. Also on his heap of rejected scripts were *Rosemary's Baby*, *Love Story*, *The Day of the Jackal* and *Who's Afraid of Virginia Woolf?* in which the second male lead made George Segal's name. However, Redford 'hated it', and that was that.

The parts he took were loners bucking the system and not necessarily coming out ahead of it, characters he identified with from his frustrating and rebellious youth. *Butch Cassidy and The Sundance Kid* wasn't his first film but it was the one that set him on an unalterable course when it appeared in the autumn of 1969. Redford was an 'overnight sensation' as the sharp shooting outlaw opposite Paul Newman's gang leader and all too soon he realised that his life would never be the same again. 'I'd walk down the street and see my face staring out at me from news-stand after news-stand and I just wanted to go someplace and hide.'

It was the beginning of a distrust of journalists that persists today. After the *Sundance Kid*, he took on some more macho individualists like *The Candidate*, the *Downhill Racer* and *Jeremiah Johnson* before he allowed Sydney Pollack to persuade him to play his first romantic lead in *The Way We Were*. His scenes with Barbra Streisand earned him a worldwide reputation as a sex symbol, which he found distasteful. So did his faithful wife, the Utah-born Lola, whom he'd been married to for close on fifteen years. 'What were you wearing in bed with Barbra?' she enquired suspiciously. 'Aramis,' he replied.

As his star status grew, so did the myths that surrounded him. In the seventies, Lola and Bob, a golden couple supposedly united in undying love, lived partly in New York, where their children, Shauna, Jamie and Amy, went to school, and partly in Sundance, the valley an hour's drive out of Salt Lake City they had made their own. Redford discovered Timphaven, a one tow-bar ski resort in the shadow of Mount Timpanogos in the Wasatch mountains, when he took up his baseball scholarship to the University of Colorado. At first he would stop off on his way through from Los Angeles to Denver but in 1962 he bought a two-acre plot for 500 dollars and built a house there. 'I'd always wanted to live in the mountains. This little canyon was the most special, beautiful spot I'd seen in the west. It was a wonderful time. No phone, no gates, no locks.' In 1969, he borrowed money to acquire 3,000 acres and the valley was rechristened Sundance. In 1973, he took on a further 3,000 acres and the place was effectively his.

Today Lola lives alone in New York and Sundance is Redford's bolthole, the base camp for the Institutes, and the place he sees as

Passing through Heathrow: Bob, Jamie and Amy head for the 1988
Cannes Film Festival.

home. The low-key, rustic development which includes a ski resort
with four chairlifts, two restaurants, two gift-shops, a cinema, rehearsal
rooms, offices and cabins, is his empire. In his valley, he is venerated
and praised, as an emperor should be, by the twenty families who live
there permanently. An equal reverence rules okay in the Sundance
offices in Los Angeles and Provo.

Whether this is good for his character is open to doubt. Paul
Newman, who shares his passion for practical jokes and knows him
better than most, has called him 'the smiling barracuda'. In the same
vein, his father, who still lives in Los Angeles, has described him as a
cross between a pussycat and Attila the Hun. 'There is always the
promise that you can penetrate his cool,' Newman told David Lewin,
'that sometime you can get through. But you can't. I haven't. I might
be his acquaintance for forty years, but still not get through to him. He
keeps his distance and perhaps that isn't all that much of a bad thing. He
is highly competitive and he wants to be first, to have power and to win.'

Only in the eighties is Redford discovering what is really worth
winning. He has always taken long breaks from acting as and when it
suited him – after *All The President's Men*, for example – but he has
made just three films, *The Natural*, *Out of Africa* and *Legal Eagles*,
since 1980. That was a watershed year: he finally decided what he

5

wanted to do with Sundance and he claimed his Oscar for *Ordinary People*, his first film as a director, two events that have shaped everything he's done since.

'Being an actor is not enough,' he told me. 'Directing gives me an outlet for my artistic talent. There are several directors I like, and respond to, but my own approach is more influenced by my background as a painter. That's what I find satisfying in film making.'

One of Redford's recurring preoccupations is the straitjacket in which he finds himself. First it was the narrow mindedness of education in suburban California, then the tunnel vision of the sports jock fraternity, then the constraints of the Hollywood system. For several of his co-stars, among them Paul Newman, Meryl Streep and Barbra Streisand, acting is a cerebral craft, requiring meticulous preparation and even the occasional rehearsal. Redford hates this approach, preferring to launch himself spontaneously into each scene as it comes up. Conflict is inevitable, the more so because of his chronic lateness. On a typical working-morning, illustrious performers find themselves hanging about while wanting to rehearse, only to have Redford turn up ready to shoot. And he is certainly selfish enough not to care.

When he was younger, Redford tried to escape through speed. He drove and rode and skied like a maniac, terrorising companions just for the hell of it. One of them was Richard Schickel, a New York neighbour whose wife went to second grade with Redford. In 1970, profiling a man he'd known for six years for *Life* magazine under the title 'Why it Isn't Easy to be a Friend of Robert Redford's', he described him as the 'cheerful anti-hero' of many brushes with disaster. He recalls 'the time he drove the Ski-Doo over the cliff, the time the motorcycle flipped out on him, the time the boat he was hauling came unhitched and appeared amazingly in front of his car, the time the accelerator on his Porsche got stuck at floorboard level as he gunned down the mountain road. He tests himself as he tests his friends – to see if the cool is still there. And the quickness. And the sense of fun.'

Another way out was going on the road. In age, Redford is a member of the beat generation. If he'd been a bit more rebellious or a bit better at painting, he might have dropped out of the mainstream rat race, just as Jack Kerouac did. In his youth, he was a drinker and an adventurer, prepared to live cheap and travel light, and there have been times when he has tried to recapture that spontaneity by riding or driving across America. Now he's given up because he knows all too well what will happen. 'I stop at a wayside diner and order something to eat. Suddenly the waitress's hand is shaking on the dish when she puts my coffee down, and I realise the jig is up. The next thing somebody gets on the phone and cars and pick-ups are pulling in and I've got to get out fast.'

Today Redford only appears privately in public places when his exits are masterminded with a conjuror's precision. He might, for example, go to a New York theatre with family and friends. Autograph hunters finger their programmes hungrily as they wait for the final curtain. The lights dim, then brighten as the actors come on stage to take their bow. Lo and behold, the Redford row is empty. In a restaurant, staff are conscripted to form a bodyguard to whisk him past the diners and out into a waiting car.

The need for this kind of vanishing act has made Redford deeply unfriendly to passing strangers and anyone who approaches him unannounced can expect a savage reception. One who got it was an amiable Australian lawyer who found himself riding a double chairlift with the great man in the ski resort of Park City, Utah. In my experience, American chairlift manners require inconsequential conversation for the duration of the journey no matter who you are, but the Australian's attempts to make it were met with an icy silence. At the disembarkation point, Redford skied off without a word.

It is hard to reconcile this boorishness with the sunny personality I met in Sante Fe, but the lawyer was telling a truth which others have confirmed. It proves two not entirely unexpected things. Number one is that whatever his unswervingly loyal aides may say, Redford is at least as capable of bad behaviour as the next man. Number two is that he has sufficient acting talent to lay on the charm when he meets strangers who may be in a position to do him good.

So what? you may reasonably ask, but Redford himself is often irritated by the dichotomy between the way he looks and the way he feels. There is an expectation that blond, smiling, blue-eyed Californians will be fun-loving extroverts who can call on natural goodwill for their fellow men in all kinds of personal relationships. 'I never felt like my colouring,' Redford has said. 'I felt like a dark-headed person. And somewhere along the line, I ran into this fellow out there, this other me. He seemed to be somebody who just got his Eagle Scout Badge. He's not someone I can relate to real well.'

Today his hair is real – only the short sideburns show traces of grey; his teeth are even and sparkling white; his blinding smile is enhanced, if anything, by the lines around the eyes. All this makes it easy to forget that he was already in his late twenties when the free-wheeling, love-thy-neighbour philosophies he theoretically subscribes to came into their own. It is not that he didn't embrace the sixties liberalism but he reserves a lot of his goodwill for causes rather than individuals. And, like many powerful idealists, his sense of humour excludes jokes at his own expense.

He will readily fight the good fight for the rights of American Indians, Inuit fishermen and New Mexican Hispanics. He will fight for his fellow American artists in film, music, dance and theatre, all now

7

included under the Sundance umbrella. And he will fight for politicians of his choice, though certainly not for George Bush or Michael Dukakis. When I asked him what political stance he would take in last year's presidential election, he replied without hesitation, 'One of desperation is the only thing I can think of.'

Within the chosen spheres, he behaves like the perfect gentleman he is not. The affection in which he is held by the people of Truchas, the mountain village where much of *The Milagro Beanfield War* was shot, is far beyond faking and even John Nichols, the socialist novelist who wrote the book and the screenplay, was pleased on this occasion to call a rampant capitalist a friend.

In the winter, Nichols writes in his kitchen in Taos at a table piled high with pans and books. 'Bob would call ahead,' he told me over a beer or so, 'then he'd turn up and have lunch with us here. He'd chew away for three hours and we'd make a plan. I worked closely with him off and on, but it requires a lot of flexibility and instinct because he's so volatile and mercurial. He seems to be moving in so many directions at once that it's hard to get him to concentrate, let alone tie him down. If I were a bit more interested in moving around this planet, I could have had a much closer relationship with him.'

If that sounds as if Redford habitually chases his tail, it is probably correct. Light on his feet, he exudes animal magnetism of the kind that suggests he rarely sits down to think things through. He has never had much time for books, preferring to learn through the experience of living life as he thinks it should be lived. In middle age, he has given up the daredevil approach in favour of a frenetic and gruelling search for a satisfying *raison d'être*.

Does he feel that time is running out? Is he lonely now that Lola is studying in New York, Shauna (born in 1960) is married with children, Jamie (1962) is working in Chicago and Amy (1970) is at Dalton? Whatever the answers, the Redford schedule is punishing even for the faithful. His staff starts work at eight a.m. as Redford, in his solar-heated house high on the hill, sips his first cup of coffee. 'He injects the stuff,' jokes Brent Beck, close friend and Vice-President and General Manager of Sundance for nineteen years.

Once he's sufficiently wired, Redford begins on a three-hour routine that may include skiing, weight-lifting, trail-bike-riding and exercises according to season: the body beautiful is still his pride, and the basis of his fortune, and he doesn't intend to let it go. By noon, he's showered and ready to join the workers; by midnight, he may not be ready to quit, and if he doesn't, nor can they. Even when he does, he likes to talk and argue with cronies far into the night over a beer or a glass of wine – he never touches spirits – in order to postpone the agonies of sleeplessness. Robert Redford is a driven man.

Good friends: Bob Redford and his elder daughter, Shauna.

But why? What makes an educational drop-out who could have enjoyed acting sinecures for the rest of his life into a high achiever who pursues a wide range of aspirations with a will of iron? The answers may lie in Redford's compulsion to come out ahead of any game he plays. As a kid, his priority was victory on the sports field. As a young man, it was making money, the ultimate yardstick of success in American terms. As an adult, it's power and influence. It has been said that his emotional immaturity indicates an inability to grow up, but his need to make his point of view stick in so many spheres is a characteristic of middle age.

'I've learned that life doesn't reflect the Boy Scout code,' he says forthrightly. 'I've learned that life isn't about how you play the game. It's about winning the game. Winning is what we celebrate.' However much he may say he hates being an all-American idol, he isn't about to give it up.

2

The Way He Was

Charles Robert Redford Jr. was born on August 18, 1937, the son of Charles and Martha (*née* Hart), second-generation Irish-Americans with some Scottish connections. Martha had another son from a previous marriage and the family lived near the beach in Santa Monica, some ten miles west of Hollywood. Nowadays houses in the area can run to several million dollars but in the late thirties, as the Great Depression dragged towards its end, it was racially mixed and anything but desirable. Charles Redford was an accountant but the job he had during the afternoons and evenings didn't bring in enough to support his small family, so he supplemented his income by working as a milkman in the mornings.

This routine meant that he and his only son were comparative strangers, an arrangement that did little for their long-term relationship. 'He'd be gone in the morning when I went to school and in the afternoon when I came home, so I felt like I never saw him and I never liked milk as a child. But even in the rough times, I never wanted for anything. He was always working so hard. I drove him crazy when I was growing up. I was terrible in school. I got F in good conduct right from the start.'

Redford has said that he felt closer to his uncle but it would have been only natural for a seven-year-old boy to prefer a soldier who died heroically in the 1944 drive for Berlin to a struggling accountant. After the war, his admiration for his uncle was intensified when the major whose life he'd saved came round to tell the family how he died. 'My uncle was riding in a jeep with the major,' Redford recalls. 'They were crossing an icy bridge outside Luxembourg when a sniper shot at the jeep and blew out a tyre. Even though the jeep was going over the side, my uncle threw himself in front of the major to protect him.'

Although he has tried to explore his roots, Redford has had little success because neither his father nor his grandfather would talk family history. He did establish that the nearest the family had ever come to show business was when his grandfather, Charles E. Redford, played the violin in the orchestra at Keith's Vaudeville Theater in New London, Connecticut but, by the time Redford knew him, the tiny old man – he called him Tiger because he was only five feet two – was deeply uncooperative.

'He had this huge nose and smoked this cigar and he couldn't let it get too short or it would burn his nostrils. I adored him. One of the great cynics of all time. He died when he was over ninety, but for the last twenty-five or thirty years of his life he was waiting to die. He just lapsed into silence. I wanted to know about the family – you know, who we were – but he wouldn't talk. The few times he did talk, he was very witty, very dry. He didn't have much use for actors. He'd seen them all at the theatre. He said he knew Eugene O'Neill when he was a kid. And he saw Edwin Booth play. "They were all hams, Bobby, just hams." I asked him what he thought of Booth. "Just a ham, Bobby, just a ham." When he was told I was going to be an actor, he said, "That's all for him," and gave the thumbs down sign!'

The old man was still alive at the time of Redford's first Broadway hit, *Barefoot in the Park*, and one of the actor's first reactions to his success was to call him in Connecticut. 'We didn't talk about the play. I asked him how he was doing and he said, "haunting houses, Bobby, haunting houses".' It was the last time they spoke.

When Redford did manage to pin his grandfather down on the question of the ancestors who came from Ireland to New England in the nineteenth century, his reply was succinct: 'They were dope addicts and horse thieves, Bobby.' That's all he would say, possibly because he felt guilty about his treatment of his own son, Redford's father, whom he conspicuously failed to provide for. 'My father was angry most of his life,' the actor told Laurence Luckinbill in 1970, 'at his parents, I think. He refused to talk about them. They were too poor to support him and his brother both, so they sent my father from New London, Connecticut to L.A. to live with an aunt. I think he must have felt rejected.'

When the Second World War boosted the job market and Charles Redford got a good position as an accountant at Standard Oil, the family moved across the Santa Monica Mountains to Buffalo Street, Van Nuys, in the Valley to the north of the city. Today that doesn't sound like a step up, but in the forties it was a solid, middle-class neighbourhood which reflected the aspirations of the Redfords very precisely.

Conforming was their number one priority, the linchpin for their existence. As the chilling bigotry of the Cold War replaced the bloodshed and gallantry of the Second World War, it was both respectable, and patriotic, to do a routine job to put groceries on the table and mass-produced clothes on your children's backs. The sacrifices were made willingly, but the children were obliged to acknowledge them. After his own childhood rejection, Charles Redford had no intention of doing his duty without proper recognition. Repayment was required above all in high grades at school, something his son consistently failed to deliver.

Redford has justified his lack of application by saying, probably correctly, that he was sent to a bad school in a dull suburb, a combination that did nothing to stimulate him. 'It was a cultural mud sea, no excitement, no romance, no edge, no nothing. The schools were primitive. We sat in our little rows with our little inkwells and pledged allegiance to the flag and bells rang to let you in and out. I hated it.'

Nor was he cut out for formal education. He has a certain restless intelligence, but he is in no way an intellectual. He has never been able to find what he needs in books and his imagination is visual rather than cerebral. At school, he used the ink in his well to sketch his peers and to forge report cards rather than to fulfil the teacher's assignments. He daydreamed, he played hookey and his grades were lousy. His parents were not amused. 'They were very straight. They were terrific, very loving. But they were part of the ethic of the fifties: you work hard and sacrifice for your kids, so they better toe the line. "I'm working so that you can have such and such . . ." Guilt! And do I hate guilt.'

In his largely misspent childhood, he worked off his guilt and his energy through physical pursuits, both legal and illegal. A natural athlete raised in the Californian sun, he excelled at tennis, baseball, swimming and football, representing Van Nuys High School with distinction and making himself very popular in the process. In the early fifties, every girl loved an athlete and the golden Redford, even with his hair dimmed by the crew cut that was fashionable at the time, was never going to be an exception. 'Sure I had a lot of girlfriends. The high school jock could always get the girl. We'd cruise down the streets in our cars, pull up alongside a girl and say nothing, but, "get in". As a group, we never treated girls like people. I didn't like that too much. When I had a date, I wouldn't take her to drive-ins like the other guys. I'd take her to the beach to explore.'

Although skiing has been a major passion throughout his adult life, Redford hated it the first time he did it at the age of twelve. 'Some of my friends from junior high asked me to come along the following Sunday. "I don't know how to ski," I said. "I've never even seen snow." "C'mon, Redford," they said, "there's nothing to it." They neglected to mention that all the other guys had skied before and not just once. I rented a pair of heavy, wooden skis that looked like driftwood, and boots that were cracking at the seams. Standing up was a major achievement. Walking was something else. I don't remember how I got on the chairlift, but I know it took the lift operator to get me off.'

Inevitably, given Redford's youthful image as a sports star, humiliation followed. 'My friends were poised for take off, then they were gone. I had two choices. Get back on the lift and be crumbled with embarrassment or have a go. I don't know how many times I fell and how many trees and other skiers I missed by the time I hit bottom: I just know it was like being on Telegraph Hill in a runaway truck. I was glad I was down, didn't know how I got there, didn't want to go again.'

Eventually his love of skiing developed out of mountain climbing, a sport he took to after preparing himself by less than legitimate means. Out of school hours, the teenage Redford, accompanied by his slightly older stepbrother, Bill Coomber, would scale landmark buildings – the Fox Village Theater, then the highest structure in Westwood, and the Bank of America were their favourites. 'It was a big, big feeling to be on top of something,' he remembers, but the ritual unscrewing of light bulbs from the illuminated signs and throwing them onto the pavement below just to prove they'd been there was something of an anti-climax.

Throughout their childhood, he and Bill were as close as real brothers. When he grew up, Bill became a respectable computer programmer at the UCLA Medical Center, but he was the inspiration for their youthful dare-devilry as Redford has explained. 'We always wanted to be soldiers of fortune. We really did. And we trained for it. We practised stunts. He saved my life, oh, lots of times. He's a great guy. He's much more of a leader than I am. He beat the hell out of me one time in high school when I tried to sneak to the head of the line in gym. We never write, but he knows I'm there if he needs me, and I know he's there if I need him. He's still a crazy son of a bitch. I don't see as much of him as I'd like to. I really enjoy spending time with him.'

One rebellion led to another and soon Redford and his mates were removing hub-caps from parked cars to sell to a fence at twenty dollars each, and breaking into rich folk's houses 'for the hell of it'. 'It was the swimming-pools that first attracted us but I'd always think, "What have they done to deserve all this?" I was fascinated too. Whenever I had a rich friend, I was always trying to wangle an invitation to his home.' Occasionally things got out of hand and Redford ended up behind bars for the night, an experience that was to influence his choice of roles.

Living in Van Nuys just a few miles from Burbank and Universal, film studios were a part of his life. He had only to walk down a boulevard to see huge backdrops depicting painted skies over the tops of the walls. Behind would be the real sky. 'It impressed upon me vividly that things in movies were unreal. How could I take them seriously?' This cynicism persisted when he went to the cinema. 'We'd sneak into the movies to make fun of the actors, yelling things like, "You tell her, lover boy," at the screen.' Only Spencer Tracy and Errol Flynn, admired for their rugged masculinity, were exempt from his disdain.

13

Scornful or not, Redford was only fifteen when he made his first attempt to cash in on Hollywood. He and Bill asked for work as stuntmen at Warner Brothers. 'Miraculously we got in to see the casting-director. We told him we were stuntmen. He was very, very polite, asked our ages, what experience we had, took our names and addresses and said that at the present, he had nothing for us, but would let us know when he had. Of course, we never heard from him.'

As his graduation approached, Redford became increasingly dissatisfied with himself, his prospects and his generation. The freedoms which had been threatened by war in the forties were in even greater jeopardy in the climate of the McCarthy witch-hunts in the early fifties, more especially because ordinary Americans, such as Charles and Martha Redford, believed that survival depended on repelling the Red Menace. With this in mind, conservatism, with all the rules it entails, was a creed, and one enforced strictly. The next generation knew only that they had to rebel, not how to go about it. That would come in ten years time when people who couldn't remember the war were old enough to lead the revolution. Meanwhile James Dean, 'Rebel Without a Cause', became a symbol of the frustrated fifties.

'It was a decade with no personality,' says Redford. 'As teenagers we had nothing to identify with. And nothing originated from us. We didn't project anything of our own. We just took what was given to us second-hand, changed it a little bit and went on. It was boring and maddening, and it bothered me. I wanted out of it.'

His chance came in 1955, the year he graduated from high school out of inertia. It was also the year his mother died at the age of thirty-seven. He'd always loved her – he describes her as 'young, full of life, a good woman, a joyous person who found the positive in everything' – and the loss hit him hard, but it also left him with 'less of an obligation to stick around'. He tried blue-collar work but was fired from a construction job for losing his tools. Then he applied to the University of Colorado in Boulder on the grounds that he could go climb the Rockies when he wasn't needed on campus. With his record, a baseball scholarship was his for the asking.

His initial intention was to get good grades just to show he could, and he joined a fraternity the better to make his resolutions stick. However, the rules, those ridiculous fifties' rules, were still there to be kicked against and it wasn't long before he was putting in the boot. 'The fraternity wanted everyone to wear a tie. My father always wore a shirt and tie and that was held up to me as the way to be taken seriously. He looked good in clothes, even though his suits were ten years old – his shoes, too – but always cleaned and shined. I couldn't cut that tie business so I shook them up by getting some California guys into the fraternity who were a little looser. But they would frown at us, and have these conferences – and those toasts at the table. Man – it was heavy stuff.'

Before long Redford was again cutting classes and baseball practice. He says he couldn't learn anything at college and he found the limited existence of a 'test-tube athlete' boring and tiresome. 'It didn't take me too long to realise that I was missing something, just going from the locker-room, to the pitch, and back. It was all training and steaks. I never knew what it was like just to enjoy a sport. The competition was exciting enough but I was always out there grovelling to win. You begin to fear not winning. When that happened, I stepped out of the arena and turned my back on the sports world.'

Skiing still didn't find favour. He had tried it a couple more times at college but too many of his fellow students were obsessed with it and Redford, the non-conformist, couldn't take that. 'It was the in thing. That put me off.' Presumably what he did enjoy at the University of Colorado were the fraternity toasts: before long he found the oblivion he thought he was looking for in alcohol. Inevitably he lost his scholarship and it was time to move on. 'It was the start of a three-year period when I was drunk every other day,' he admits. 'I don't remember much of 1956.'

He spent that year on the road, initially criss-crossing America taking jobs when he needed them. One was on the El Segundo oil-field in California. He worked as a jackhammer man daylighting pipes – shovelling oil-slick to clear them – and he 'never felt better in his life'. This was the start of a voyage of self-discovery, that took him to Europe and prevented him from becoming just another Californian surf-head. Until this point, he had been hemmed in by family values and pack values. The high-school Redford was never a loner and, indeed, can rarely have been alone. He basked in the praise thanks to his sports skills and he ran round familiar tracks: home, beach, school, streets, dates. His rebellion was always within the framework of known territory. It never tested him. He never tested himself.

In Europe, it was different. In mid-1956, he arrived in Paris to study painting, the one thing he'd felt passionate about during his youth. At Van Nuys High School, he'd been a member of the Art Club, his only voluntary contribution to his education, and he'd always liked sketching. No one had suggested that he had any kind of outstanding talent but he believed that he had something to say that could best be expressed on canvas. Paris, a Mecca for beatniks and jazzmen in the fifties, had been recommended by fellow students at the University of Colorado; as soon as he'd saved up enough money, Redford was prepared to give it a try.

As it turned out, his days in Paris were geared to acting as much as to art. It may seem absurd for a blond Californian with no French (whatever Redford had learned at school, it certainly wasn't foreign languages) to try to pass for a Parisian, but that is what he did. Wearing a beret stolen on his way through New York, he set himself up, sketchbook to hand, as a pavement artist in Montmartre, 'generally looking like a fool'.

With no props department to outfit him, he got the details wrong but he was certainly the prettiest pavement artist on the block and American tourists crowded round to photograph what they assumed to be a fetching heir to the Impressionist mantle. Redford remembers one man who took thirty-four pictures before he realised he wasn't for real. 'What tipped him off were my Argyll socks. He was furious when he noticed them.' Do these photos now have pride of place in some family album in middle America? Or did the frustrated photographer tear them up? If so, it is a pity; fifteen years later, they would have been worth a fortune.

At the time, Redford would have been glad of a fraction of it to pay for food. In Paris, he became a genuine soldier of fortune, surviving on wits and charm. He cruised the markets on a regular basis to cadge carrots and other vegetables, no easy task in the face of Parisian commercial acumen. Another haunt was Harry's Bar, a favoured watering-hole for American tourists. 'If you hung around long enough, someone would buy you a meal.'

When the academic year started, he found himself involved in student demonstrations. 'I thought of myself as a revolutionary,' he recalls. 'I got clubbed by policemen who didn't know I was just a kid from Van Nuys. It didn't radicalise me; it sobered me up. I realised I didn't know what I was doing there. I was just hungering for action.' Twenty years later, Jane Fonda would attack Redford for deceiving her over a radicalism he didn't feel; this statement shows that he never deceived himself.

As the days began to draw in, he went on the road again, hitch-hiking through England and Germany and down to Greece. By New Year's Eve he was in Rome, a solitary drinker in the American Bar. Suddenly the door opened and in walked Ava Gardner with five escorts. To Redford, she was the most gorgeous creature he'd ever seen and, drunkenly, he resolved to walk over and kiss her as midnight struck. 'All the courage went out of me like steam from a valve,' he remembers. 'I could hardly walk. I got all the way to her table and lost everything, nerve, courage, memory, vocabulary. I just stood there like a dope in front of her.' While the escorts looked anxiously, or perhaps enviously, at the silent intruder, Gardner rose to the occasion. 'Happy New Year, soldier,' she said and kissed him warmly on the lips.

Eventually he regained his sense of purpose by attending art school in Florence. In retrospect, one of the things Redford liked best about painting was being his own man. 'Nobody comes in and tells you that you can't use the colour red because the network doesn't like red. The decisions are totally your own, and there is a satisfaction in that. That, for me, still tends to outweigh the great satisfactions in acting.'

When he was working on his own in Paris, he'd been reasonably satisfied with the results, but as soon as he had to expose his soul to his teachers, things began to go badly wrong. Living in a tiny room with no change of clothes, he was up against it in a way that suburban Californians of his generation rarely were. Given the exchange rate between the lira and the dollar, living in Italy in 1957 was dirt cheap, yet Redford, whose parents had denied him nothing during childhood, had to fast for long periods because he couldn't afford to eat.

And he was lonely. 'It was an atmosphere of no resources, no hopes, no expectations, just an absolutely neutral place to spring from. It was such an open time – your mind was so open, you had no predispositions. I didn't know anything. I didn't know anybody. I just had a lot of energy and wanted to learn. I always learned more from the streets, from meeting people, or from experience, than I did from any books. I spent a lot of the time alone – I mean, really alone. I didn't eat because I didn't have the money, but I enjoyed the fasting. I was wilfully putting myself in a bleak situation.'

It would all have been worth it if he'd found the recognition he needed, but he didn't. His canvases were dark and brooding, reflecting an increasingly disturbed mind, and his favourite professor, a Frenchman, refused to be impressed by them. This presumed rejection made Redford retreat further into himself until he was spending most of his time smoking and drinking in his room. Without food to dilute the effects, he would stare at a patch of ceiling for hours on end while his mind ran wild. Strange creatures formed in his brain and he started to hallucinate to the point of imagined madness. 'So much was happening to me mentally that I couldn't handle it. At first it was exciting, but then it got frightening because I felt I was losing control of it. And it certainly wasn't anything I could share with anybody. I didn't feel any of my friends would understand.'

Matters came to a head in mid-1957 when he showed his teacher a painting he'd been working on all summer. 'I got a very bad put-down,' he recalls. 'He came through Florence with some students he was taking to Palermo, and I grabbed him and sort of unveiled the thing – kind of grandly – and he almost laughed. He said, "You haven't progressed at all – you've been standing still. You're imitating me." And he was right, of course. He was a strong influence and I really respected him, and I guess I was imitating him. I was really crushed. And when he put it to me with that great French intellect and great education, I just . . .'

His words tailed off but what he just did was give up. He sold what canvases he could for 200 dollars to pay his fare back to California, not because he wanted to be there but because the instinct to lick your wounds in the place you know best is deeply engrained. Today he believes both that he could have made a decent living as an artist, and that one day he'll go back because he has unfinished business to attend to, but at the time, he was too 'messed up' to know what to do next. 'I'd hit a terrible low in Italy and I felt as if I'd aged and become an old man. No one I knew could relate to the feeling of isolation I had so it all went back inside me. I started drinking worse than ever because I didn't have anyone to share that experience with. I was just dying a little bit each day. Heading right downhill, and almost enjoying it. The worse I got, the more I kind of liked it. I really didn't have the energy to come out of it. I might have gone under in some way.'

That he didn't was thanks to Lola Von Wagenen, a nineteen-year-old Mormon girl from Provo, Utah. The slim, long-legged, wasp-waisted blonde was in Los Angeles for the summer, sharing an apartment in Redford's building with girlfriends from home. It was inevitable that they should meet but she has never forgotten her first encounter with the magnetic drop-out. He was sitting on a brick wall wearing jeans and a vest with nothing on underneath, no shoes, a big red beard. 'Bob was my biggest rebellion,' says Lola. 'He was number one on the list of forbidden items my parents gave me when I left home. I thought he was the greatest thing I'd ever seen.'

When the demi-God invited the girls up to see his paintings, they accepted with alacrity but Lola was the only one who understood the pain behind canvases covered with eyes gouged out and images dripping blood. As acquaintance grew into friendship, she was clever enough not to force the pace. Mostly she listened night and day to tales of frustration and humiliation. Redford needed to talk about what he'd been through, what had gone wrong, and Lola showed genuine interest. 'She was just out of high school and her attitudes were so fresh and responsive,' he remembers. 'There were nights when we would walk around the Hollywood Hills and start talking like after dinner. Walk down Hollywood Boulevard to Sunset, then up Sunset to the top of the hills, then over to the Hollywood Bowl and back to watch the dawn come up, and we'd still be talking.'

Initially, Lola insists, these intense discussions were in no way romantic. 'We were friends from the beginning, but we didn't date for the first few months. We didn't want to, so our relationship got off to a better start because we were honest with each other. All that stuff that comes with dating just wasn't there. You know, when you date, you want a guy to think you're neat, so your true personality doesn't come out until the third or fourth time because you're trying to be nice. And you don't get to know each other because you're both so busy doing your numbers.'

By the time Bob and Lola had talked their way into love, she had persuaded him to take a grip on his future. Acting still wasn't a part of the equation, but he did consider advertising before deciding to continue his art studies at the Pratt Institute in New York. By the time he got there, he'd come to terms with the fact that he wasn't going to be a career artist and decided to take a course in theatre design instead. A friend suggested that if he were serious, he'd be better employed studying acting on the grounds that he'd learn how theatres worked and make the necessary contacts. Why didn't he audition for the American Academy of Dramatic Arts? Redford had lots of answers based on his childhood prejudices, but this was one of only very few occasions in his life he allowed himself to be overruled. 'The trouble was, I never liked actors. But I didn't really care so I went to audition.'

When it came to rehearsing the two monologues, one comic, one dramatic, required by the admissions committee, he slunk off to Central Park to avoid the embarrassment of being overheard declaiming in his room. On the day, he started with the comic piece and decided it was going badly wrong. One member of the committee made him mad so he vented his anger on him throughout the second piece. As he was supposed to be ticking someone off, it worked out pretty well and all the members, including the 'victim', gave him straight As, the first time that had happened during his patchy academic career. In their notes, they said he had 'a natural ease of expression, good imagination and flair'. On the negative side, they agreed that his Californian accent would have to go, and he would have to learn how to project his voice. Fortunately they compared him to the young Spencer Tracy, one of only two actors Redford could stand the sight of.

Predictably his early days at the Academy did not go smoothly. 'I went into acting predisposed against the life, and it took a long time to get down through all the muck and all the hang-ups. I hated the Academy until one day in movement class, we had to put choreography to a poem. I was damned if I was going to. But the teacher kept calling on me, and I finally got up without even thinking and went right into "The Raven", the only poem I knew by heart, and I used the entire room. I was all over it, flipping and twisting, running out into the hall, grabbing people out of their chairs. I got to the end and the teacher said, "Fine, now do it again". And I did it again! I was so free, I could do anything!'

Even before this breakthrough, he'd been pleasing his teachers. In his own opinion, he was lazy but one of his mentors assessed him as, 'hard working, creative, responds well to direction, shows fine promise, thoughtful interpretation of character'. Another noted 'an excellent stage presence. He's learning an actor's discipline. He should develop into a very fine talent', while a third considered him to be 'leading man material. Excellent sense of use of feelings. Impressive ability and potential, especially considering complete lack of experience.' And they were all correct. It is to the Academy's credit that they were able to be so positive about the very things that Redford, the movie star, has consistently been praised for, in such a raw, and reluctant, recruit.

Redford had always promised himself that he wouldn't get married until he was thirty-five, but he soon discovered that carrying on a romance at a distance of 3,000 miles was deeply unsatisfactory. 'My instincts told me Lola was a person I'd like to go through life with. The first time I proposed was from a pay-phone in New York. I said, "I have thirty-two dollars in quarters. Let's decide whether we're going to get married or not." But she wouldn't make up her mind. The second time was months later in California. I asked her, "Are you going to marry me or not?" She said, "I don't know." And I said, "I'll give you until tomorrow to decide. If not, I'm going back to New York." She said, "Okay."'

The wedding was in September, 1958, just after Redford's twenty-first birthday. Lola's parents were horrified by the kind of match they'd specifically warned her against. What was their beautiful blonde daughter, a decent practising Mormon girl, doing marrying an actor, and a student actor at that? The newly-weds escaped from such questions as fast as possible by spending their honeymoon hitch-hiking east for the start of the academic year. They lived in an apartment without a lift on Columbus Avenue, to the west of Central Park in the eighties, a quiet residential district even today. Lola worked in a bank to support them but as she only earned fifty-five dollars a week, they were chronically short of money, so much so that when their wedding presents arrived from California, they exchanged them for cash. Bob displayed his first liking for carpentry by cobbling together some rudimentary furniture and Lola learned to bake bread.

During the second of his two years at the Academy, Redford found himself cast in classical plays, albeit much against his will. From the start, he preferred contemporary American works like *A Streetcar Named Desire* and *Bus Stop* to *The Seagull* and *Antigone*. Certainly classical drama was one of many educational blanks, but ignorance wasn't the only reason he rejected them. Even at this early stage, he saw acting as a means of exploring his own heritage and culture rather than a showcase for European values. He may have found his parents' beliefs inhibiting, but he certainly adopted their patriotism.

At this point, however, he had no choice but to go along with what his instructors ordered. Francis Lettin, one of his strongest supporters among the teachers, put him down for Chekhov's *The Seagull* because he reckoned that his talent warranted casting him in top-class plays. 'He wasn't happy about it,' he told James Spada in *The Films of Robert*

Redford. 'Ron Liebman, one of his classmates, said, "That's a great part." Redford just looked at him and said, "I never heard of it."'

Another classical role was Creon in *Antigone*. 'I believe Bob has a very big talent,' Lettin wrote at the time. 'He has grace of movement, courage. Seems full of a deep anger, and uses it constructively. Has an appreciation of beauty – an awareness of ugliness – and is not afraid of either. Has quick personal identification. I feel he has an expression of freedom and should not be pinned down – yet.' When Redford returned to the Academy years later, he repaid his debt to Lettin. 'He told the students he had come to realise that being put into that kind of work was one of the greatest compliments he'd ever had,' the teacher recalls.

Despite the widely held belief that Redford just plays himself on screen, Lettin has never wavered in his support for his ex-pupil's acting. Today he rates him among America's finest actors and expects that proper recognition will come belatedly, as it did to Spencer Tracy, another graduate from his school. 'The public tend to think of actors as flamboyant, but Bob is just not a flamboyant person. He's very much like Spencer Tracy in that he deals with the reality of a character, the reality of human behaviour, what people do. There's a certain subtlety in that, of course, which the layman doesn't see, but people did grow to accept Tracy as one of the finest actors there was in this country and Bob is still relatively young in his profession.'

Redford himself says that he didn't learn to act at the Academy but agrees that it was there that he discovered the kind of actor he was going to be: imaginative, intuitive, unrehearsed. 'They taught me that you can only be as good as you dare to be bad. I learned not to be afraid to do things in front of people. They called it "stepping outside of yourself". They had a lot of clever terms for things like that. It was a question of taking whatever was there and bringing it out. It wasn't really learning. The best thing an actor has is his instincts, and I don't think you can learn them. I've worked with actors who've studied with Strasberg and stuff and they're mechanical people. They work technically off of a formula that I don't think works very well. I don't think you can technicalise acting. At the Academy I got the space, and the opportunity, to expand and form myself as an actor but I didn't learn how to act. Acting being institutionalised academically is a turn-off to me. I really wasn't happy in the school.'

Maybe not but he stuck with it and survived. 'Acting is important to him, even though he may hide it with a certain nonchalance,' another of his instructors wrote, and by the time he was through with Pratt, Redford spoke no more of stage design: he was hooked. Even before that, he had his first taste of Broadway thanks to Mike Thoma, another of those supportive teachers at the Academy. He doubled as the stage-manager on a hit called *Tall Story* and when its director, Herman

Shumlin, put in a request for 'high school students' who could dribble a basketball in a crowd scene, Thoma saw to it that Redford was one who was asked to audition.

He put on a sweater in the belief it made him look younger and, despite never having played basketball, dribbled sufficiently well to take his place in the line-up. As one of a group of players protesting against the suspension of the team star because of bad grades, Redford wasn't stretched – his only line was, 'Hey, they're in here!' – but apparently the athletic Californian with the sparkling white teeth and the James Dean quiff stood out. 'He stuck in my mind because he had an excellent stage presence. He was extremely believable,' Shumlin commented.

For the director, he may have been just slightly more than another bit part player but for Redford, *Tall Story* was 'a life-saving deal'. 'Lola was pregnant,' he recalled many years later, 'and – talk about sexism – the bank had a four-month cut-off point for pregnant women, and she had about two more weeks to go. And we had nothing in savings. I'd been up for parts before, unsuccessfully. I had this early image of myself as not being acceptable, in terms of looks and personality. So I was really desperate for this one-line job in a Broadway comedy. Inside the theatre, the director, producer and writer all looked bored and impatient, standing there saying nothing but "Next", "Next". I went in, grabbed a basketball and just went crazy on stage. I was dribbling and hook-shooting off the wall and doing set-ups while I babbled some incoherent high school chant I remembered, just jiving and generally doing a gorilla number on stage. The director finally put up his hands and said, "All right, fine, hire him, as long as he'll get off the stage." It was eighty-two dollars a week, and I couldn't believe my good luck. It was such a big deal. I took Lola to the Copacabana and we had our picture taken. If you looked at that picture now, you'd throw up, such a dope sitting there. But it was very important at the time.'

Mike Thoma was also instrumental in getting Redford an agent. Normally these hawk-eyed predators were barred from Academy plays on the grounds that they might tempt the cream of the students with fat contracts before their studies were finished. However, Thoma allowed his friend, Stark Hesseltine, into a performance in which Redford was a silent member of a group at a party. 'I saw such a presence, such a look of concentration, that I literally couldn't take my eyes off him. He had no lines at all, nothing to say, you see, but I just knew . . .' he recalls. When he saw his quarry again in *Antigone*, he realised what it was he knew. 'It was an incredible performance. I knew I had to have him.'

But when the hotshot agent summoned the newly-graduated Redford

Let no one say Robert Redford doesn't have a sense of fun.

to a meeting at the Music Corporation of America (MCA), he found himself faced with someone who seriously doubted whether he needed Hesseltine's services at all. The man who was used to tyros grovelling in order to get onto his books laughs at the memory. 'He was a very independent boy. He sat in my office and asked me why I thought he needed an agent. He challenged me to convince him.' Convince him he did and so began an association that lasted through Redford's short, but glittering, stage career.

3

The All-American Boy Next-Door

Today *The Highest Tree*, a play about a dying physicist who uses his last months to atone for his nuclear guilt, is remembered only because it launched Robert Redford as a professional actor. As the scientist's nephew, Frederick 'Buzz' Ashe, he wore a neat suit and tie and spoke barely half a dozen lines. However, even they caused him considerable pain. According to Natalie Schafer, who played his mother, he was extremely nervous, a situation that wasn't helped by the playwright, Dore Schary, directing his own work. His experience as a director was as limited as Redford's as an actor, which made both men insecure and, in Redford's case, uncharacteristically unwilling to argue over how he should interpret his role.

While the play was on the road prior to its New York opening, his artistic problems were compounded by tragedy when Scott, his and Lola's first child, died mysteriously in his cot, at the age of two months. Later they discovered that the death was caused by a virus rather than any lack of care on their part but at the time their sorrow was exacerbated by guilt. Redford was allowed a long weekend off to comfort Lola and to come to terms with his grief. The couple spent it driving round Pennsylvania but the young actor showed a true trouper's spirit by returning to the play a few days later.

The Highest Tree opened on November 4th, 1959 at the Longacre Theater to reviews that could politely be described as mixed. This came as no surprise to Redford who instinctively thought the play was 'pretty bad'. Nor was he too impressed with the hype that greeted its opening. 'The cast was getting wires and messages connected with the play, all reading "good luck to a wonderful guy" or "to a swell fellow, nice having you with us in the company", etc. None of them mentioned anything about being a good actor.'

On the opening night, he was told to go to Sardi's because that was what people did. To his astonishment he was embraced by strangers in the street, so much so that he began to think the show must have been all right after all. In the restaurant, everyone was in a congratulatory mood until the papers came. 'The critics said it was a bomb,' Redford remembers. 'I'd ordered a turkey sandwich and by the time it arrived the crowd had disappeared. I figured I'd better eat because I'd probably have to go on rationing after all these glad hands slunk away.'

When *The Highest Tree* closed twenty-one nights later, this prediction looked like coming true. Although the acting had been praised by several critics and Redford himself had been picked out for special mention by Alta Maloney of the *Boston Traveler*, he received no further offers of work. He'd spent the money the cast had collected for him when Scott died and now had no alternative but to return to Los Angeles to chance his arm on television.

Over the next five years, he served his apprenticeship faithfully, swapping coasts on demand and appearing in thirty small-screen dramas and three more Broadway plays. Gradually a pattern developed so that he spent most of the year in Hollywood, then returned to New York in the autumn to prepare a play for the winter season. When he first arrived in California at the start of the new decade, Lola was pregnant again and the family finances were desperate enough for him to try to get work in the lucrative commercials market. 'They were very poor,' Hesseltine recalls. 'We shared countless meals together, I loaned them money, that sort of thing. But there was never any doubt in my mind that Bob would become a star. He's the only actor I never got tired of watching.'

It was not a view shared by those who cast commercials. Jean Thomas, a powerful agent in the field, believed he would make an excellent clean-cut American presence and put her considerable muscle behind his cause. However the response was always the same: good looking but nothing special. 'It got so I was embarrassed to call him,' says Thomas. 'Finally I gave up. I knew he was special, but advertising guys are idiots. They're the last people who can appreciate a new talent.' Nearly thirty years later, Thomas is bombarded by requests for 'a Redford type'. 'You asshole!' she roars. 'When I had him, you didn't want him. If I had a new Redford now you wouldn't appreciate him. And I certainly wouldn't waste anybody that good on commercials.'

Fortunately the gods smiled more willingly in other areas. Redford made an impact during his first Californian stint in a Playhouse 90 production, *In The Presence of Mine Enemies*. It was a Warsaw ghetto story, with Charles Laughton as Rabbi Adam Heller, the head of an orthodox Jewish congregation who tries to pass on his own courage and belief to his people. Redford played a sympathetic Nazi, Sergeant Lott, but only after his West Coast agent, Monique James, had pulled out all the stops to secure him the role.

She also represented George Peppard, already on the road to stardom and the number one choice of Ethel Wynant, the Playhouse 90 casting director. In the belief that he was too old and not really right for the part, James persuaded him to turn it down, then suggested Redford instead. Wynant was adamant she wanted a star but James stood her ground and got Redford in. 'I drove them crazy until they finally agreed to let him read,' she told Spada. 'It was set up and I was more nervous than I'd ever been for a client. I was so sure he was right, but you never know what they're going to think.'

When the audition was over, Redford came to her office to tell her that it had gone fine, but they still wanted a star. He'd decided to leave Hollywood and drive back to New York. His car was packed and ready. Then the phone rang and she picked it up. It was CBS offering him the part, albeit on the lowest union pay-scale. Elated, he researched the role by following a friend's gardener round for days in order to copy his accent. 'The gardener came from Bavaria,' he remembers, 'so that's where I said I came from in the show.'

When it aired on May 18 1960, the reviews in the prestige press were raves. 'As the young Nazi lieutenant with a conscience, Mr. Redford, a newcomer to the ranks of TV stars, made an exceptional contribution in his depiction of a man trying to reconcile a personal code with military brutality,' wrote Jack Gould in the *New York Times*, while the *Hollywood Reporter* suggested that the newcomer had almost stolen the show.

In The Presence of Mine Enemies marked Redford's coming of age as an actor who could hold his head up in any company. As is only natural for someone just starting out, he was often somewhat in awe of his distinguished co-stars until a cataclysmic moment of truth with Charles Laughton. 'What finally cured me was when I slapped him,' he recalls. 'I was supposed to slap him on the show and during rehearsals I just went through the motions. When it came time to go on the air, he wanted to know what I planned to do. I said, "Well, I'll just give you a light slap," and he said, "No, I don't like to be hit. You'll have to work something out. I can't be touched, I hate it. I'm sorry, but it's your problem, you'll have to work it out."'

The show was just about to go out live, as was the custom in the early days of television, when Redford presented his quandary to the director. He panicked but came up with no solution so Redford was still undecided as to what to do as the fateful moment approached. To hit or not to hit? With a final apprehensive look at Laughton, he raised his hand and slapped him full on the face. 'It shocked him and me and the people on the set. It was very effective for him dramatically, I must say. He didn't miss a beat. He played to the moment beautifully. When it was over, I went to apologise and he stopped me. "You did what you had to do," he said, and that was the end of it. He was very nice and I stopped being in awe of people.'

And, Hollywood being Hollywood, he stopped being out of work as television producers rushed to jump on the bandwagon. Popular series such as *Perry Mason*, *Dr. Kildare*, *The Untouchables*, *The Twilight Zone* and *The Virginian* were keen to have a Redford presence and his name crept up the cast lists. He also appeared as the doomed alcoholic in Sidney Lumet's production of *The Iceman Cometh* before being re-called to New York in the autumn of 1960 by Herman Shumlin, the director who'd been so impressed with his basketball work in *Tall Story* during his student days.

The play was *Little Moon of Alban*, a drama written for television by James Costigan and opened out not entirely successfully for the stage. Julie Harris repeated her small-screen role as Brigid Mary Mangan, a fresh-faced nurse in the Irish Revolution whose lover, Dennis Walsh, is killed by a British soldier, Lieutenant Kenneth Boyd. Later the fortunes of war bring Mangan and Boyd together. Redford played Walsh, a naïve and winsome patriot, but his relations with Shumlin and Julie Harris were often strained. On the one hand, Shumlin directed Redford down to the tiniest detail while leaving Harris, already experi-enced in her part, to her own devices; on the other, Harris, an actress from the over-prepared school that Redford so mistrusted, left him no room to breathe.

'I had a difficult time early in my career because I got angry very easily,' Redford admits. 'I didn't like to be told. I've always hated being over-directed. I don't respond to it at all. I remember not thinking much of Shumlin as a director, thinking he was old-fashioned.' How-ever, Redford's irritation was not reciprocated: Shumlin was delighted with the man he saw as his protégé. 'Bob had impeccable acting taste and was totally believable in the part. Once I told him, "I think you can be what Spencer Tracy was in theatre. When Tracy walked on stage, the theatre disappeared, he was so entirely in possession of the stage. I think you have that same quality." Redford just stared at me.'

The conflict between them was mainly over Redford's scenes with Harris. Both Shumlin and Harris thought Redford was too much in awe of her to do himself justice. The actress described him as 'very timid', and says she overdid the affection in their love scenes in order to help him 'get the point'. Redford admits that he was in awe of her – it seems that his breakthrough with Laughton didn't extend to partners in romance – but insists that the wall between them had different founda-tions.

'I'll never forget it – it was the most extraordinary thing. On the first day, she came into the rehearsal without a script. She had the part down cold. I like to stay loose and allow things to happen, allow characterisa-

28

tions to grow and relationships to evolve on stage. But her responses were all set in cement. There wasn't any room for any chemical interaction between us. The lines were all worked out, the moves were all worked out, the emotions were all worked out from the first day. There was nowhere to go. It was intimidating to me because this was only my second speaking-role on Broadway and it was a big deal for me.' It was also the shape of things to come. Lola has confirmed that Bob never prepares for a part but he is an exception to a great many actor's rules and the conflicts he had with Julie Harris would be repeated with most of his future screen partners.

When *Little Moon of Alban* opened on December 1, 1960 at the Longacre Theater, Redford, now the father of baby Shauna, got excellent reviews. 'There is a splendid performance by Robert Redford in the brief role of the slain Irish Republican,' wrote Richard Watts in the *New York Post*, while *Newsday* thought that he 'emerged as a winning and attractive young actor', and regretted his early death. The play itself was less praised and it closed after twenty performances.

In January, 1961, Redford was back in Hollywood to resume his uneasy relationship with the small screen. In the early sixties, television was a knife-edged business and Redford, with his liking for putting himself under pressure, was well suited to its breakneck pace. In later years, he has come to see it as an excellent basis for future operations. 'You had to realise that at best you could only give about fifty per cent of yourself because of the time factor, the limitations, the speed. So my attitude was that I used it as a training-ground to make me learn to work quickly and deliver the maximum in a short amount of time, achieve full characterisations with very little to work with, and very little time in which to do it. I guess I'd say I learned a lot of my craft for film in television. I was fortunate to get in at the very end of live, because there was a stimulation to going live on camera. It was very edgy, and challenging, and good.'

During his second Hollywood phase, he began to find his feet and with them his inalienable right to complain. Typecasting and directing – or misdirecting – were major causes for discontent as he learned how to bend the industry to his will. The direction was always too little or too much. 'Someone who did nothing made me nervous. I thought, "Well, why aren't they directing me? I should be getting direction because I'm new." If I got too much I hated it and if I got too little, I'd get paranoid. It was very contradictory.' Nor did he allow himself to be comforted by Hesseltine's sycophantic comment, 'Nobody knows how to direct you because everything you do is right.'

The typecasting he blamed on the nature of the business, correctly assessing that the agencies gave priority to buttering their own bread as effortlessly as possible. 'They weren't interested in versatile actors

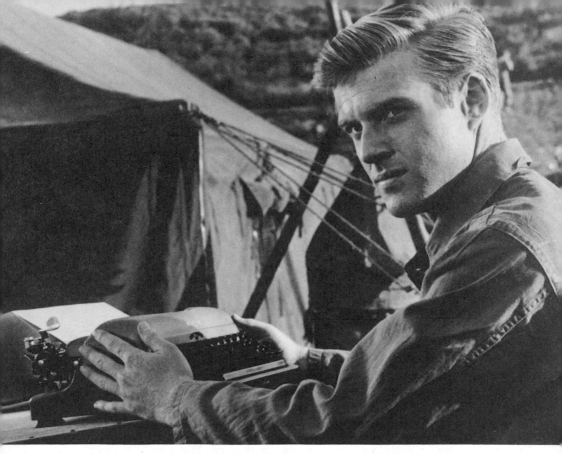

And the camera loved him: Private Ray Loomis launches Redford's
screen career in *War Hunt* (1962).

because they couldn't make any money with versatile actors. Music
Corporation of America, the gigantic agency, put tags on everybody
who came through, like cattle: this is the All-American Boy, this is the
Boy Next-Door, and this is a freak so we'll give him all the freak parts. I
was labelled All-American Boy Next-Door, but since I never cared
much for those kinds of guys, I started to play killers to get away from
that. But then suddenly I was just this neurotic guy and wasn't being
sent any other scripts.'

When *War Hunt*, his first film script, arrived, he assumed he would
play the leading role, Raymond Endore, a character he summed up as
just another killer. Nettled by what he saw as typecasting, he turned up
rather unenthusiastically at the studio, only to discover that John Saxon
was to be the protagonist while he was to be Private Ray Loomis, the
man who observes him at work. This caused a lightening of the spirits
and he unwisely signed a four-movie contract with *War Hunt*'s young
producer and director, the brothers Terry and Denis Sanders. His fee
for *War Hunt* itself was a modest 500 dollars.

War Hunt is a Korean tragedy about an American squad in action just before the cease-fire. The psychopathic Endore, a man apart who believes implicitly in his mission to kill, is unable to accept the decision to end hostilities and it falls to Loomis, among others, to prevent him endangering the peace. It was a low-budget affair, shot for 250,000 dollars over three weeks in the summer of 1961, with the Hollywood Hills standing in for Korea. Redford, of course, was doubly unimpressed. 'I grew up around Hollywood and it was never the end of the rainbow for me. I knew there was no real rainbow. No one looked the way they did on screen. Anyway *War Hunt* didn't seem like a movie. It wasn't at all what I imagined movies would be like. It was like a bunch of film students together. It really was a good feeling, but it wasn't a feeling of Hollywood.'

What he means is that the actors and such hangers on as Francis Ford Coppola and John Houseman took it in turns to cook the lunch and drive the army trucks to the location. Also in the cast was Sydney Pollack, another recruit from Broadway making his first film, and in retrospect the friendship that grew up between him and Redford is *War Hunt*'s most significant legacy. 'We were trained on Broadway,' Pollack explained to James Spada, 'where you sat down and discussed the parts and then rehearsed for four weeks. Now we were on a movie set where someone stands you someplace and you quickly go through a scene, they shoot it and then they reshoot it, again and again. It was such a different way of working, neither one of us knew what was going on. Neither Bob nor I thought much of the movie while we were making it. We couldn't see how all this was going to come out as a good film. But when we saw the finished product, I remember we both thought it was good.'

When it opened in 1961, the critics agreed. 'A happy instance of stunning achievement on the part of two young film makers is evident in *War Hunt*, a tightly-packed, tensely-drawn war drama . . . in which there is not one conspicuously conventional GI type. It reaches a rare emotional level – a kind of poetry – for this type of film,' said Bosley Crowther in the *New York Times*. Rival publications had warm praise for the clean-cut Loomis as well, among them the *New Yorker* – 'Robert Redford is appropriately all thumbs, good looks and milkfed intentions' – and the *Hollywood Reporter* – 'Robert Redford has a translucent quality as the idealistic young soldier, whose few resources are nearly shattered by his exposure to the barbaric. A fine performance.' But Redford himself, remembering himself as a wild child who joked at movie stars, never dared to see his screen début in a public cinema. 'I was afraid of overhearing some killing comment from the audience, the kind of crack I used to make.'

Redford's autumn play for 1961 broke new ground on two fronts: it was his first lead and his first comedy. When he told Stark Hesseltine he wanted to get away from heavy drama, he got the reaction experience had taught him to expect. He was told he needed special training, that comedy was a whole new ball-game, that he didn't have the style to pull it off. Redford disagreed. 'It all sounded like nonsense to me. Acting is acting. I pressed for them to find a comedy I could at least read for.'

They did. It was *Sunday in New York*, produced by David Merrick and directed by Garson Kanin, but unfortunately Merrick too believed that Redford lacked the light comedy touch. 'I won't pay his way from California to read because I don't think he's right,' he said. Redford replied by buying his own ticket. At the reading, Kanin too thought he looked so like Spencer Tracy that he asked him if he was a relation and gave him the part. Perhaps Merrick disagreed with the decision because he never refunded the plane ticket.

Sunday in New York was a limp, sexually-oriented farce about a part-time critic, played by Redford, who gets involved with a dashing young virgin who may or may not agree to sleep with him. Essentially it was pretty silly, but not silly enough for a teacher from a Catholic girls' school who removed 150 pupils from its corrupting influence in the middle of a Washington try-out. On another occasion, a water-heater caught fire on stage, leaving Redford and co-stars Pat Stanley and Conrad Janis ad-libbing furiously as they tried to put out the flames. When they succeeded, the audience burst into spontaneous applause at the virtuoso performance. 'As usual, Redford remained completely unflappable,' was Janis's comment.

The show opened on November 29, 1961 at the Cort Theater, New York and once again it was thumbs down for the play, thumbs up for the star. 'Mr. Redford has personal charm; he will be a matinée idol if he doesn't watch out,' warned Howard Taubman in the *New York Times*, but others emphasised the excellence of his acting. 'Sandy-haired Robert Redford is a marvellously skilled farceur,' said Richard L. Coe in the *Washington Post*, an opinion enlarged upon by Walter Kerr in the *New York Herald Tribune*. 'Appealing Robert Redford, who is really first-rate, no matter what the evening is doing, can dart in and out of an all-too-evident bedroom, begin to lash his tie around his neck without having a shirt to go under it, listen with his own private radar to the confusing undercurrents that keep changing the room temperature, and finally propose solving the whole dilemma by a mass lie with a bland bafflement that is always precisely triggered.'

Sunday in New York was the kind of feather-light fare which theatre audiences loved and it ran for several months after Redford left it to return to California. By now he was involved in long-term litigation with the Sanders brothers as a result of the injudicious contract he'd signed the year before. Whenever they sent him a script, he turned it down with the inevitable result that they put the affair in the hands of their lawyers and prevented him making films for anyone else until it was sorted out. Meanwhile he continued to work for television, winning an Emmy nomination for Best Supporting Actor for his portrayal of George Laurents in *The Voice of Charlie Pont* and turning down 150,000 dollars for a five-year contract for *The Virginian*. 'The money is nice,' he commented, 'but I don't want to be out of the theatre for five years. I want to build slowly and become a dramatic star.'

With money less tight than it had been, he was able to take a firmer line on the direction his career should take. It was in the spring of 1962 that Bob and Lola Redford, now the parents of David James, nick-named 'Jamie', as well as Shauna, realised their long-term dream of buying a plot of their own. Timphaven, just thirty minutes drive from Lola's home town of Provo, was an unspoiled paradise under the shadow of sickle-shaped Mount Timpanogos.

Most of the land was owned by the S. Paul Stewart family who bought it in 1901 from the Federal Government for one dollar an acre as sheep pasture. In 1945, one of the brothers installed a rope-tow so he could ski there. By 1962, it had developed into a 'momma and poppa' operation. It had one chair lift and a Polynesian-style snack-bar called Ki-Te-Kay ('come and get it' in Maori) modelled by Paul Stewart on a Latter Day Saints mission house he'd seen in the South Pacific. Both were shut on Sundays in deference to Mormon sensibilities.

It was here and in neighbouring Alta, 'one of the foremost powder-snow areas in the world', that Redford took to skiing in the early months of 1963. 'I finally got hooked. I listened to the natives talk with glowing reverence about the area and the sport – this was without pressure or salesmanship – and I became interested in skiing in my own terms. Once I had been taught how to ski, instead of pointing the skis downhill and yelling a lot, it became wholly different. I had always loved speed. Here was a scene that, to me, was using speed in the purest form; nature's own gravity – very little between you and the mountain, just two boards and some straps. You weren't bound to the dependence of a mechanic or a piece of machinery or an asphalt strip.

'I began to go after it. It was raw fun. Everybody began to take a hand in seeing that I learned the sport – friends and strangers. The motivation was simple. They wanted to see someone else enjoy the sport. Also, everybody loves a good crash! At first, I went too fast. I was anxious to attain a supersonic boom. But there was no technique to support the desire. I fell a lot. I raged against everybody from lift operators to lift towers. But things eventually came together, though I still swear a lot.'

When he'd paid for his plot with money from the sale of a piece of property he'd inherited in Texas, he didn't have anything left to hire builders, so he decided he and Lola should put up their own house. 'I was dubious when Bob said he wanted to buy land there,' Lola recalls. 'It seemed crazy to sink everything we had into land when we couldn't even afford to build. We finally saved up enough to put up a triple A-frame and did a lot of the work ourselves. One wall is made out of stone; it goes up three storeys and has a twelve-foot fireplace. Bob found out from an expert just how to lay the stones, and we lugged all the rock ourselves. I think we used about eight tons altogether.'

Over the summer of 1963, the house went up on a rectangular platform built high on the mountainside. It had rock walls, rough wooden beams and huge glass windows to let in the view. Bob and Lola worked uninterrupted for four months while the real world conspired to give him the part that would make his name.

The man behind the plan was Mike Nichols. In October 1962, he'd been asked by playwright Neil Simon to direct his latest romantic comedy, *Barefoot in the Park*. The request came on the day after Nichols had seen Redford in *The Voice of Charlie Pont* on television and he made his acceptance contingent on the young actor taking the part of the stuffy Wall Street lawyer, Paul Bratter. 'Redford was remarkable in it,' Nichols remembers. 'He had great authority and was extremely interesting. He was really right, really accurate. It was immediately apparent that he was an unusual actor.' Neil Simon didn't know who Redford was but Elizabeth Ashley, already set to play Bratter's tear-away bride, Corie, had liked him in *Sunday in New York* and soon the deal was done.

But would the man leave the mountain? The first time the question was asked, the answer was yes, but only just and only on economic grounds because Redford already had doubts as to whether Ashley's acting would mesh with his. 'Lola and I were broke. We had everything in the house. I was really into that rock wall. It was like sculpture, that rock work. I stayed with it until 3.30 in the morning before catching a 6.30 plane to New York for rehearsals. I just didn't want to be there, but there I was. They were all talking so fast and it was all about the theatre. It seemed so unreal to me. I was thinking, "I built a house". I couldn't get those rocks out of my head.'

Nor did he try to do so during rehearsals and his reservations about Elizabeth Ashley came to a head as soon as they started their pre-Broadway tour. She had a flashy part and she spent most of the time in her slip so it was easy for her to milk the audiences to her own advantage. Meanwhile Redford tried to become Paul Bratter and to relate only to the other characters on the stage. This worked well enough with the older Mildred Natwick but not with Ashley. 'She had a very affected way of acting but it worked for the audience and who am I

Family man, with Lola, Jamie and Shauna.

to say it was wrong? But sometimes I'd realise I just wasn't getting through to her, so I'd deliberately blow the line – say something like "habufizish" – and she'd say, "Of course," just as if I'd said the right line. I liked her, but the trouble was, I got lonely. It was lonely acting all by myself.'

Figuring that if the play flopped, he'd be back in Utah all the sooner, Redford slept in 'flea traps' instead of the first-class hotel accommodation provided by the company and sent the difference, plus all his salary, back to Lola so she could finish the house. As the tour continued, he wanted to quit but Nichols was determined not to let him go. 'I was lousy in the part, really bad, I just couldn't get with it. Nichols took me to dinner across the street from the theater in New Haven and said, "I know you want out and I know what the problem is. I can't explain it to you, but I know what it is. And I'm not letting you out. You can go on in New York and be lousy – worse than you are here – and I won't fire you. So make up your mind."'

Nichols, who'd once suffered a similar eclipse at the hands of a girl-partner in a comedy team, went on to explain to Redford that he couldn't win the battle with Ashley until he acknowledged its existence. The spur of competition was just what the actor needed, as Nichols recalls. 'That night he very slightly, and almost invisibly, increased the size of what he was doing. He didn't play up to the audience because I don't think his pride would permit it, and someone with his talent doesn't have to do that anyway. And just that slight alteration on the performance made a spectacular difference. That night you couldn't even see Ashley on the stage, it was all Redford. As the weeks progressed, we balanced it out, and we never had that problem again.'

Redford's recollection is rather different, but the end result was the same. 'One night – I don't know, something clicked, and I changed everything around, tore things up, changed the lines, everything – and it was really bad, but that broke the spell, and I guess I was able to believe the thing . . .'

So the show went on, but always fraught with acrimony. The differences between the two leads were presented in the press as a full-scale feud and Ashley replied to quotes that Redford says he never made, by airing her hurt on television. He thought of trying to smooth things over by writing to her, then rejected the idea. 'I didn't think it would do any good, but I feel badly that all this has come about. I liked her – there was something very sympathetic about her, even with all her harshness and bravura.'

Years later Ashley herself took a lot of the blame. 'I was already in analysis, but I just couldn't connect. At twenty-four, I had become a raging schizoid. All the frustration I had inside me I turned on the people around me. Neil Simon was incredibly kind to me, and believe me, I wasn't an easy girl to be kind to. Robert Redford and Mildred Natwick . . . I was bitchy to both of them. I can't ever make it up to them, but I hope they understood.'

Barefoot in the Park opened on October 23, 1963 at the Biltmore Theater to notices that hardly suggested it would be a runaway hit but the public disagreed – the ticket queues were so long that the management supplied coffee and doughnuts as an antidote to the bitter New York winter. Redford himself had no great liking for the play and none at all for Paul Bratter, a man in a tie pressed in a dictionary, with whom he had absolutely nothing in common. Though he came to know both inside out during his eleven months on Broadway, his interest in the proceedings lasted for just ten weeks, his maximum attention span for a stage role. After that he survived narrowly by enlivening the proceedings with practical jokes and fake accidents. 'If you came out with one shoe off one night, at least it made life happen on stage. Otherwise, it got pretty stiff.'

Elizabeth Ashley apart, the actors developed a great rapport during their long months in harness. Mildred Natwick and Redford, in particular, spent time and money taking the mickey out of one another on and off stage. Natwick would mutter witty asides to Redford under the cover of the audience's laughter to try to make him crack up. She failed until his twenty-seventh birthday when she hired a stripper to stand behind a door he had to open in order to say something to his 'wife'. He reciprocated on her birthday by replacing her nightly limousine with a horse-drawn carriage, then staging an ambush by another member of the cast so that the horse reared and plunged off into the night.

Although *Barefoot in the Park* ran for four years, Redford handed Paul Bratter over to Robert Reed on September 5, 1964 without regret. His television career had ended the year before, much to his agents' sorrow. 'What do you want to go back to Broadway for when you're carving out a career in TV?' they'd enquired plaintively. 'You can go on to the movies from TV if you stick with it.'

But Redford had been adamant. Now he was equally firm in his rejection of the theatre. As with live television, it had had its day. 'There was a revolution in the New York theatre at the time of *Barefoot*,' he explained. 'It was really the twilight of the romantic sex comedy. The commercial aspects were drowning the theatre's good qualities. I was looking for something with some literary quality and there wasn't anything for me in that revolution. Nothing has come along in the theatre since then that has interested me enough to attract me. It was the success of *Barefoot in the Park* that helped me break into the movies. It all happened pretty much the way I wanted it.'

Quite so. In five short years, he'd established himself as an actor in comedy and drama in front of audiences and cameras on both coasts. Stark Hesseltine, the man who dared to claim that he was 'responsible for his career', the father-figure who helped the Redfords out when funds were short, had run out of Redford time. 'He left me, of course, when he went to California. I used to drop in on the last fifteen minutes of *Barefoot* once or twice a week on my way home, just to see him, because he amused and stimulated me and made me laugh! Even when I knew where the laughs were, he never failed to surprise me.'

If Redford felt a debt of gratitude, he chose not to pay it. 'Stark was a great theatre agent. He lay down like Leningrad and let himself be used for anything, and everything, that would serve his people. But that kind of devotion and loyalty I don't want. The loyalty, yes. The devotion, no. I don't like people who try to get too close.' The apprenticeship was over. The real Robert Redford was ready to stand up and be counted, but only on his terms.

4

The Gates Of Hollywood

By 1964, cashing in on Robert Redford was a game everyone wanted to play. Everyone, that is, except the man himself. 'When I was young, I didn't know what the hell I wanted to do, except get out of California,' he told *Time* magazine. 'I'd grown up there, but I always had this image in my head of living in New York. Now California is only a place to work. Let's face it, if you want to get anything done in Hollywood, you've got to fight. It's just one big battle out there, and I don't need that.' But from the start, he showed that he was prepared to do whatever it took.

Terry and Denis Sanders, the brothers who made *War Hunt*, were the first, but by no means the last, to fail to put one over on Robert Redford. Like many others, they assumed that the charismatic golden boy was as biddable as he looked. The contract they'd made him sign was a bummer, as Sydney Pollack recalls. 'It gave him a pittance and he became hot pretty quickly after that. And the material they wanted him to do, he didn't want to do.' So he didn't do it. Let them wheel in the lawyers, let them keep him out of the movies for three long, litigious years: he had his bolthole in Utah where he could live cheaply, and he wasn't going to budge.

Once he was off the Sanders hook, he headed for Germany to make *Situation Hopeless – But Not Serious*, a title as inept as the movie it belongs to. The fact that Redford accepted third billing in this weak and sentimental comedy suggests that although he knew what he didn't want to do on the large screen, he wasn't yet sure where his true bent lay. On the plus side, the script was based on *The Hiding Place*, a popular satirical novel by the late multi-talented Irish actor, Robert Shaw, and the cast was headed by the inimitable Alec Guinness. On the minus side, there was the director, Gottfried Reinhardt, who had a leaden way with comedy. The thing that tipped the balance was probably the trip to Germany, which Redford hadn't visited in seven

Still fighting when the war was over: Michael Connors and Robert
Redford as captive flyers in *Situation Hopeless – But Not Serious*
(1965).

years. The chance to show some of his old haunts to Lola and the
children, now walking and talking, was too good to miss.

The film was made in and around Munich and he was able to move his
family into the same apartment he'd stayed in during his previous visit.
He claims – rather improbably – that he picked up the language well
enough to discuss local culture with a number of interesting people.
With the generous daily expenses paid to film actors at his disposal, he
was able to travel around and try out restaurants that had been beyond
his means before. 'Going back there just allowed me to sort of do things
with a little more comfort, not with my back against the wall and the
wolf at the door and all that. It was a nice chance to continue what I'd
started. The actual film experience, though, was the least of the
virtues.'

Situation Hopeless – But Not Serious is nothing if not contrived. It tells
of two airmen, Hank (Redford) and Lucky (Michael Connors), who are
shot down over a small German town in 1944. In order to escape their
pursuers, they hide out in a cellar belonging to a mild-mannered clerk
(Alec Guinness). He enjoys his dominance over them so much that he

40

tells them Germany is winning the war and keeps them imprisoned for six years after it ends. When he is forced to set them free, the prosperity they see around them persuades them that he was telling the truth and they attempt to fight their way to 'freedom' in Switzerland. Eventually it ends happily, with the trio locked in long-term companionship.

Redford is the wealthy intellectual captain to Connors' sexy, blue-collar sergeant, with Guinness in one of those soft-spoken oddball roles he masters so effortlessly. The three men got on well together and the seasoned Englishman had words of wisdom for the transatlantic new-comer in his first film comedy. 'I'm afraid you'll find it particularly difficult and frustrating,' he told an unusually respectful Redford. 'One's performance is fragmented up into so many little twenty and thirty second bits and pieces. It's immensely difficult to sustain a properly balanced comic character throughout the three months or so it takes to make a film. In fact, doing a film comedy can be rather an ordeal.'

Redford agreed and again, not for the last time, he had unkind words for the director. 'He was heavy-handed and had a rather Teutonic sense of comedy timing which may have been right for some things but it wasn't the kind of humour I felt was applicable to that film. And what he was doing with the camera seemed static, conventional.'

When the picture opened the notices were so bad that Paramount shelved it. 'Quite right,' said Redford. 'I guess I felt as we were doing it that it might not be releasable. But I didn't trust my feelings because it was just my second film.' Four years later, when *Butch Cassidy and The Sundance Kid* had made him famous, Paramount had a second shot but that too went wide, sabotaged by Robert Shaw's much publicised request that his name be removed from the advertisements. 'Typical,' Redford commented. 'It's all part of the "cash-in" syndrome round here.'

His low opinions were confirmed in several ways on his next picture, *Inside Daisy Clover*. The lures included 75,000 dollars and the current honey-pot, Natalie Wood as Daisy, the teenage singer whose meteoric career ends in tears. However Redford's agents told him not to touch the part of Wade Lewis, Daisy's film star husband, with a barge pole. The problem, as written by novelist-screenwriter Gavin Lambert, was that he was a homosexual, always a snag at a time when pretty actors who played gays were apt to be more than typecast.

Redford decided to get round this dilemma by reinterpreting the character as a narcissist. After all, Wade Lewis was a movie star and most of the movie stars he saw in the Hollywood he was coming to know and loathe were narcissists. It was logical, it fitted. And Redford was prepared to fight for his artistic rights by telling producer Alan Pakula that if he couldn't do it his way he wouldn't do it at all. 'I'm interested in

Sitting comfortably as screen idol, Wade Lewis,
in *Inside Daisy Clover* (1965)

playing, if anything, someone who bats ten different ways: children,
women, dogs, cats, men, anything that salves his ego. Total narciss-
ism.' And that is what he did.

The shooting of this supposedly heart-tugging saga of the poor little
poor girl who becomes a poor little rich girl went off smoothly as far as
the personalities were concerned. Wood and Redford had a rapport that
turned into a lifelong friendship and their scenes together were effective
enough. Crisis came briefly out on the ocean when rough seas separated
their sailboat from the boats carrying the film crew. 'One of the crew
members broke his leg as a cable snapped and we had to rush him to a
hospital,' director Robert Mulligan told James Spada. 'All the time we
were worrying about Bob and Natalie, and it was obvious that she was
terrified and he was having a great time. He was laughing like hell and
turning the whole thing into a wonderful adventure. When he found out
about the broken leg, of course, he didn't think it was so funny, but I
think his sense of fun kept Natalie from having a heart attack.'

Early on in the filming, Mike Nichols flew in from New York to try to talk Redford into playing Nick in *Who's Afraid of Virginia Woolf?*, opposite Richard Burton and Elizabeth Taylor. Redford knew how determined Nichols could be from his experiences with him in *Barefoot in the Park* so he said, 'No,' from the outset, and this time he meant it. Nichols also spoke of Redford's 'star quality' and the way it jumped right off the screen in *Inside Daisy Clover*, a topic he claimed was the talk of New York. Strange, Redford replied, because at that stage he hadn't even been in front of the cameras.

His opinion of the industry took another nose-dive, but not so steep a one as it did when he learned that the completed *Inside Daisy Clover* had an extra scene explaining that Wade Lewis was a homosexual. 'Since I hadn't played it that way, it knocked hell out of the character, the interpretation,' he explained.

Years later, he spelled out his disillusionment at such behaviour. 'The film makers weakened in regard to the commitment they had made. They wanted something strong that wasn't in the film they'd made, something shocking to juice it up. And I remember being quite upset about it because it was done without my knowledge and it was reinterpreting the role, which isn't fair. It isn't fair to an actor to direct him and agree on a concept and play it all the way through and have the film finished, and then come around from behind without telling him and put something in that reinterprets the role. It was another of those little incidents that made me not very anxious to continue in movies.'

Nor were his doubts alleviated by reviews that were generally hostile though personally excellent. 'There are redeeming moments in the performances of Christopher Plummer, Robert Redford and Katharine Bard. Together they cannot save a picture trying to be too many things at once, but they do make it intermittently enjoyable,' said *Life*'s Richard Schickel. Pauline Kael had even warmer praise. 'Robert Redford, in one of the most cryptic roles ever written, gives the only fresh performance.' Hollywood's Foreign Press Association agreed and gave him their Golden Globe as 'Star of the Future', a prize he didn't bother to collect. Not that it mattered much because they didn't bother to televise his category either.

His own view of the film was that half of it was doing one thing, half another, so confusing both itself and the audience. At the time, he still wasn't sure enough of himself to fight the good fight on this delicate front but his instincts told him it would be a failure. 'I didn't feel qualified. I was just there as an actor and I was hired and that was it. I wasn't really sure what was wrong. I just thought, "This is strange". Now, looking back, I can articulate what it was that I felt. But then I didn't know.'

Credentials don't come much smarter than *The Chase*: produced by

Going it alone as Bubber Reeves in *The Chase* (1966).

Sam Spiegel, directed by Arthur Penn, scripted by Lillian Hellman (returning to Hollywood after years on the blacklist), starring Marlon Brando, Jane Fonda, Robert Duvall, E. G. Marshall, Angie Dickinson, James Fox – and Robert Redford. He plays Bubber Reeves, an escaped convict who returns to a small, mean-minded south western town where his wife (Fonda) is having an affair with Jason Rogers (Fox), the son of the local cattle baron (Marshall). Brando is Sheriff Calder, the good guy who tries to save Bubber from a lynch mob of teenage excitement seekers and wealthy vigilantes.

Hellman's political stance ensures that Bubber emerges as the wronged and sympathetic hero, the catalyst who brings out the worst in his prejudiced fellow citizens. They are prepared to condemn him without fair trial for a crime which he didn't commit. Essentially it is a political parable which presents the extremism in a blinkered community as a microcosm of American attitudes. Although this is a worthy

44

aspiration, and one the liberal Redford might be presumed to support, he was not impressed. 'It did have a lot going for it on paper, but I was never that taken with the script. I thought it suffered from the kitchen-sink syndrome, it tried to do too much. I think it could have done well with a quarter of the relationships. Essentially the hub of that film was centred around four people, the character I played, his wife, the father on the hill and the sheriff. And it was a chase. But the movie wasn't a chase. It just tried to bring in all the liberal concepts of civil rights.'

Its shooting was marked by overt antagonism between Spiegel, still riding high after his associations with David Lean on *The Bridge on the River Kwai* and *Lawrence of Arabia*, and Arthur Penn, still a year away from his great success with criminals on the run, *Bonnie and Clyde*. In Sam Spiegel's case, being run around the Congo's equatorial rain forests by the maverick John Huston during *The African Queen* may have made him cautious over the amount of freedom he gave his directors. Penn's opinion was that it wasn't nearly enough. 'I have never made a film under such unspeakable conditions. I was used merely to move the actors around like horses.'

One actor he rarely got to move around at all was Redford. It was rumoured that he was offered both Sheriff Calder and Jason Rogers, but turned them both down in favour of Bubber Reeves, a part that had a special meaning for him after his teenage stints in prison. 'I understood what made Bubber what he was. I felt close to him.' Bubber's part, though crucial, was pretty small: Redford worked for seven days in the first two months, and just four weeks in all in a twenty-two-week schedule. Much of his spare time was spent hunting and fishing, so much so that he had to reintroduce himself to the other actors each time he turned up on set. Not that he cared: he was being paid handsomely for doing nothing much. When he did work, he was mostly alone on the run through the outskirts of the town. These scenes were shot by the second unit in the rice fields of Chico, California far removed from Penn's struggles with principal photography in Hollywood.

This may be why Redford was so unsympathetic to his director's predicament. 'He didn't have to work under unspeakable conditions. He could have changed them – or left. I don't think retrospective criticism was very admirable in this case. If it was me, I would have said, "Either let me direct this film my way, or I'm leaving."' His relations with Brando were altogether better. On the rare occasions they shared scenes, they spent the warm-up time talking about American Indians, a subject of enduring interest to both of them, and trying to outdraw each other with flashlights.

Penn didn't get final cut on the film, but the reviews were so negative that it might not have helped him if he had. Rex Reed rated it 'the worst

A coffee break with Jane Fonda before the call to work on *The Chase*.

thing to happen to movies since Lassie played a war veteran with amnesia', and *Life*'s Richard Schickel concluded that *The Chase* was no modest failure. 'Thanks to the expenditure of a great deal of time, money and talent it has been transferred into a disaster of awesome proportions . . . A valiant minority of the cast – Miss Fonda, Robert Redford, James Fox, Angie Dickinson – try to keep their heads while all about them are losing theirs. But their isolated moments of lucidity are no more effective against the fever than cold compresses; they relieve, but they cannot cure.'

Variety topped this review, from Redford's point of view, by saying he gave the film's best performance and his own best performance to date. 'He has an instinct for economy of dialogue delivery and, alone on the screen during much of the earlier action and by-passed for lengthy sequences when the story deals with other plot elements, he so imprints his character on the viewer's mind that, upon re-entering the scene, his last-seen action is still clear in the memory. Even when he finally

46

becomes involved with other cast members, his own performance dominates.'

As with *The Chase*, *This Property is Condemned* had almost too much going for it in theory and not nearly enough in practice. It was 'suggested' by a one-act play by Tennessee Williams, but twelve scriptwriters, among them Francis Ford Coppola, were unable to translate his suggestions into a viable script. The original intention was for Richard Burton to direct Elizabeth Taylor as Alva Starr, an exotic piece of white trash who uses her mother's boarding house in Dobson, Mississippi as a base for serious flirtation during the Depression. When the Burtons pulled out, the screenplay did the Hollywood rounds: John Huston and John Frankenheimer were approached to direct, but neither had accepted by the time Natalie Wood was signed for Alva Starr.

Wood had enjoyed working with Redford on *Inside Daisy Clover* so she asked for him to be cast as Owen Legate, the stranger who comes to Dobson to sack some of the railway-workers and falls in love with Alva Starr. It was a first leading role for Redford and he set about finding himself a director he wouldn't need to complain about. Sydney Pollack, his fellow thespian on *War Hunt*, had started building a reputation with *The Slender Thread*. When he came under consideration for *This Property is Condemned*, Redford enlisted his support. 'I sure hope you do it, because we're really in trouble, and it's a crummy script,' he told him. Pollack believes that Redford may have put in a good word for him with Ray Stark. In any case, he got the job.

As locations in the deep south were appropriate for a steamy Tennessee Williams melodrama, Bay St. Louis, Mississippi was chosen as the centre of operations. Resenting the playwright's view of their lives as over-sexed, bigoted and obsessive, the citizens banded together against the production, circulating a petition and enlisting the help of the mayor to expel the film makers from their town. This he failed to do and shooting continued in an atmosphere of mounting animosity.

On set, things weren't much better, especially between Redford and Charles Bronson. He played a sacked railroad worker who marries Alva Starr after he and his colleagues have driven Owen Legate out of Dobson. He felt his part should be upgraded to match Redford's and to create a genuine triangular conflict between the three principals. Pollack could see the sense in this but with Ray Stark constantly on his back and the script in shreds, he 'couldn't deal with it' so he just left Bronson to glare at Redford. 'Their scenes together were mostly silent. There were a lot of evil looks that passed back and forth but that's all really.'

This Property is Condemned set the tone for the Redford–Pollack working relationship that would develop during more distinguished films over the next decade. In *War Hunt*, the men had been equals. Now they were director and directed, a situation Pollack approached rather warily. 'I was going to be telling him what to do and I thought, "this is gonna be rather weird".' In the event, it worked out okay, but only after each had had his say. 'We argued like crazy on the set,' he told James Spada. 'He'd say, "Now wait a minute, Pollack, you're way off on this", and I'd say, "Now don't tell me how to do things!" The first time he got personal with me on the set I really was too insecure to handle it very well because I was nervous. It was a big cast on location and Natalie was a very big star at the time. When he'd say, "No, no, I think I should do it this way", I'd stop and look around to see if anybody had heard him say that. I thought, "God, there goes my image as a director!"'

Gradually they got the balance right. Pollack was struggling with the script, chopping it up and stapling it together again in an attempt to make it work, and Redford supported him both in this and with Ray Stark. 'He kept trying to change things, seldom for the better,' the actor recollects. 'As for the script, we'd end up improvising, just making things up as we went along, hoping they'd add up to something.'

Redford, with co-star Natalie Wood, awaits direction from his favourite mentor, Sydney Pollack, on *This Property is Condemned* (1966).

As far as Tennessee Williams was concerned, they never did and he asked, unsuccessfully, for his name to be taken off the picture. However some of the critics were not uncharitable. Bosley Crowther, writing for the *New York Times*, said the film was 'As soggy, sentimental a story of a po' little white-trash girl as ever oozed from the pen of Tennessee Williams', adding that Wood and Redford were 'wholly implausible' in this cheap environment. But Joseph Gelmis in *Newsday* considered that Redford was 'too good for the movie' and *Variety* felt that 'his outstanding performance' would result in 'a significant leap to stardom'.

No doubt the Hollywood oracle was right because demands for Redford's services arrived by every post, but again he broke the rules without hesitation and without regret. He'd made four films back to back, all of them commercial and, in his eyes, artistic failures. He was already committed to the film version of *Barefoot in the Park* several months ahead. Many actors believe that if they turn down an offer they're in a position to accept, they'll never work again, but Redford always wanted the studios slightly less than they wanted him. When they talked about 'career momentum', he knew he could afford to laugh in their faces.

'They said, "You gotta work, kid, you gotta move out here, you gotta do a lot of pictures". Well, I didn't like that. I'm not a rebel, but I'm not gonna be dumped on the assembly line. After the first three films I did in Hollywood, I wasn't too enthused about continuing on as an actor. Things seemed unreal. I wanted to take a break and take it easy for a while.'

Escaping eastwards across the Atlantic was becoming a habit. This time the four Redfords spent several months in a village near Malaga. Shauna and Jamie played on the beach while Redford sketched and painted. He and Lola travelled around southern Spain, just as they had in Germany, picking up the language and absorbing the European way of life. When their village was invaded by tourists in the high season, they moved on to Crete. In the spring of 1966, those who were prepared to look could still find relatively unspoilt stretches of Mediterranean coastline and Redford was prepared to look. 'I was trying to find some parts of Europe that were still European, not Americanised. It's not easy to do any more.' In fact, this would be the last time he tried before his obsession with the American west replaced his youthful fascination with European culture.

As he'd given his word on *Barefoot in the Park*, he had no choice but to travel back to New York in the autumn to make it, but he did so unenthusiastically. He hadn't been asked to make the film of *Sunday in New York* (Cliff Robertson took the role Redford had played on stage) and he hadn't expected to be approached for *Barefoot*. 'I thought it was the rule for the Broadway actors to be ignored for the film.' Anyway, he didn't like repeating himself, he didn't much like the shallow frivolity of the play, and he certainly didn't like the uptight Paul Bratter. He did like Mildred Natwick, who'd also been in the original production, and he liked what little he knew of Jane Fonda, signed for Corie Bratter, from *The Chase*. He also liked the near certainty that the film would be his first commercial success. It was a close-run decision, but in the end he said yes.

As Neil Simon had adapted his play for the screen and the characters were only too well established after the long Broadway run, the shooting was pretty straightforward. At this stage in their careers, Redford and Fonda had a lot in common. Born within six months of each other, they both warmed to the free-wheeling spirit of the mid-sixties. Both were searching for ways of preventing their remarkable good looks from dictating their careers but neither had defined their beliefs nor found ways of expressing them in their work. Once they did, they would be on different tacks and the highly-politicised Fonda would have harsh words to say about the self-serving Redford.

Meanwhile they got on well together and Redford, with his greater knowledge of *Barefoot in the Park*, was able to help Fonda with her interpretation. He showed his contempt for Paul Bratter by adorning the hated blue suit and button-down shirt with a black stetson and cowboy boots whenever the cameras weren't actually turning. In between times, he amused himself by terrorising the director, Gene Saks, who is on record as saying he'll never drive with Redford again after a wild night-ride. 'I was terrified, but Bob was having a great time. I was sure the jig was up for both of us.'

The theatre critics hadn't liked the stage production of *Barefoot in the Park* nearly as much as the customers had, but the cinema critics were better versed in recognising public appeal and they didn't hesitate to deliver the goods. 'The amount of fun writer Neil Simon can wring out of these rather tired situations is astounding,' wrote Archer Winsten in the *New York Post*. 'The cast is a big help. Fonda and Redford work together wonderfully.' *Variety* again praised Redford as 'an outstanding actor' and predicted a long and successful career in the Cary Grant mould.

Only the *New York Times*'s Bosley Crowther had reservations. 'If you are for a certain measure of intelligence and plausibility in what is presumed to be a take-out of what might happen to reckless newly-weds today, if you expect a wisp of logic in the make-up of comic characters which is, after all, what makes them funny, instead of sheer gagging it up, then beware.'

As few heeded his words of caution, *Barefoot in the Park* fulfilled its destiny as Redford's first screen hit. Unwisely he had signed a three-picture deal with its backers, Paramount, in the wake of its success but

A moment of liberation for the normally inhibited Paul Bratter in
Barefoot in the Park (1967).

he promptly put their backs up by taking refuge in Timphaven and
rejecting every script they sent him, among them the part of the satanic
husband in *Rosemary's Baby*. When that hit the dust, his agents,
irritated at their inability to cash in on their gold mine, offered him a
Viking movie. 'They said, "Listen, champ, this is it." I said I didn't
want to run all over Yugoslavia in horns and a bear fur, so they said,
"Okay, that's the end." They couldn't work with me any more.'

Mike Nichols, defeated over *Who's Afraid of Virginia Woolf?*, tried
again with *The Graduate*. This time Redford went so far as to read the
script, which he liked, and to take a screen test for the Californian
prototype yuppie lead. 'Bob thought he wouldn't look the part,' said
Nichols. When the result came through, they both agreed he didn't.
Much of *The Graduate* is taken up with its hero's difficulties with
women; anyone could see that they would fall at Redford's feet.
According to Pollack, Redford regretted not being suitable. 'He complained he might be stuck all his life playing good-looking golden boys.'

In the end, Redford agreed to do a western called *Blue* for Paramount, but only when they'd agreed to rewrite parts of the script along
the lines he suggested and shoot it up in Utah near his home. On day

one, when he showed up for work to play the dreamy-eyed adopted son of a Mexican bandit, he discovered the rewrites hadn't been done, so he quit. 'You notice he wasn't walking out on *Gone With The Wind*,' said Al Ruddy, the producer who would employ him on *Little Fauss and Big Halsy* in 1970. 'The script was a piece of crap, that's all.' This opinion was reiterated by the critic, Rex Reed, when the film was finally unveiled, with Terence Stamp in the lead. 'I don't know which is worse – bad cowboy movies or bad, arty, cowboy movies. *Blue* is both.'

Predictably Paramount were not amused by the defection money had changed hands and their immediate reaction was to hit Redford with a 253,000 dollar law suit. 'I was kind of excited about that. How could they be suing me, a little kid from Van Nuys? I kind of liked the idea!' While he wondered how the people who knew him back home would react, he divided his time between his New York apartment and his mountain retreat, occasionally leaving Lola to make forays into the wide world to combat what he has called 'the Irish furies'.

It was a time for stubborn pride, for going obstinately broke, but he never wavered. 'People said I wasn't tending my career when I walked out on *Blue* and turned down all that other stuff. I thought I was.' Richard Schickel, Redford's New York neighbour at the time, remembers how unmelodramatically he reacted to the crisis. 'Until then, he'd been choosing parts, not films,' Schickel wrote in *Life* magazine. 'Now he was insisting on having something to say about the property surrounding him on screen. "They throw that word, star, at you loosely, and they take it away loosely if your pictures flop. You take responsibility for their crappy movie, that's all it means. So what I said was, since you say I'm responsible if my name's above the title, then give me responsibility. That's all."'

Schickel remembers that Lola, who had thought to spend some of the proceeds from *Barefoot in the Park* on completely renovating the New York apartment while her husband was off on location somewhere, bore the brunt of his resistance. As the furniture moved out and the workmen moved in to tear down walls and coat every surface with fine dust, Redford sat on one of the few remaining chairs, snapping his rejections down the phone.

When he got fed up with being in the way, he went on the road for the last time as an ordinary man. 'I walked the Big Sur once. I'm really proud of that. I was back in California and things were kind of bad – we were broke – and I had wanted to do it for a long time, so I just took off, walking. It took me two weeks. I'd walk awhile and when I got tired, I'd hitch a ride up the road a bit. And you know, nobody ever asked my name or where I was going or where I came from. That really impressed me – everybody just accepting me for what was at that moment. It was the greatest feeling I've ever had. The most peaceful thing.' For Lola, it was less peaceful as the phone went on ringing. 'I'm sorry,' she'd reply. 'Bob went out for a walk to Big Sur. He'll be back in a week.'

It was as well he went when he did because his anonymity was coming to an end: after *Butch Cassidy and The Sundance Kid*, Robert Redford would never be faceless again.

The Sardonic Renegade

'Redford's got guts. Nobody wanted him in *Butch Cassidy* except me, in the beginning. We sat around Allen's hamburger joint one night and got bombed, and he gave me his word that he would wait while I tried to get him in the picture.' The speaker is George Roy Hill, unaware at that time that waiting – and keeping others waiting – was Redford's stock-in-trade. Born a midwesterner and educated at Yale, the sophisticated, lanky Hill had spent much of his early career as an actor and a theatre director in Dublin. After serving in Korea, he became a television writer-director, graduating to Broadway in 1957 and to Hollywood in 1962 at the age of forty. His success with the unusual New York comedy, *The World of Henry Orient*, in 1964 put him in line to direct *Butch Cassidy and The Sundance Kid* from the screenplay that William Goldman had sold to Twentieth Century-Fox for a record 400,000 dollars.

Goldman had spent six years meticulously researching the lives of the two bandits, Robert Leroy Parker and Harry Longabaugh, better known as Butch and Sundance. They were respectively leader and side kick of the Hole-in-the-Wall gang which terrorised the south-west at the turn of the century. Goldman's story was true in essence, but not in fine detail: Cassidy's relations have confirmed that the bank robber returned to the United States in 1912 under an assumed name after his exploits in South America rather than dying in a Bolivian gun battle. However, Goldman caught the spirit of the man: genial, daring and high-spirited. Much less is known about Longabaugh: The Sundance Kid probably owes a lot more to Goldman's imagination than to his investigations.

Although the western had given America the opportunity to bask in the glory of colourful heroic roots since the cinema began, the late sixties were a time for reassessment of accepted screen norms. Abroad, faltering imperialist ambitions in Vietnam cast doubt on the ritual slaughter of Red Indians. At home, hippie culture's rejection of the 'pigs' (police) in a whole series of campus revolts reduced the status of right-wing law-enforcers in the John Wayne mould. What was wanted was a new type of western hero, a tough, rebellious outlaw whose appeal lay in his refusal to accept conventional conservative attitudes. And this is exactly what Goldman provided in his slick, jokey script.

Once Redford had completed his own reassessment, it was inevitable that he would wait for Sundance. From the start he got on exceptionally well with Hill: 'Both of us have that black Irish thing. We understand one another.' And there were other pluses: the mustachioed sharp-shooter was as far removed as possible from *Barefoot*'s pompous Bratter and he fitted in with the actor's view of himself, on screen and off, as a sardonic renegade with emotional roots in the American west, an image that would dominate his private and public lives from now on.

'I had a strange identification with Sundance that I can't quite put my finger on. There was a time, when I was very young, that I didn't think it would be so bad to be an outlaw. It sounded pretty good to me. The frontier wouldn't have been a bad place to be in the 1880s, it seemed to me. You didn't turn your back on too many people, but the atmosphere was free and you carved out what you could make of it. One reason I liked the script was that it pointed out the fact that a lot of those people were just kids, doing what they did – robbing banks, holding up trains – as much for the sheer fun of it as anything else.'

There were, however, some fairly massive flies in the ointment. Goldman had written his screenplay for Jack Lemmon and Paul Newman, as Butch and Sundance respectively. Richard Zanuck, head of Twentieth Century-Fox, rejected Lemmon on the grounds he lacked box-office clout. 'Bring me Steve McQueen as Butch,' he demanded, and McQueen agreed to consider it. George Roy Hill didn't want him for either role, and especially not for Butch, so he set about persuading Paul Newman that he was the one who should play the bandit chief. 'He wasn't confident he could do it,' he recalls. 'He saw it as a comic part and said to me, "I just proved I couldn't play comedy doing *The Secret War of Harry Frigg*." But I told him it wasn't a comic part. Butch was a totally straight guy in sometimes comic situations.'

Newman began to see things Hill's way, but only if he got top billing, a proviso that put a resentful McQueen out of the hunt. Hill had met Redford back in 1962 when the actor read for the director's first film, *Period of Adjustment*. Later he'd seen him on stage in *Sunday In New York*. On both occasions he'd liked what he saw. 'I thought he was a very rugged guy, quite physical, with a great deal of underlying warmth. I knew he could handle comic situations, and that's exactly what I needed.'

On the famous night when the two men got bombed together, Hill started by asking Redford if he could play Butch. 'Sure I can,' the actor replied, 'but I'd be much better as Sundance.' By the time the bottle had circulated a few more times, Hill had come round to Redford's point of view. 'I was convinced that it had to be Newman as Butch and Redford as Sundance.'

Once he'd made up his mind, Hill proved to be admirably tenacious in sticking to his guns. Newman still wasn't sure about Butch, and even less so about Redford whom he saw as a boring Wall Street lawyer called Paul Bratter. He'd never met him and, at this stage, he wasn't prepared to back him, but he was persuaded to remain neutral while Hill tackled Zanuck and the film's producers, Paul Monash and John Foreman, at the conference table. Zanuck too thought Redford was an indoor type and, worse still, a failure after several flops, plus one totally unsuitable success – *Barefoot in the Park*. He was prepared to consider almost anyone except Redford, with Marlon Brando at the top of his list.

'It was a joke,' Hill remembers. 'First McQueen, then Brando and finally Warren Beatty – disaster all of them. We'd sit around in Zanuck's office in these goddamned conferences and it would go around the circle and everybody would say, "Brando", or whoever it was that week, and Zanuck would say, "How about you, Hill?" and I'd say, "Redford". Finally I thought Zanuck would explode. He said, "Redford has been to the post too many times, and never made it, what the hell do you want him for? I'll tell you what, I'll pay you off and shelve the picture rather than use him."'

Hill's prospects of getting his own way took a nose-dive when Monash announced that Brando had agreed to play Sundance. 'I was scared to death of him in the first place, and I didn't think he was right for the part,' he told James Spada. 'But they were proceeding, and Paul said Brando was eager to do it so I stopped my kicking and screaming and relented.' To his relief, Brando, who was holed up in Oakland with the Black Panthers at the time, refused to return phone calls or meet the studio's emissaries. A Twentieth Century-Fox vice-president, sent to tell the actor that the role was important for his career, was summarily dismissed. 'America's important too,' said Brando, 'and I'm working for America.' But it was only when the studio received a call from Elia Kazan asking Brando's whereabouts that Zanuck gave up. 'He wanted to talk to him about *The Arrangement*,' Hill explained. 'Well, we figured if Kazan couldn't find him, what chance did we have? I thought it was pretty odd for a guy who was anxious to play a role.'

With Brando out, Zanuck switched to Beatty, currently riding high after *Bonnie and Clyde*, but Hill fought on. 'I made one entire trip to the coast just to needle them about Redford. Finally, I used up all my muscle and I asked Paul Newman to step in, and by that time he was convinced about Redford too so he used his muscle.' So did William Goldman who considers that 'Redford is infinitely creative as an actor, the closest thing we have now to a romantic-comedy type like Cary Grant in his prime. He can be graceful and virile at the same time, and he's got that marvellous comic sense.' When Hill enlisted his support, Goldman sent a six-page telegram to Zanuck asking why the hell management couldn't go along with the wishes of the whole creative team. Finally Zanuck relented: Redford was in.

'All this while, he sat tight, and waited, and turned down other work, knowing that nobody wanted him in the picture but me,' said Hill. 'That takes guts, because it must be a hell of a blow to an actor's ego. But Redford is a stubborn son of a bitch. He's a great competitor. He hates to lose.' Redford shrugged. 'I put it out of my mind. I just stayed out of it until somebody told me the deal was made.'

With casting completed, *Butch Cassidy and The Sundance Kid* was ready to roll. In the public mind, Newman and Redford have a lot in common: they like fast cars and liberal causes and, for many years, they were said to have marriages that could withstand any pressure that Hollywood could throw at them. Because of all this, and the way they relate to one another on screen, it is easy to think of them as the best of friends rather than the best of colleagues, but it isn't true. Newman, twelve years older than Redford, is extremely relaxed. He'll sit down in a room full of journalists, cross one leg over the other and answer questions slowly and thoughtfully. He leavens the intellectual's approach with easy jokes and he shows no inner tension. Redford is another matter. Face to face, he is a coiled spring, fidgeting with his watch, his ear lobe, his hair, and he treats himself and his issues with deadly seriousness. There is no doubt that he has a sense of humour, but it stops far short of laughing at himself – or letting others do so.

Ask Paul Newman about Redford and he smiles, as if the joke were on him in some way, before he speaks. 'I guess we get along because we each have a streak of larceny. It takes one criminal to recognise another. He has a tremendous ego; so do I. He has that marvellous kind of relish for life. But he's reserved, in a way. He's the one who determines how much of himself he's ready to declare.'

And there too Redford stops some way short of total commitment. 'I like people I work with, I feel close to them, but five years might go by before I'd see them again. I like Paul Newman, for instance, and it was a great experience doing *Butch Cassidy* with him. For that very reason, I wouldn't want to seek him out too much. I wouldn't want to run the risk of jeopardising a relationship. You have to keep your professional and your personal lives separate.'

Both the differences and the shared sense of fun emerged when they met for the first time for the making of *Butch Cassidy* in Utah and Mexico in 1968, but it was the differences that were obvious from the start. Newman and George Roy Hill, both sticklers for punctuality,

Bolivia is the end of the line for Butch and Sundance.

were always early. Redford, who has said that appointments and time schedules bug him, was always late. Newman, who had a classical acting training at the Yale Drama School and the New York Actors' Studio, was always prepared, but he hated to shoot a scene until he'd 'talked it to death'. Redford, who preferred to fly by the seat of his pants, was impatient with what he saw as unnecessary shilly-shallying.

Hill was on Newman's side, so Redford, as the new boy, had no choice but to do it their way, but he didn't have to like it. 'Paul really is a good guy. I really like him. Otherwise I would have balked at the whole rehearsal thing. I believe rehearsal cuts into the spontaneity of what you're doing, and spontaneity is vitally important in films, since films are essentially about capturing life as it happens. That's the illusion they try to create, anyway. But I rehearsed. Newman was calling the shots so I rehearsed.'

The story of *Butch Cassidy and The Sundance Kid* is simplicity itself. It starts in a saloon where Sundance is accused of cheating at blackjack, then moves to the mountains where Butch repels a takeover for the leadership of the Hole-in-the-Wall gang by an upstart rival. The current game plan is to rob a Union Pacific train twice – once on the outward trip, once on the return – a ruse they reckon will confuse the men who run the railroad. It doesn't: not only do they blow up the train and the money by using too much dynamite, but they find themselves on the run from a posse. With the help of Sundance's girlfriend, a schoolteacher played by Katharine Ross, they leap off a cliff into a mountain river in full flood and escape. The three of them then pursue their calling as bank robbers in Bolivia until death do them part – which it soon does.

Given the credibility gaps involved, the film would only work if the two heroes played it fast and loose. The screenplay interspersed sharp one-liners with rapid action, leaving the audience little time to think. If they'd had more, they might have noticed the fundamental immorality in the outlaws' tale. Butch and Sundance were not latter-day Robin Hoods, but self-seeking adventurers; they didn't celebrate the land-owning zeal of the original frontiersmen so much as the corporate greed of contemporary America, even of Hollywood itself. Only the quickness of the actors' hands would deceive the public's eye.

Paul Newman reckons that George Roy Hill appreciated this only too well. From the start, he needled his stars, and Redford in particular, with a view to making them compete with each other so as to get the performances he wanted. 'George has such an uncanny sense of story, and character, that there's a reason for everything he does,' Newman explains. 'With the little con games, he was effectively getting Redford, and me, into the spirit of the picaresque guys we were playing.'

Redford took Hill's tactics rather more personally. 'George Roy Hill

Bang on target: Sundance the Sharp-
shooter draws again.

is a crazy bastard. And a military goddamn director. Oh, you can fight
with him, you can have an idea about something, but you'd better have
about four reasons to back it up, and be able to fight for it, because he
will fight like hell.' One of Hill's favourite running jokes was over
Sundance's quickness on the draw, as demonstrated in the opening
sequence when he shoots off a man's gunbelt. 'I really worked on the
being-fast-with-the-gun business,' Redford claimed, 'and every time
I'd screw one up, Hill would be over there with his hand over his
mouth, going "Heh, heh, heh, what's the matter, Redford?" He was
always telling me to be careful not to shoot myself in the foot!'

The tone for Hill's mockery over Redford's screwing up was set early
on. The actor was supposed to jump off the train the gang was robbing
and then, when it rolled to a stop, give an arm-signal to the others and
run back to the door of the pay-roll car. 'Well, Redford works so
physically,' Hill states gleefully, 'and he was so concerned with this
arm-wave he was doing and the graceful way he was running, and
stopping, and turning, that he didn't notice that the train had rolled
right past him. When he looked up and didn't see it, and looked around

for where it had gone, the expression on his face was incredible.' Hill was speechless with laughter for the next five minutes but, hard though he tried, he was unable to fit that sequence into the finished picture.

Redford had always enjoyed practical jokes but he was to learn that he wasn't yet in Hill's class when it came to arranging them. 'I like a caper. A really good joke requires careful planning. Of course, you've got to be on your toes if a joke comes along ready-made, but my favourite kind is the set-up. Hill really hustled me once on set. He saw that I'm hung up on being physically competitive, so one night after we finished shooting, he said, "You name the sport, and I'll find a match for you from the movie company. Name any sport you want."'

Redford can't quite remember how, let alone why, he chose fencing, but Hill decided to take up the challenge in person, and the two men bet 100 dollars on the outcome. 'I looked him over and, you know, it seemed like an odd sport for Hill to be confident at because he had a bad back. In fact, he looked like a spaz.' Then again Redford thought he could have been one of those guys who'd trained in just one sport at college and reached an improbably high standard. Hill confirmed this impression a couple of nights later when Redford surprised him in his trailer with a load of fencing equipment. 'Épées, rapiers, sabres, electric tips – gee, it was impressive. He tried to hide it all under a blanket, but I'd got a good look at it. By now there was 500 dollars riding on this in side bets. Newman was making some bets of his own.'

When the company moved down to Mexico, Hill set the time and place: five p.m. on the local tennis courts. Each chooses his second and the village police chief is asked to be the judge. By now Redford is getting worried. 'Hill is using jargon on me about rules and weapons, and I'm trying to pretend I know what he's talking about.' On the day of the match, Redford is on time for once in his life, but Hill doesn't show. The money is Redford's by default. Or so he believes. 'Half an hour later, they bring him in, and he's in real pain. He's barely walking, his face is white, because he's hurt his back on the hills somewhere. I said, "Hill, you really blew it!" He said, "Sure, take the money. If you don't mind winning by default, take the money." I thought that over, and it didn't seem right, so I offer to postpone the match. Hill gets charitable about the whole thing and tries to choose a stand-in on the spot. I knew I had him then because there wasn't a chance he'd pick a winner!'

Hill looked around vaguely, then asked the two stuntmen. Both refused. Other heads were shaken as he went through the crew. Finally he came to his assistant, Bobby Crawford, who was making a documentary about the shooting of *Butch Cassidy*. He was a young graduate, just out of UCLA, and Redford was confident – until they clashed swords. 'I knew I'd been had. That kid turned out to be a Junior Olympic champion fencer. Hill had worked for weeks to set it up, but what made it a really beautiful hustle was that he knew my weak spot so well, he could risk the whole thing by offering me cash for the default. I didn't know I'd turn it down until I did, but somehow Hill knew all along. But, you know, I didn't do too badly that day. Of course I lost to Crawford, but not by much. At one point, it was five to four. I came that close. I almost had him.'

Back in Utah, Hill set up a race between himself, Newman and Redford: his own biplane versus Newman's Porsche-powered Volkswagen versus Redford's Porsche. Hill would have to land and refuel somewhere which should have made the times about equal. 'Redford was so goddam serious about it that I finally had to call it off. It was the hunting season, see, and I was really afraid that he'd kill himself, or some damned hunters, trying to win!' In fact, it was Newman who had this encounter sewn up. He'd worked out that if he chartered a transport plane to fly his car to Provo, he could unload it with ample time to sit drinking beer at the winning-post while his rivals struggled to get there. But he never got the chance.

There were times when Newman joined Hill in the Redford-baiting, especially on the knotty question of time-keeping. 'You know Redford's left-handed,' he once said. 'I wanted to change the name of the picture to *Waiting for Lefty*. He should be clubbed for this deformity. I'd just tell him he had to improve and he really did try. George Roy Hill and I would see him coming down the highway at 125 m.p.h., and sometimes he got to the set almost on time – and would immediately vomit into the nearest portable toilet.' Later in their friendship, Newman gave Redford a piece of needle-point that reads, 'Punctuality is the courtesy of kings.' No one suggests that the hint has ever been taken.

Another Redford trait is that for a self-styled mountain man he is uncommonly afraid of heights. Again Newman was quick to capitalise on the weakness. The spectacular scene when the outlaws jump off a cliff into a river was staged on a very much less impressive scale with the actors landing out of sight on a platform six feet below the lip of the gorge. Even so, Redford hesitated on the brink. 'Look at the old lady up there,' Newman chortled. 'Look at her.'

On another occasion, Hill recalls that their ganging-up tipped Redford over the edge. 'He got furious. "I worked damned hard on this picture" – Christ, he nearly burst, and we laughed like hell. But, you know, acting is really a kind of babyish thing to do. They push you and pat you and dress you and do practically everything but defecate for you. I don't think Bob particularly wants to do that all his life.'

If all this banter were designed to create joviality on screen, it worked. Long before the film was completed, Richard Zanuck's doubts about Redford had evaporated and he now believed him to be the perfect Sundance. So too did Hill who felt completely vindicated by

Headed for stardom: Robert Redford, Katharine Ross and Paul
Newman in *Butch Cassidy and The Sundance Kid* (1969)

his performance. 'He is a leading man, a man's man, strong, terse, sardonic. I think he brought a great deal of his own personality to the part. Bob is a very hard-nosed, independent, private person. And he has a tendency to be very cool on the exterior, and very distant. Yet he has a tremendous warmth underneath it. If you have a cold man playing a potential killer, it's repulsive. Redford was able to play against the underlying warmth and make the character full-bodied. It was exactly what I wanted.'

And, as it happened, exactly what the public wanted, although the critics complained about its lack of centre. 'It would be hard to think of a more thoroughly determinedly entertaining film,' wrote John Russell Taylor in *The Times*. 'It has had a vast success in the States, and no doubt will do the same here. Deservedly so: it is hard to fault anything so patently eager to please. The only trouble is that, in their eagerness, the makers seem rather too ready to be swayed this way and that by whatever quirks of style and subject-matter are apparently at present most pleasing to audiences, at the expense of any internal coherence the film's subject may have.'

The *Guardian*'s Derek Malcolm agreed in essence and praised the 'impeccable' acting. 'The basic trouble is that almost everybody lays on almost everything just a bit too thick,' he summed up. 'The charm eventually turns to whimsy. We learn to love those boys just a little too much for comfort. The laugh lines get progressively uneasier. But the film remains a genuine achievement, an exercise in corporate style that is as good to listen to, as to look at. Newman gives a beautifully relaxed performance, as if he knows that Redford is so good that he doesn't have to lift the scenes of his own accord.'

When *Butch Cassidy and The Sundance Kid* opened in late 1969, Robert Redford became a victim of mass media, his face on the cover of every glossy magazine in America. The exposure made him a superstar and the film made him seriously rich for the first time. On its back, he became a landowner and a film producer, but he also became a wanted man. From now on, he would never walk alone.

One of his first actions was to buy 3,000 acres at Timphaven from the Paul S. Stewart family. 'He put together a 2.5 million dollar deal that made no financial sense to anyone,' says Brent Beck, Vice-President and General Manager of Sundance and Redford's friend since he was employed to upgrade the ski resort in 1969 shortly after the new purchase went through. 'Everyone advised him against financing it over thirty years. It was not a wise thing to do at the time but he loved the canyon and he was prepared to pay his dues to get it. From the first, Bob said, "I don't want to build or develop here. I don't want to ruin this thing." He used his own money to bury power lines, re-route the creek and landscape the area at the bottom of the lifts.' And, reluctantly according to Beck, he changed the name to Sundance, not only because of the film, but because of the way the sun dances on Mount Timpanogos. Maybe, maybe not, but it is unlikely that the link with the movie that made Redford has done the resort any harm.

In the early days, Redford and Beck cruised the area on skis planning where the new runs and chair lifts should be sited. The towers to carry the cables were designed to fit in as far as possible with the topography and broad swathes were cut out of the forest and reseeded to form the basis of groomed pistes. Runs were named after Shauna and Jamie and another was christened Redfinger. 'Bob tripped by those trees,' Beck pointed out, 'and fell all the way down that slope. He was so furious he gave it the finger. That's why we called it that.'

The Stewarts' Polynesian-style snack bar was replaced with two adjoining restaurants, the Grill and the Tree Room, plus a shop selling local artefacts. The walls are made of untreated local spruce planks to blend in with the environment and the Tree Room has the second Robert Redford fireplace inspired, it is said, by the work of Frank Lloyd Wright. It was made up, just as the one in his house was, from lumps of Utah limestone set in a concrete wall, stretching from floor to ceiling. Redford likes high ceilings so, once again, it was a mighty task and once again he did it himself. The walls of the Tree Room are hung with items from Redford's extensive collection of Indian art, among them some handsome and very valuable Navajo rugs. It also has a tree, though not the original one which died during the first year of operation. The Grill Room has candid photos of celebrated visitors – Paul Newman, Karl Malden, Sydney Pollack, David Puttnam, Alan Alda – by way of decoration.

Even today only 400 acres are given over to skiing and numbers are limited by the size of the car park. Once it is full, everyone else is turned away. 'We're trying to keep it informal and fun, and it's got a nice family feeling,' Lola commented at the time, 'but we have less privacy than we used to and have to work harder to find time for ourselves.'

Some time before the *Blue* fiasco, Redford had set up his own company, Wildwood Enterprises, to develop projects in his own image. The first of these was *Downhill Racer*, about a conceited American skier who comes to understand the emptiness of his obsession even as he receives his Olympic gold medal. Redford's partner and ex-agent, Richard Gregson (then married to Natalie Wood), shared his enthusiasm for the subject and agreed to produce it.

Paramount, at the height of their euphoria over *Barefoot in the Park*, were willing to put up the money provided Roman Polanski, in favour after *Rosemary's Baby*, despite going seriously over budget, was the director and the story was based on Oakley Hall's *The Downhill Racers*. Scorning the novel which he described as 'an *après-ski* book', Redford presented Paramount with his own screenplay commissioned from James Salter. Even before he riled them over *Blue*, they hated it. Given the perfect excuse to withdraw, they didn't hesitate to take it.

However, Redford was not to be deterred from what had become his pet project. It had never been the skiing component that appealed to him so much as the concept of an athlete seeking worthless goals for the purpose of self-glorification; the kind of person he himself might have been if he'd stayed with his baseball scholarship and graduated to the major league. The actor had seen films about athletes and they were always clean-cut farm-boys, backed all the way by apple-cheeked mothers and fathers with brows furrowed by honest toil. In other words, they represented America as it wished to see itself as surely as the John Wayne vigilante cowboy had done during the Cold War. Like him, Redford concluded, they had had their day.

'What about the athlete who is a creep?' he demanded. 'We tend to tolerate creeps if they win. Who remembers who came in second? I wanted to see that in a film, and it only happened to be skiing because I was into it at the time and thought it was something very beautiful, and visual, that hadn't been dealt with in film before. It was inevitable, in a way, that I became interested in competition. I had been in competitive sports most of my life as a kid, and while I had never ski-raced, I was convinced that the drama of racing was worthy of a film.' He has also believed that his kind of film could make a comment about sport that would carry far beyond the confines of the four-million-strong American skiing fraternity.

Few shared these convictions, and the studio chiefs were not among those who did. Having been turned down all over Hollywood, Redford took the typically confrontational step of returning to Paramount. By this time, the dispute over *Blue* had been settled – Redford had agreed to do three films for the studio at his old option figure – so they had nothing to lose when they welcomed back the man 'they'd had machine-gun turrets set up on the lot for' just a year before. Not that the going was easy. They still wanted a commercial script about romance on the ski circuit rather than Salter and Redford's vision of the flawed athlete as a media tool, and they still wanted the novel's title, *The Downhill Racers*.

Redford found a champion in Charles Bluhdorn, founder and President of Gulf + Western, the company which owned the studio. In an inspired fifteen-minute one-man show, he acted out the part of David Chappellet, a loner from Colorado who was digging for Olympic gold in the men's downhill, the blue riband of the Games. As a further sweetener, he promised to bring in his picture for less than the three million dollars originally agreed with Paramount. The problem was time: the real Winter Olympics, the Grenoble Games in which Jean-

Claude Killy won all three men's disciplines, were set for early 1968. Redford and his crew had to be there to record the event.

'I'm pretty good on skis but we had to shoot the actual Olympic skiers because those few men are the only ones in the world who can race that downhill course authentically. You're skiing eighty miles an hour; one false move and goodbye, Charley.' As all skiing, even when done by professionals, films much slower than it really is, and as the timed descent doesn't have the excitement that is built into man-to-man competition (a sprint or horse-race, for example), this was a realistic viewpoint, and Bluhdorn gave Redford the green light to get as much footage as cheaply as possible. Once he had permission from Bob Beattie, the American Olympic ski coach, to travel with the team up to and during the Games, he left for the European warm-up tour with Salter, a cameraman, and a group of ski bums.

'We were all holed up in one room in this dive by the river in Grenoble. The French weren't letting people film the Olympics, so we had to use disguises to get by the guards. The photographer was pretty well known, so I fixed him up in a hairpiece and a false nose so he could get out on the slopes with his camera. He loved it. The ski bums shot a lot of footage too, but they couldn't get by the officials, so they swiped a sign from a refreshment vendor, put it in their car window, and got through that way. Every night we met at the room to see who was still alive.'

With 20,000 feet of film in the can, Paramount agreed to finance the non-documentary part of the film at 1.8 million dollars, a figure that meant Redford had to use a British crew and work without a salary. It had to be called *Downhill Racer* but otherwise he was given *carte blanche*. 'I inherited the whole enchilada,' he said cheerfully, and enlisted a first-time feature director, Michael Ritchie, whose two-hour pilot for *The Outsider* television series had impressed him. 'I was very flattered to get the call,' Ritchie remembers. 'I had known Redford from his earliest days on television. I saw one of the first things he did on TV, *Moment of Fear*, and I'd seen him on Broadway, so I knew he was terrific and somebody I'd like to work with.'

So it turned out to be. The Harvard-educated Ritchie, who would build a career out of chronicling America's dubious attitudes towards competition in films such as *Smile*, saw eye to eye with the actor from the start. He agreed that their movie should be 'as gutsy, as realistic, as harsh and as documentary as possible'. He also agreed to travel to Europe with Richard Gregson to scout for locations that would match the Olympic footage. Immediately the new snow fell for the 1968–9 season, the cameras were to turn on Redford as Chappellet. And they would have done if Redford the Unwary hadn't tried to kill himself by driving a Snowmobile over a cliff in Utah ten days before he left for Europe.

'It was a dumb move,' he admits. 'I thought I could manoeuvre the vehicle but pretty soon I was just blasting through big powder drifts. I stayed with the machine rather than jump clear and I was literally flying through the air. When it landed, my knee went right into the motor. That cooled me down a little. It was bad, seven stitches and a lot of pain. The doctor did a good job sewing me up, but I walked with a limp through the first part of the film. A cheap way to get close-ups. All the while, of course, was the hovering suspicion that the gods were trying to tell us something.'

While Redford fretted over his inability to get on skis as the unit moved round Austria, Switzerland and France, Paramount breathed a sigh of relief. Indeed they would have been happier if they could have persuaded their dare-devil star to leave all the skiing scenes to his stand-in, but of course they couldn't. 'We were too far up the mountains for the studio to reach us so there was really no way they could force me to control whatever it was I was doing. But the question becomes, "What is dangerous?" I think driving around Hollywood is dangerous. I think some meetings in some offices are dangerous. I'd rather be on the mountain any day.'

It would have been against Redford's character to turn his back on a challenge when expert skier-cameramen were hurtling down mountains at breakneck speeds in order to capture the thrill of the descent. Inevitably there were injuries, mostly broken bones during the action sequences and frostbite in between. Nor did the shoestring budget help. Camilla Sparv, who played Chappellet's love interest, didn't even have a hairdresser. 'She did her own hair,' Ritchie recalls. 'Every bit of her wardrobe was off the racks. We didn't have a wardrobe mistress, make-up, dressing-rooms, folding director chairs or even toilets. If you had to go to the bathroom, you went behind the trees. I think it improved the quality of the film. We didn't have a chance to introduce anything phoney.' 'We worked, at one point, for seven weeks straight, without a day off,' Redford adds. 'A lot of mumbling and remarks like, "I didn't know there was snow on Devil's Island!" And so it went.'

Downhill Racer follows David Chappellet's obsessive search for gold through three winters of competition and two summers of training. It begins when he is summoned to Switzerland as a replacement when America's top skier is injured on the eve of the Olympic trials. It ends when he stands on the winner's rostrum two years later, secure only in the knowledge that he has paid too high a price for his fleeting, inconsequential victory. In between, he wins or wipes out, suffers or celebrates, rises or falls in the crucial starting order as ski racers do.

It is no part of Redford's plan that the audience should like David

A passion shared: Redford plays spoiled world champion, David Chappellet, in his own production of *Downhill Racer* (1969).

Chappellet. He is ignorant, stupid, antagonistic, arrogant and a bad team member. He is also incapable of sustaining a relationship with his girlfriend when it stands in the way of personal glory. On the slopes, he may be a king for a day; off them, he is invariably a bastard. His only redemption is his realisation that he wins by default, and that winning isn't all that important anyway. However Redford and Ritchie do want us to understand that Chappellet doesn't bear sole responsibility for his behaviour: the battery sports factory which turns athletes into pawns, must share the blame. And so must the media: in a medal-hungry country, and all countries are medal-hungry, journalists habitually dehumanise sportsmen to the point at which they no longer exist as people, only as potential winners. Is it any wonder they begin to believe their own myths?

Although Redford's cover wasn't fully blown in these final months before *Butch Cassidy* was released, it is easy to spot the shape of things to come in this anti-media message. Before 1969 was over, he would be taking journalistic interference personally, a stance he maintains today. Even those who don't much care for skiing as a film topic can admire the way in which *Downhill Racer* blends the documentary Olympic footage with the fictional footage. This required Ritchie to shoot his actors with natural, rather than flattering, lighting and camera angles. Fortunately Redford and the glamorous Camilla Sparv looked good no matter how they were presented and Gene Hackman, who plays the beleaguered Olympic coach, neither expects, nor wishes, to be glamorised. Nor, of course, did the other members of the cast, most of whom had never acted before.

'They would have been put ill at ease by an enormous amount of hot lighting equipment, or by being told they had to hit marks,' Ritchie has explained. 'I wanted to have a certain freedom, a looseness, the opportunity to shoot rehearsals and use them, the facility to have the camera searching out the action, rather than anticipating it so that, ultimately, the audience wouldn't be able to tell where the dramatic material left off and the documentary ski footage began.'

Again it is easy to see how this spontaneous and flexible approach would have appealed to Redford, fresh from his encounters with George Roy Hill and Paul Newman. As executive producer on *Downhill Racer*, he called the shots literally and figuratively. The only thing Ritchie checked him on regularly was his liking for working while chewing gum: when the cameras were about to roll, the actor would slip a wad into his mouth. 'Just as he took his first chomp, I'd always yell, "cut",' Ritchie recalls.

Even with Redford and his crew safely back in America, Paramount's problems with *Downhill Racer* weren't over. Unwisely they decided to preview the film in Santa Barbara, a retirement haven for millionaires fleeing from bitterly cold winters back east. 'Those people had come out here to get away from the snow and the last thing they wanted was to see a lot of skiing,' Redford said disparagingly. Apparently he was right because half of them walked out, leaving Richard Gregson, Natalie Wood and Redford sitting limply in the back row. Fortunately the quitters were too polite to throw things at the screen but Redford, after a drastic re-think, took the film back to the cutting-room, tightened it up and removed most of the music, leaving only the spare dialogue and the natural effect of the skiing.

The film was appreciated by people who knew what they were seeing, among them most of the critics. 'If, on occasion, it takes a spill or two, *Downhill Racer* still comes through as a perceptive, unsentimental portrait of a young athlete on the make,' said *Time*. 'A thoroughly engaging and offbeat little film which tracks through well-trodden ground but stops, nose aquiver like a labrador retriever, every time it scents a cliché, and flushes quite a few unexpected gems in the process,' wrote Tom Milne in the *Observer*.

The public, however, stayed away in droves. 'It took two years of my life, but it wasn't very successful commercially,' Redford admitted later. 'Really the films that I've wanted to make, and have really been behind, haven't made much money. That's the way it is. But you end up with the satisfaction of doing something that you have a kind of passion for.'

One way and another, 1969 was a landmark year in Redford's development. It brought him stardom, which he didn't want, and the muscle to do his own thing, both at Sundance and in Hollywood, which he most definitely did want. He would spend the next five years balancing the equation. Only after that would he be his own man.

6

If Only The Directors Knew Their Jobs . . .

' Let's face it,' Robert Redford told *Time* magazine in December, 1969, 'if you want to get anything done in Hollywood, you've got to fight. It's just one big battleground out there, and I don't need that. I work it this way. If I don't like it, I don't do it.' That may sound great, but in the early seventies, it was only partly true. In five years of leading roles, his most productive screen period, Redford made films for love, money, liberal principles and fun. He made them for George Roy Hill, Michael Ritchie, Sydney Pollack and others rather less in thrall to Hollywood. He made them for himself and for his family. By 1975, the all-American loner with the cold eyes and the radiant sex appeal would be strategically and economically secure.

In the process, he turned down *Love Story* and *The Godfather* and *The French Connection*. As a result of these and other sacrifices, he chooses to present his career as uncompromised. If that were so, it would make him the worst assessor of material ever to hit the big time. After all, there aren't many film enthusiasts who would place *Little Fauss and Big Halsy*, *Hot Rock* and *The Great Waldo Pepper* above *The French Connection*. Is it taste he lacks, or merely judgment? Or does he, as actors must, accept an occasional ideologically impure character out of expediency? Of course he does, but he rarely admits it: Redford's *modus operandi* is to rationalise his decisions as plausibly as possible and to insist that he has no regrets. But an obstinate, competitive go-getter would say that, wouldn't he?

It is not difficult to see why he made *Tell Them Willie Boy Is Here*. Once the *Butch Cassidy* dates were set, it filled a gap in his 1968 schedule between the Grenoble Olympics footage for *Downhill Racer* and the start of shooting in late summer. And it marked his first rather muddled attempt to adopt the cause of the American Indians on screen. Adapted from Harry Lawton's novel by Abraham Polonsky, emerging

72

after twenty years on the blacklist following his refusal to testify to the House of Un-American Activities Committee in the late forties, *Tell Them Willie Boy Is Here* had its heart in the right place.

'I like things clear-cut,' says Redford. 'Take the problems of the Indians. They got cleaned, done out of their land by loophole deals. It's an injustice. I wanted to work on *Willie Boy* because it was about the white man's relationship to the Indian. I think the problems of the Indians can only be resolved by education, and I thought the film would work towards that. Gee, this is heavy stuff. I hate to sound like a fifty-year-old sage. I like to operate from my instincts. I like situations where your behaviour counts rather than how you say something.'

Willie Boy is a Pauiute Indian who works as a cattle hand on a Californian ranch in 1909, a career which ends abruptly when he accidentally shoots his prospective father-in-law while claiming his daughter for his bride. When the unhappy couple go on the run, Cooper, the local sheriff, enlists a couple of locals and follows, with a view to bringing back the girl. Enter President Taft; exit Coop, designated as a bodyguard to the great man. Meanwhile the posse contrives to start a small genocidal battle which triggers rumours of a major Indian uprising and an attempt on the Presidential life. Re-enter Coop to kill Willie Boy and emerge as the winner in a duel that turns out to be meaningless because the Indian's gun is empty. As in *Downhill Racer*, Redford–Cooper is left regretting a pyrrhic victory.

In that it presented the Indian as a victim of white prejudice, *Tell Them Willie Boy Is Here* was very much of its time, a time when black – and by implication red – was beautiful. However no one connected with it, not even Abraham Polonsky, was prepared to go all the way by casting American Indians in the main roles and therein lay the roots of considerable controversy. Polonsky claims that he got the actors he'd wanted from the outset: Redford for sheriff, Robert Blake for Willie, Katharine Ross – pre-*Butch Cassidy* and *The Graduate* – for his wife.

Redford disagrees with this. He says he was offered Willie first, but turned him down and urged Polonsky to hire a real Indian. He then accepted Sheriff Cooper because he liked his neutral stance. 'It was in the grey area that I'm rather fond of in films. He saw the good and the bad on both sides and that's the character I thought I should play. He's a loner who can't make the adjustment to modern society. He was raised with Indians, but around 1909, the Indians were about to be squelched. He has no respect for the white community, for the attitude of "I think I'll go out and kill me a few Indians", but he has to maintain law and order. In the process of the chase he discovers a lot about himself. In the beginning, he's an uncommitted man; at the end of the film you should feel he's a man committed. He learns, he grows. I was attracted by the idea of playing a simple man who grows.'

Teamed again with Katharine Ross in *Tell Them Willie
Boy Is Here* (1969).

In the rump of the studio system, it made economic – though not
artistic – sense for Universal to use their contract players in as many
roles as possible. As the available paid talent didn't include Indian
actors, Redford's complaints fell on deaf ears. 'I was sick and tired of
seeing Indians, many of whom I had known personally and been
friendly with, depicted on the screen in a way that really annoyed me,'
he commented, 'and I thought what better opportunity than this, a real
Indian story, to let the Indians play themselves.'

Universal ignored him and, in due course, cast and crew assembled in
Southern California in the hope that the wrangling was behind them. It
wasn't. The most persistent difficulties were between Abraham Polonsky, directing only his second film (the first was *Force of Evil* in 1948)
and considered out of date by the crew, and cameraman Conrad Hall, a
cool and highly professional customer who was about to make a film
himself. 'That's the toughest time to get a cameraman,' Redford
explained, 'just before he's going to fly the coop and be a director,

because he disputes everything.' Polonsky tried to exert his authority by behaving 'like Rommel'. 'A lot of times he was being definite when I don't think he had a clue what he wanted to do,' Redford summed up.

Much of his own attention was taken up with his deal with Paramount for the completion of *Downhill Racer* and with his preparations for *Butch Cassidy* so he stood coolly by while others quarrelled. 'Nothing affects my performance,' he stated arrogantly. 'I don't really work within the confines of the set anyway.' Nevertheless he found the energy to fuel the flames on the question of Indian representation. 'It wasn't real. Indians don't talk that much, and they don't talk like that. Polonsky was still carrying forth the liberal causes from the thirties and he put dialogue in the mouths of Indians that didn't really fit. Indians don't talk like people out of Hell's Kitchen. They don't say, "Your hand is white, mine is red – does that make you any different?" That kind of stuff gives you a little cringe.'

Later there would be bigger cringes. Universal looked unfavourably on the finished picture because it didn't fit into any of the right slots. 'They were afraid, they weren't sure what it was,' Redford claims. 'A lot of distributors, unless you hit them between the eyes with a sledge-hammer about what the movie is, a big label, they look the other way. They're afraid to have to use their imaginations and come up with something creative to characterise it.'

It took *Butch Cassidy* and *Downhill Racer* to persuade Universal to stop looking the other way: the belated release of *Tell Them Willie Boy* was greeted with widespread praise, tinged with nervousness at its bleak depiction of white American attitudes. *Variety* suggested that it was 'the most complex and original American film since *Bonnie and Clyde*', a viewpoint endorsed by the *Los Angeles Herald Examiner*. '*Tell Them Willie Boy Is Here* is an admirable motion picture – taut, clean, precise in scene and image, cinematically cogent,' wrote Winfred Blevins, adding praise for 'performances of really exceptional skill' for Blake and Redford.

However, it was Pauline Kael who pinpointed the cause for Universal's neurosis over the release. 'If Americans have always been as ugly and brutal and hypocritical as some of our current movies keep telling us, there's nothing for us to do but commit geno-suicide. That's what *Tell Them Willie Boy Is Here* suggests we should do . . . here's a movie that goes all the way – turning white Americans into a race carrying blood guilt, a race whose civilisation must be destroyed.' No wonder Polonsky felt the film went over better in Europe where anti-Americanism over the Vietnam war was at its peak.

Redford himself seems to have liked the movie, then changed his mind. According to Polonsky, this was because his associates told him that the Indian was the real star. 'His ego got in the way, so he's been going round saying he hates the film now,' the director said gloomily. Not surprisingly, Redford denies this vehemently, even to the extent of claiming that it was he who promoted Robert Blake as Willie in the face of opposition at Universal. 'That's totally wrong. Jesus, that's incredible. In fact, it was sort of the opposite as I recall. Blake was going around on talk shows at the time, really bitter and hostile towards me, feeling he got screwed in the release of the film. I didn't have anything to do with the movie's release or how it was promoted. As a matter of fact, I got him the job. I fought to get him when the studio didn't want him. It was a strange gratitude on the part of Blake, but then he seemed to be fairly bitter all around.'

Given Redford's antipathy to a white man playing Willie, his championship of Blake's cause is implausible. As for his eclipse in the marketing of the film, it was surely inevitable. Pre-*Butch Cassidy*, *Tell Them Willie Boy Is Here* was ethnically chic but unreleasable according to studio lore; after it, it was a Robert Redford film. Universal would have been crazy not to sell it as such.

'I had reservations but they had nothing to do with Blake or anyone stealing the picture,' Redford concluded. 'Again it was the Indians. I felt they were being portrayed as whites. And I thought Polonsky – through insecurity because he hadn't made a film in so long or because of pressure from the studio – backed off from the kind of film he wanted to make. The script was terrific. I don't think the movie realised fifty per cent of its potential as a script. Had Abe been left to his own devices, he probably would have made the movie I thought he was going to make.'

In two of his next three films, *Little Fauss and Big Halsy* and *The Candidate*, Redford reinterpreted the ambivalent Sheriff Cooper in contemporary terms, firstly as a dirt-track rider and secondly as a politician. When he received Charles Eastman's screenplay for *Little Fauss and Big Halsy*, he still owed Paramount on their original three-picture deal so he was only too happy to find himself deeply impressed by its originality. 'It was the best screenplay of any film I've ever done. It was without doubt, the most interesting, the funniest, the saddest, the most real.'

The protagonists in a picture blatantly designed to cash in on *Easy Rider* are out and out losers, not the Chappellets who learn who they are through the hollowness of victory, but the small time competitors who come face to face with reality through repeated failure. Little Fauss is the short, ugly son of cloying parents, a mechanic and would-be motor-cycle racer; Halsy Knox is the arrogant trickster, a man who sells everyone short and most especially Fauss, his devoted, if deluded, disciple.

Redford had been a motorbike freak since his Van Nuys days, often to the point of danger or beyond, so he identified effortlessly with Halsy,

Big Halsy takes time out from drag racing.

even to the extent of feeling that there were circumstances in which he himself could have turned out like that. 'It was a very different role from what I'd been doing. He's very verbose for a next to illiterate type of guy. He's a rake, an absolute cad, scroungy and raunchy. There was nothing subtle in that role. It was fun to go that way for a shot. You could say my love of motorcycles has something to do with sexual drive, but if you try to analyse why you like things, you take the sense of fun out of them.'

Charles Eastman wanted to direct his own screenplay, but the powers that be appointed Sidney Furie – wrongly, as many eventually admitted. Furie knew very well what he was reading – 'the best dialogue and some wonderful scenes' – but he always had doubts about the ending. 'I got talked out of my feelings. I started the picture and talked myself into thinking it was going to work.'

Furie had no hesitation in casting Redford as Halsy and Michael J. Pollard (from *Bonnie and Clyde*) as Fauss, but he soon discovered that the two men had absolutely nothing in common. From their first meeting, Furie thought Redford was unlike any other actor he'd ever met. 'If you didn't know he was an actor because you recognised him,' he told James Spada, 'you'd think he was a young executive. He's personable, matter of fact, no bullshit, no small talk, no talking about girls or drinking or what he did last night.' Pollard, on the other hand, enjoyed a reputation as a free spirit. The relationship between him and

Redford when they went on location in small-time south-west America, with occasional brushes with civilisation in Los Angeles, San Francisco and Phoenix, Arizona, stopped far short of communication. 'All I got to say about Redford is he's got a great smile. He's got a great laugh,' Pollard summed up a few years later.

Meanwhile they had a movie to make together and, given Pollard's alleged predilection for exotic substances, it was never going to be easy. Nor did Furie and Redford see eye to eye. There was, for example, the occasion when Furie was trying to line up a long shot and Redford kept on moving. When Furie said he was having trouble, the actor snapped, 'too bad', forcing Furie to take a firm line. 'You're right, it's too bad,' he told the recalcitrant star, 'because if you ever do that again, I'm leaving. I don't need to stay and hear that and be embarrassed in front of people. I'm trying to make this picture. If you don't think the shot's a good idea, let's talk about it. But if you do, don't tell me, "too bad". I don't treat you that way. He respected that I put my feelings on the line and didn't harbour it. After that, he was very sensitive to my feelings.'

During filming, perhaps, but Furie was another victim of Redford's post-production scorn. Although he says he was 'beat' and 'very detached' when he was playing Halsy as a result of his on-going preoccupation with *Downhill Racer*, he later accused Furie of not understanding the screenplay. 'He kept making cartoons out of it. He didn't shoot the ending that was written because he didn't understand what the movie was about. And he had a big ego problem – he didn't want to listen to suggestions. Things were dealt with in a large, splashy, cartoon way rather than in the sensitive, finely-tuned way of the script. There was a terrific ear that went into writing that script and it was a bad ear that went into making it. The author was done a disservice. Furie can't blame anyone but himself for the way the picture turned out. It was his interpretation. He made it.'

In fact, he didn't because his hands were tied by producer, Al Ruddy, who prevented Eastman from directing and Furie from changing Eastman's script. 'I was just showing up and telling people where to stand. I wasn't in on the storytelling, and the director should always be in on that.' Despite Redford's criticism, Furie kept faith with him, perhaps because the actor lent him his house in Sundance when the film wrapped. Furie has always thought Redford put up one of his very best performances in *Little Fauss and Big Halsy*, and regretted that the film's lack of commercial success prevented him from getting proper recognition. 'People criticise him and say he's always Redford. Well, he isn't. He might always look like Redford, but he really does become the character he's playing. There's a certain unreality about acting, but Redford is the realest actor I've ever met. He's just a guy who happens to be an actor.'

On the critical front the *New Yorker*'s Pauline Kael delivered the first of many vicious personal attacks on an actor she'd initially admired: 'Robert Redford is symbolically wounded, and has a great big scar running down his spine to prove it. The scar is much in evidence, because Redford, playing a swaggering oaf, rarely wears a shirt. (This will not, however, do as much for his career as it did for Paul Newman's.) Redford can't seem to keep his pants up either, and he's constantly fiddling with his zipper and juggling his genitals (on one occasion, in what is possibly a movie first, in a close shot). Trying to be cute and raunchy, Redford also flashes his teeth like Kirk Douglas, keeps a toothbrush stuck in his mouth, wears funny hats, and wiggles his behind. Was it only a few months ago he seemed a promising actor? He's already an overripe star, smirking on lines like "Cycles is a mean toy, lady".'

When their new baby, Amy, was born on October 21, 1970, the day after *Little Fauss and Big Halsy* opened, the Redfords decided it was time to buy a bigger New York apartment. Urban Redford has always been a dedicated New Yorker. 'The pace is fast. It's dirty and gritty, but at least it's honest,' he says by way of favourable comparison with Los

Little Fauss and Big Halsy (1970) unveiled the Redford chest.

Angeles and indeed all other cities. The Redfords chose a penthouse on Fifth Avenue in the nineties overlooking Central Park – prime Kennedy territory and by no means cheap.

The new place was done out Redford-style which always means simply and ecologically. The spacious, open-plan rooms had white stucco walls and beamed ceilings. The dominant features in the living area were a tan leather sofa and a brick fireplace adorned by antique rifles. A tiled sideboard separated it from the dining-room in which the whole of one wall was given over to a giant wine-rack. A heavy refectory table separated this from Redford's study area where he kept his classical records and his books. As a child, he'd risked the scorn of philistine peers to read Fenimore Cooper and Edgar Allan Poe, but not much else; by 1971, he was becoming aware that things he wanted to know about history and politics could be found in books. Another feature of the apartment was a life-size cardboard cut-out of Paul Newman as Butch Cassidy, gun at the ready. Was it a memento of good times past or a goad to Redford's competitive spirit?

The two older children, freckled strawberry blonds like their father, attended an exclusive Manhattan private school a short walk away. They returned home for lunch and were escorted on all occasions by a West Indian maid. 'Too snobbish,' said Lola, 'but what can you do? We liked the other kids there – they're sort of cool – their parents are actors and politicians and opera singers. Bob can't wait for the kids after school any more without getting mobbed. It's trauma time!'

The need to pay for this smart lifestyle was becoming critical when Redford was offered *The Hot Rock* and he deigned to accept a job with money as 'a principal consideration'. Although he was earning between $250,000 and $300,000 a picture, he was flat broke: 'I really had financial problems at the time.' Another consideration was that the film would be made in and around Manhattan over a three-month period, which meant that he could be at home with Lola and the new baby. Though these are valid reasons for going to work, they provide no guarantees that the results will be good, and they weren't.

The Hot Rock is a caper comedy about a newly released prisoner (Redford) who teams up with his brother-in-law (George Segal) to steal a priceless diamond. The property of an African nation, it is on display at the Brooklyn Museum. With assistance from emissaries of a rival African nation, who want to own the stone, the thieves set up an elaborate robbery which goes seriously wrong. At this point, the film degenerates into a series of near misses as the Redford team thinks up increasingly silly ways of reclaiming the prize.

With a script by William Goldman of *Butch Cassidy* fame and a studio, Twentieth Century-Fox, which hoped it would succeed on a similar level, *The Hot Rock* looked very much better on paper than it did on celluloid. Again, Redford blames its failure on the director, Peter Yates, an Englishman in vogue after *Bullitt*. 'Yates was essentially an action director,' he explained, 'and being English, he had an English humour. *The Hot Rock* was a very American movie, with a very American humour about it. Yates was in the process of being Americanised, but the movie suffered because he didn't really understand American humour.' There may well be elements of truth in this, especially as Yates has rarely recaptured the inspiration he found in *Bullitt* in the string of mundane movies he has made since.

Making *The Hot Rock* was an occasionally hairy business for Redford because he did his own stunts. These included scaling a twenty-foot prison wall and dropping out of a hovering helicopter onto the roof of an abandoned house in Greenwich Village. Though the manoeuvres were tricky rather than dangerous, there were times when the actor had 'a slightly panicky look in his eye', according to publicist Monroe Friedman. He remembers too how much Redford enjoyed the robbery scenes set in the Brooklyn Museum, not so much for the acting as for the time between takes when he could prowl the halls to study the masterpieces.

One of the greatest problems for most film actors is filling these periods of inactivity when all around them is chaos. However, Redford's passion for art gave him an excellent on-going solution which left him relaxed while others fretted. 'I'll do some sketching. I'm very happy then. No tension and I lose my sense of time. Appointments, time schedules bug me. When I get rolling along on a sketch, I almost make myself high. Hours pass and I think it's minutes. It's a very private thing; the people around the camera all fade out.'

So too did *The Hot Rock*, but not before it earned Redford some of the worst personal reviews of his career. 'Redford's supercool poise of *Butch Cassidy and The Sundance Kid* and *Downhill Racer* has sunk to the inexpressiveness of catatonia,' said Joseph Gelmis in *Newsday*. *Life*'s Richard Schickel thought that Redford and Segal presented themselves with 'consumer-approved charm, but not much more'.

Typically the actor himself admits to no doubts over this blot on his résumé. 'It's certainly not the most substantive piece of work I've done,' he assesses correctly. 'But I don't regret it. I don't regret anything I've done. If I had my life to live over, I'd do exactly the same things. I'd turn down the things I'd turn down. And the ones I did, I'll stand by even though they may not have turned out quite right.'

7

A Highly Political Animal?

Redford's political stance was, is and probably always will be am-biguous. He claims to be apolitical but the truth is that he uses politics in much the same way he uses Hollywood: as and when he needs them. When he doesn't need them, he speaks out against them vociferously. He is so confident of his power that he knows he can bite hands that feed him with impunity.

On a local level, he fights the political fight to protect his beliefs and privacy at Sundance. If need be, he operates from within the existing framework as he did when he served as President of the Provo Canyon Sewer District when it was set up in the mid-seventies. Apparently one of several candidates, he was elected unanimously for three years. 'That made him Number One in the Number Two business,' jokes Brent Beck. During his term of office, Redford manipulated the system adeptly. He dealt with pollution and septic tank regulations. He met with town and county officials and raised funds to make sure waste was properly handled. According to Beck, he conducted the meetings as if he knew what he was doing.

Even before the sewerage stint, he'd saved Provo Canyon from a six-lane highway. Though his quota of speeding tickets for his hair-raising descents down the winding mountain road is legendary, he is not in favour of being able to go even faster. 'I think the road commission-ers, if they had their way, would pave the country. What bothers me is there's almost a fatalistic attitude about it. Well, it took a long time, but that road didn't go in. Ah, it sounds like a lot of bull, but I just believe in doing things that are effective, not marching around the country and shouting in the wind.'

His views, as stated over the last twenty years, suggest that it is politician rather than politics which is the dirty word. Redford has vivid recollections of his first meeting with a major figure, Richard Nixon, then Vice-President in Eisenhower's administration, and the memories are not happy. 'He presented an athletics award to me when I was a teenager. I had no pre-judged attitude towards the man. But when the award was presented, he shook my hand and said a few words to me; it was almost chilling how hollow it was, and I never forgot it. That had a lot to do with my attitude towards politics.'

His experiences on the road in Europe in 1956 broadened his mind wonderfully on the question of how other nations' problems are presented to the American people. He was visiting Vienna when the Russians crushed the Hungarian uprising, sending thousands of rebels into exile on the other side of the Danube. Some of them stayed in the same youth hostel as Redford and one of them told him how he'd lost his whole family – mother, father, sisters and brother – during the river crossing. 'He was going back,' the actor recalls. 'I said, "What for? You've only just escaped." And he said, "You don't understand, you've never had blood spilled in your own country and your own family." I said, "What are you going to do, beat on tanks with your bare hands?" He turned me off.'

It was only when he got back to America that he understood that the Hungarian was right: with the Korean conflict ending just before he was old enough to fight, Redford had no way of understanding the violations inherent in war. 'When I got back, I'd try to tell people, but they'd say things like, "Hey, it was kind of tense there for a minute, wasn't it?" In this country, all that was covered over. Politics is a game. It's full of crap. They press a button – it's war. And they press another button – and it's anything they want it to be for the economic system. It's a game like chess. Move this here, that there. I can't stand games, and screw it.'

In the highly politicised sixties, Redford 'bought Jack Kennedy', but balked at buying Bobby. 'I couldn't. Did you see his eyes? He was on TV, quoting this thing, "I dream of things that never were", and he was looking around to see if reporters were getting it down.' The next politician he approved of was Eugene McCarthy, the candidate who tried unsuccessfully for the Democratic nomination in 1968. Lola and Bob went to a McCarthy rally in Salt Lake City, a poorly-attended affair where they were trying to auction things off to raise money for the campaign. Redford remembers a girl putting her beads up for sale. 'Somebody offered two dollars, and suddenly I hear Lola on her feet, absolutely blazing, "One thousand dollars", and I said, "Stop her".'

With Nixon in the White House, Redford had more to say. 'I can't talk about him. I get sick to my stomach. And Agnew. That fool! Those fools! But, you know, I think this country is pretty great, and it's possible, if we keep talking it down, to bring it down. I'm buying up all the acreage around my house to sort of wall us in, but also because I want to keep anybody else from screwing it up. The one cause I am interested in is this conservation thing. I don't think I'm very patriotic about the country, but I am patriotic about my family, my wife and kids.'

During the Vietnam War, for which he was rather too old and much too famous to be drafted, he resisted pressures to speak out for the anti-war movement. 'I do care about individuals,' he said at the time. 'I can't stand injustice at any level. I'm not an activist, though I am against the Vietnam War. I don't know, maybe I'm too selfish or too lazy to get really involved. I want to be honest about this, I don't want to seem better than I am. Anyway, say I stood up at an anti-war benefit with a lot of celebrities who do that sort of thing. Right in the audience there'd be any number of people who knew more of the facts and could make a better case against the war than I could. Just because you're in the public eye for something like acting doesn't mean you're an expert in politics. With Paul Newman, it's different. He's really into the issues and he speaks out because he has to if he's going to stay honest with himself. Paul's a thoroughly good man.'

This then is the political background of the man who made *The Candidate*, the story of a holier-than-thou Californian lawyer, Bill McKay, who is persuaded to enter a hopeless race for state governor by the Democratic campaign manager. McKay, chosen because his father has already served as governor, has a dislike of politics stemming from over-exposure to the system during his childhood. However, he goes along with the scheme in the knowledge that he has no chance of beating the reactionary incumbent, Crocker Jarmon, and in the belief that he will be able to give welcome exposure to the issues that concern him during the six-month campaign.

Of course it doesn't turn out like that at all. Once the outspoken, dazzlingly handsome McKay goes on the road, he attracts a ground swell of support which suggests that he could be in a match winning position. But only if he silences his father, who threatens to come out against him, and replaces his outspoken demands for justice on civil rights matters with the kind of flim-flam voters want to hear. With the scent of victory in his nostrils, he capitulates: he is metamorphosed into a politician, a plausible shell of the idealist he once was.

The idea of making a film about the political process came to Redford as he sat watching the Nixon versus Humphrey telethon in November, 1968. 'What I saw frightened me. It was so absolutely staged. Nixon's looked like it was being broadcast from Madame Tussaud's Wax Museum, so lifeless. Bud Wilkinson was feeding the questions to a confident Nixon. The young audience was polite, neat, plastic. It was all so phoney, and the people were eating it up. Then I switched over to Humphrey and watched him destroy everything he once stood for, trying on his new image, and I resented him. He also had this strange

A word of advice for 'The Candidate' (1972) from his father
(Melvyn Douglas).

end-of-the-line fatigue. I thought to myself, "This would make a
movie".'

With Nixon, the old enemy, unsafely installed in the White House,
Redford started to research the electoral process. He went to the
Kennedy archives and spoke to senators, political columnists and
television announcers to 'get the feel of it'. He then contacted Michael
Ritchie, whose political activities included campaigning for the liberal
John Tunney. Ritchie eagerly agreed to help Redford put flesh on the
bones of his idea. There are enough elements of *Downhill Racer* in *The
Candidate* – another man who learns that winners are losers too – to make
it logical that the two men should work together again on what would
become a Wildwood–Ritchie Production.

The first step was to commission a script from Jeremy Larner, a
speechwriter for Eugene McCarthy in 1968 and fairly bitter about the
experience if his subsequent book, *Nobody Knows*, is anything to go by.
He wrote the screenplay for *The Candidate* along lines suggested by
Redford. 'I was a McCarthy supporter and I was disillusioned because I

85

was naïve enough to think – maybe because I'm Irish – that he could force a change of system. We discussed whether to make a film about that. I did not want to. It could have been about the Kennedys too. I didn't want that. Lazy people will try to pick out real-life characters. There are no real-life characters. We worked very hard to create this character, Bill McKay, and it wasn't easy.'

'There are no villains in the piece,' he continues. 'The family tree all comes down to one thing: the system itself. I don't think the political professionals can be blamed. They're doing their job. It's just that it all results in a grey, computerised mess of . . . whatever . . . and it's wrong.'

The film is primarily about dehumanisation. A candidate finds himself in a world of special effects: the crowds are created, the image is created, the commercials are created. Only the policies are diluted because to be specific is to make enemies. McKay is asked about legalised abortion. He has no doubts. 'I'm for it,' he replies. 'How about just say it's worth studying?' his campaign manager advises. 'Okay, I'll think about it,' says McKay, and he does. And he thinks about bussing and taxes and other issues. In future speeches, commitment to causes will be replaced by flannel. When he is elected, he can only look around him and ask, 'What do we do next?' He has stepped into the vacuum; now he has nowhere else to go.

Redford finds striking parallels between politics and sport: both are male-oriented, chauvinistic activities which rely heavily on locker-room team-spirit. Both brutalise relationships, yet attractive women lay themselves on the line to be cheated on and abandoned by sportsmen and politicians. When Redford did the studio circuits once again to raise money for *The Candidate*, he discovered that the moguls too had some comparisons to make: political movies, like sports movies, were death at the box-office. As with *Downhill Racer*, no one wanted to play ball.

Once again the actor had to do his piece for the benefit of cynical producers. Stanley Jaffe, the president of Paramount, nearly fell asleep during one such Redford 'rug performance'. His rivals were equally negative but the trail ended at Warner Brothers, run at that time by Richard Zanuck, the man who hadn't wanted Redford for *Sundance* during his Twentieth Century-Fox days. At this point he did, which was fortunate because time was running short if the film were to be ready for a 1972 release, to tie in with the next presidential election. Redford had wanted to set it in New York, mostly for the pleasure of being there, but the more politically-experienced Ritchie had convinced him that prototype Bill McKays are Californians to a man: only there would such a campaign be taken seriously.

A high-class cast was assembled – Melvyn Douglas for McKay senior, Peter Boyle for the campaign manager, Karen Carlson as

McKay's wife and Natalie Wood as the girl he meets at a fund raiser – and shooting began on November 29, 1971. Redford surely believed in what he was doing because McKay, suited and charismatic, was not the way he presented himself out of choice. Nor did he like the crowds, the rallies and the endless handshaking which the role required.

Towards the end of filming, he found that there was something he did like about politics: the buzz of adulation was irresistible even when it was play-acting. The notion didn't please him, but nor did he try to deny that it was so. This snippet of self-knowledge came about during a ticker-tape parade down Montgomery Street in San Francisco. It was midwinter and Redford had only had four days off in the whole film. He wished he could be skiing in Utah. Instead he was surrounded by cheering crowds in the middle of a huge city.

'I had to come back to do it. Resented it. I was down. Anyway the scene was set up by an actual advance man who went around arranging for all the secretaries in the area to tear off their calendar pages and throw them out of their windows at twelve noon. And when I was in that car, with all those people reaching for me, and all those thousands of calendar pages coming down – well, in five seconds, I was on a high. You feel you could go for days without eating or sleeping, and at that time you would believe anything good about yourself. It's like finding a piece of kryptonite, you feel so powerful.'

The Candidate was largely improvised, with Redford and Ritchie giving inspiration free rein as and when it came to them. Redford thought up the opening and closing sequences while Ritchie drew on his Tunney experiences for the scene where the rival candidates race to reach a fire in Malibu: exposure on television, no matter what the cause, is every candidate's bottom line. Larner provided the behavioural detail for McKay, especially his relationship with his father and the way he is overtaken by his own vanity without realising it.

Though not nearly so jolly as *Butch Cassidy*, the filming was enlivened on one notable occasion by Peter Boyle and friends. On a chilly winter's morning, Redford was slated to go swimming, not generally considered too wise as he had a bad dose of flu and a temperature of 102. However he insisted. Meanwhile the sixteen-year-old groupie who was supposed to strip off and join him was digging her heels in. She'd never done a nude scene before and it took all Ritchie's powers of persuasion to convince her that nakedness was dignified and, in any case, the crew were so accustomed to it that they wouldn't leer at her. Fortified by a few drinks, she eventually lowered herself into the pool and the cameras turned. At this moment, Boyle and five stark-naked fellow performers, male and female, dive-bombed the pool, then vanished back to their dressing-rooms as quickly as they'd come, leaving everyone except the girl creased up with laughter.

Camera and sound at the ready as Redford awaits the director's orders on *The Candidate*.

The Candidate was unveiled in July, 1972 to notices that suggested the critics were running out of superlatives. 'Political themes have never been any more successful on the screen than, say, movies about the American Revolution,' wrote Rex Reed. '*The Candidate* blows that old taboo sky high. Not only is it the most interesting and entertaining movie I've ever seen about American politics, but it also achieves the provocative distinction of probably getting Robert Redford a nomination for President. I have seldom seen a performer so firmly entrenched in the nuances of a role; even when the film is not being improvised into moments of throbbing realism, it soars with the sweat and sweetness of total naturalism in scenes that never seem rehearsed.' Reed even forgave the film its opportunistic timing and ended his rave with, '*The Candidate* certainly gets my vote.'

Art Unger thought that Robert Redford, 'the king of cool', had come up with 'the coolest political film ever', while Dilys Powell admired his versatility in *The Sunday Times*: 'Robert Redford as the candidate – nobody's fool but cornered into accepting shifty and vulgar ways of campaigning – gives a beautiful performance; for once a character who really changes in changing circumstances.'

There were some voices of dissent, however. Andrew Sarris of *Village Voice* missed the rapturous opening, caught up with the film a month later and delivered not so much a review as a personal attack. 'Have my fellow scribes been duped by Redford cultism?' he asks, and answers himself at length. 'Redford seems to have convinced a great many people that he has more integrity than any other thirty actors put together. He comes down from his kingly mountain top in Colorado only rarely and only reluctantly to mingle in the madding crowd for the sake of his muse. He never hangs around at Sardi's with all the other phonies trying to make the scene. No, he's too pure for that. Of course, he does take options on film properties, and currently he is campaigning for his slice of the profits in *The Candidate* with all the meditative monasticism of a Fuller Brush salesman. But we never hear about this side of his soulful nature in all the interviews he manages to squeeze into his spiritual days. All we hear is how hard the corrupt world is trying to rape pure Robert, and how manfully Robert is resisting the rape.'

Predictably the politicians were not amused either. *New York*'s Bella Abzug complained about the film's possible effect on young people. She suggested they would find their worst fears confirmed by what she considered to be a simplistic film. 'There's still room for men and women with passion and principles in our society,' she concluded. 'They just need staying power and more confidence in the electorate than *The Candidate* is willing to concede.'

Redford himself was mildly amazed at the seemingly serious suggestions that he should actually run for office. 'I've thought about it and I've thought about how I wouldn't like it. I can't imagine any politician surviving the campaign process and remaining totally his own man. I think a politician has to sell a little piece of himself, and I don't want to.'

Instead he headed back to Utah to make his one and only movie in Sundance, *Jeremiah Johnson*, the perfect antidote to corruptible politicians on crowded hustings. Like *The Candidate*, it was a film close to his heart, indeed the one he has picked most frequently as his personal favourite. The project originated in two books on Indian lore in the early part of the nineteenth century: the novel, *Mountain Man*, by Vardis Fisher, and the story, *Crow Killer*, by Raymond W. Thorp and Robert Bunker. Both narratives grew out of exhaustive research: *Crow Killer*, in particular, benefited from its authors' delvings into the Bureau of American Ethnology for authentic details of Indian life in the 1830s.

The marriage of the two books resulted in a screenplay called *Liver Eatin' Johnson* which eventually came Redford's way. He and Sydney Pollack had been looking for a second collaboration ever since *This*

Property is Condemned. Redford had turned down a role in Pollack's overblown Burt Lancaster war movie, *Castle Keep*; Pollack had rejected *Downhill Racer*. Now he agreed to read *Liver Eatin' Johnson*. 'I don't think it's your kind of thing,' Redford warned. 'It's a bawdy comedy about a guy who eats livers.' 'Sounds pretty shitty,' Pollack replied. In the event, he thought it had potential, especially the first fifty pages – 'one of the best beginnings I ever read'. The liver-eating scenes towards the end turned him off, but he agreed there was enough to work on to go ahead.

As the idealism of the sixties faded into the nihilism of the seventies there was a timeliness about the man who was rechristened Jeremiah Johnson. At the outset, he is a neat, clean-shaven easterner who wants to go it alone. Unlike many western heroes, he is not a homesteader or a cattle-rancher or a lawman. He isn't even a man with a mission to 'civilise' the Indians. He is just an ex-soldier who can't take it any more. Surviving in the mountains is his means of salvation, solitude his only purpose. He believes he is giving up killing for good. For Redford, the suburban child who'd grown into a mountain man with a passion for all things related to the American west, the ingredients were all in place.

At home in the wilds as the mountain man in *Jeremiah Johnson* (1972).

In his ignorance, it is inevitable that Johnson should be wrong about many things. He survives his first winter only because he falls in with a more experienced mountain man, Bear Claw, played by Will Geer. By his second year, he is capable of living on his own, although a bushy red beard and heavy fur clothing make him almost unrecognisable as Robert Redford as he tramps through deep snow. His peace of mind ends abruptly when he finds two survivors of an Indian massacre, a wife and a son. The wife runs off into the wilderness leaving Johnson to bury the dead and take care of the silent son. One thing leads to another and soon our hero has an Indian bride and a mountain love-nest as well.

Can the ill-assorted trio live happily ever after? Of course not. Johnson must soon answer another question: will he violate Indian burial-grounds in order to help a troop of cavalry save some lost settlers? Military training dies hard and he agrees. The Indians retaliate by murdering his wife and the boy; he retaliates by going on the rampage against the Crow Indians, suitable targets as their habit is to attack singly rather than in bands. Dubbed 'Killer of Crows' and constantly pursued by them, his quest for solitude ends in the loneliness of bloodthirsty revenge.

This format evolved gradually through discussions between Pollack and Redford while the film was being made. Before that their friendship almost ended owing to pressure put on them by Warner Brothers, enthusiastic about the film at the start, less so later when they tried to pull the plug. The problem was that Redford signed early on and received a 200,000-dollar advance which he spent immediately. As usual at this stage of his career, his financial affairs were in a mess. On the one hand, he was legally committed to making films for Paramount at mid-sixties prices; on the other, he was desperately overstretched. The combined costs of Wildwood Enterprises, improvements at Sundance and prime real estate in Manhattan far exceeded his income. By the time Warner Brothers rethought *Jeremiah Johnson* and concluded they could only afford to make it on the back lot at Burbank, the 200,000 dollars was gone beyond recall.

Neither man was prepared to make a film about a mountain man on a concrete wasteland in California so Warners offered Pollack a sum of money to withdraw from the project. When Pollack told Redford, the explosion was inevitable. 'He couldn't give them back the money. He was stuck. But I wasn't. I had an out. At that point, he said, "You son of a bitch. If you walk away from this picture . . . I wouldn't do this to you. We went into this together!" I mean he was really furious. And he was right.'

After this wavering, justice was seen to be done because Pollack had to put his own neck on the line to get *Jeremiah Johnson* rolling. Warner Brothers only gave him the green light when they had his personal guarantee that he would bring the film in from its locations in Utah for the same money it would have cost at Burbank. This meant strict adherence to a very limited budget, a comfortless procedure at 12,000 feet in midwinter. *Jeremiah Johnson* was in no way a Hollywood film. Redford had no dressing-room and, half the time, there wasn't even a lavatory. Cast and crew disappeared briefly – usually very briefly – into the nearest trees. There was no money for a wardrobe designer so the clothes were cobbled together from what was available locally, a necessity which probably added authenticity to the end result.

Money was also saved by basing the production in Sundance, with Pollack staying in Redford's house. Night after night they held story conferences as they tried to find a device to turn Johnson into a Crow killer. Legend has it that the Crow attack on Johnson's family was purely arbitrary, but Redford, the Indians' champion, wasn't prepared to present the massacre as unmotivated brutality.

And brutality there had to be, as an economic as well as a narrative necessity. With a loner, a terrified Indian woman and a mute child as its main characters, *Jeremiah Johnson* is a film of few words and much scenery, hardly a sure-fire box-office winner. Warner Brothers backed it only if it cashed in on recent hits such as *The Wild Bunch* and *Dirty Harry* by turning into a bloodbath over the last hour. But how to change a man who walked away from military life to look for tranquillity in the wilderness into a dedicated Indian-killer? Not too difficult. Have the Indians kill his dependants. But why would they do that?

It was a question that took a long time to answer. Every evening, Redford would build a fire and Pollack would do the cooking. After dinner they'd sit down in the firelight over a pitcher of beer and mull over the dilemma. 'We can't kill all those Indians. How can we make a picture killing all those Indians?' Redford would demand. 'I know, I know,' Pollack would reply, 'but what are we going to do? I mean, we've got to get it so that when the Indians kill your family, it's not their fault. You've gotta screw up, you know.' 'Well, how am I gonna do that?' With each failure to come up with an answer, their depression deepened.

In the end it was Pollack and co-scriptwriter Ed Anhalt who worked out a solution. What if Johnson screwed up by violating Indian burial-grounds? Then they'd have right on their side in killing his woman. And he would have a revenge motive for killing them. 'The whole picture took on a meaning for me then,' says Pollack. 'That was the little bridge I needed to make the end work.'

Despite the beauty of the surroundings, shooting was never going to be easy. Filming in snow has built-in problems. There is often too much or too little and even when there is the right amount, it only looks virgin once. For each subsequent take, the equipment must be moved to a new patch and beware the person who leaves footprints in the wrong place.

The difficulties are exacerbated when you need horses because they sink in and lash out in panic. Pollack solved this one by buying a thousand yards of chain-link fence from Sears Roebuck and laying it on the surface, then waiting for it to be snowed over to an appropriate depth for a horse to walk on. 'It was murderous moving an arc-light around,' Pollack recalls. 'We were convinced we had a disaster because we didn't know where to turn or what to do. The weather was wrong every day. We were going crazy.'

So were many members of the seventy-man crew. Marooned in what they saw as wilderness, and worn out by working at high altitudes, they weren't always in sufficiently good shape to finish each day's work. On one such occasion, everyone had quit with the exception of Pollack and the helicopter pilot. The plan was to film Johnson from the air, a tiny lone figure in a vast white landscape. 'Sydney and the pilot dropped me off in the snow,' Redford remembers. 'While I was walking across the snow, the 'copter disappeared. I didn't know where they'd gone or if they'd come back. I wondered whether Sydney was mad at me. I finally figured out he had gone for more film. There was something wonderful about that day. While they were gone, it was quite an experience. I lay back in the snow and savoured the soundlessness of every moment, nothing but an occasional echo over the tip of a glacier.'

This, and an earlier experience of being lost in the mountains while climbing alone, took Redford deep into the soul of Jeremiah Johnson, a fusion of characters that resulted in what Pollack thought was a wonderful ending. His original intention was for the Indian killer to climb higher and higher into the mountains until he froze to death while Redford thought he should just disappear. What finally happened came about by chance when Johnson, blood on his hands from many encounters with the Crow, comes across another potential victim. Both men are on horses and they watch each other from a distance, wary and uncertain. Then Johnson raises his hand in a respectful salute.

It didn't work the ·first time and Redford suggested he try again. 'When he did it, I got chills just watching him,' says Pollack, 'and I said, "O.K., that's it." That's what I ended the film on. The gesture had grief in it, it had anger, it had respect, it had sadness. Everything that had gone before. I didn't tell him how to do that. It was from within himself.'

When *Jeremiah Johnson* opened to generally favourable reviews in December, 1972, it was unfortunate that Pauline Kael thought that Redford was giving the finger in response to a peace sign from a Crow chief, a judgment that brought a tirade from the actor. 'She misinterpreted it in a way I never thought possible. It was absolutely mind-boggling. The gesture was an ad-lib response to the frustration of the pain and confusion the character was experiencing in just continuing. It

93

Struggling against alien elements in *Jeremiah Johnson*.

indicated a respect for the enemy – what Rommel and Patton might have done if they had met. The criticism was especially painful to me because of my feelings and concern for the American Indian. The remark seemed to me far-fetched and personal beyond the limits of responsible criticism.'

Nor can he have been too pleased with the rest of Kael's review. After mourning the loss of the old-style Western hero personified by Gary Cooper, she went on: 'Probably young audiences can no longer relate to what the Westerner stood for, but are they supposed to like Redford because he's so sheepish and silent and straight? Hell, so was Lassie. The cool silence of the Coop archetype implied depths. There are no depths in Redford he's willing to reveal; his cool is just modern, existential chic, and it's beginning to look sullen and stubborn rather than heroic. When Redford is in a competitive buddy-buddy co-star relationship, the cool can be a put-on but in this fake-authentic Western setting it's cool gone dank and narcissistic.' Some hundreds of words later, she concluded that *Jeremiah Johnson* 'seems to have been written by vultures'.

94

She was not alone in her doubts; Joseph Gelmis of *Newsday* was one who shared them. 'Let's get it straight, Bob,' he wrote. 'Blue eyes aren't enough. Steely looks won't win any prizes in these pages. If you've got a big brother, send him out and let's see what he can do. Because, Bob, to us you'll always be the aging *ingénu*. Redford is one of those lightweight talents who go a long way on looks, on knowing when to turn up the thermostat on his clean-cut, boyish California-surfer sex.' More positively, Judith Crist of *New York* saw him as 'triumphant in his near-silent portrayal of a quiet man in a world where survival depends on the sound and the stillness'.

Warner Brothers showed its lack of faith in *Jeremiah Johnson* by refusing to promote it, so Redford went on the road instead, taking it to the Cannes Film Festival and attending selected openings in small towns across the United States. The strategy worked and the film did good business. 'I loved *Jeremiah Johnson*,' he says. 'I loved doing it and I loved the overall film. But I don't like looking at myself on film. So if I'm stuck with myself, it's very bothersome. I'm just thrilled that people seemed to like it.'

8

Never Say Never Again

Why did Robert Redford make *The Way We Were*? An honest answer to that question would cast a lot of light on the mixed motives of the man who'd said he'd never be a matinée idol. For years Hollywood producers had wanted to get the gorgeous hunk with the flashing teeth into a more than fleeting association with a girl. They'd dreamed of feeding women's fantasies by stripping Redford's shirt off his hairy chest and his jeans off his sports-muscled legs, but the answer had usually been no. One thing the film parts he'd selected had in common was a lot of conspicuously bulky clothing – ski suits, politicians' suits, mountain raiment, cowboy kit. As his principal screen-partners had been men – Paul Newman, Gene Hackman, Robert Blake, George Segal – there was no reason for him to take it off, and he didn't. The women in his films had been little more than bimbos designed to move the story along and establish that the hero is emotionally locked into adolescent buddy-buddy relationships rather than actively homosexual.

Bimbo is not a category in which it is possible to put Barbra Streisand, the little lady with the big nose for whom *The Way We Were* was written. Arthur Laurents, who'd worked with her on her first Broadway musical, *I Can Get It For You Wholesale*, back in 1962, devised the Jewish radical heroine, Katie Morosky, to fit the feisty Streisand persona. Katie spends her college years in the late thirties promoting causes that include The Young Communist League. Along the way, she meets Hubbell Gardiner, a privileged Virginian jock and would-be novelist. They would get on well together were it not for his scornful brain-dead chums who mock plain Katie's unworldly aspirations.

Cut to 1944. Hubbell is a drunken sailor perched precariously on a Manhattan bar-stool. Katie, now earning a living from radio while continuing her work as a political activist, finds him there and whisks him back to her apartment. Will their union be consummated at last? No, he passes out. Nevertheless it is the beginning of a relationship that leads to marriage and takes them to Hollywood just in time for blacklisting to influence the saga. Hubbell, now turning his first novel into a screenplay, feels he is selling out, just as Katie said he would, while she remains true to herself by travelling, when heavily pregnant, to Washington to protest at the hearings of the House of Un-American Activities Committee.

The cracks in their marriage begin to show and the usually non-confrontational Hubbell widens them by spending the night with his ex-girlfriend. In 1948, such behaviour was reasonable grounds for divorce, and that is what the Gardiners do, despite still being in love. The tear-jerk ending takes place when they meet by chance in a Manhattan street in the early fifties. Katie is handing out Ban the Bomb leaflets, Hubbell is a television hack, Katie has remarried, Hubbell and Katie are still in love. Under the surface, nothing has changed, or so we are asked to believe.

The Way We Were was – is – a load of rubbish, as Redford agreed from the start. 'Aw, that piece of junk. Yeah, they sent it to me a long time ago in treatment form. I passed,' he said when Sydney Pollack first approached him over playing Hubbell Gardiner. But Pollack, hired by producer Ray Stark following his Oscar nomination for another period piece, *They Shoot Horses, Don't They?*, was not so easily put off. 'I found the script very moving and I thought right away, "Gee, this would be great for Bob,"' he recalls.

He also recalled that, metaphorically speaking, Streisand ate her leading men for breakfast – Omar Sharif in *Funny Girl* and Ryan O'Neal in *What's Up Doc?* come to mind. As befits a star-vehicle, *The Way We Were* was tilted fatally in her favour. Katie is the one with commitment, passion, balls and a sense of destiny. Hubbell, though pretty and slickly intelligent, is her sounding-board, more a person hired to suggest an opposing point of view than a character in his own right. He relates rather than creates. His belief that people are more important than causes, though widely held and essentially likeable, seems soggy when compared to his wife's blazing certainty. The actor who played Hubbell Gardiner looked like being a loser all the way to the bank. Redford was determined it shouldn't be him.

Pollack was determined it should. Whenever he met Redford, he niggled him. The chemistry between him and Barbra could be great, he told him, very unusual, very striking. When the script was completed, he sent it to him. 'What are you doing this for?' Redford asked by way of reply. 'I don't know what you see in this. You must see something in this.'

But the seeds of doubt were sown. 'I wish he'd make up his mind,'

Lola told Pollack. 'He's driving me crazy. He sits up at night and says, "What should I do? I don't like it. Pollack is really turned on by it. I trust him. Maybe he sees something I don't see but I don't see it."'

Meanwhile Ray Stark was losing patience. Ryan O'Neal would do it; Ryan O'Neal would have to do. Stark gave Pollack just one hour to get Redford to sign; otherwise the part was O'Neal's. 'I was ready to pull out of the picture unless I could get Bob,' Pollack remembers. 'I knew we needed someone strong enough to counterbalance Barbra. The only guy who could just show up and stay with her was Redford. I knew it had to be him. That final hour I was in Ray Stark's apartment and he was fuming. He said, "Who does he think he is? I'm not gonna chase my life around Robert Redford. We got Barbra. What do we need Redford for?"'

By way of a last throw, Pollack went round to Redford's office to try bribery: the film would be delayed by four months so he could spend the summer of '72 at Sundance, then return to New York to shoot it in the autumn when he'd have to be there anyway for the school term. 'But what is this picture about?' Redford asked plaintively. 'This guy is just an object. He runs around saying, "Aw, c'mon Katie, c'mon Katie." He doesn't want anything. She wants everything. What does this guy want, Pollack? What does he want?'

Only when the deadline had passed and Stark's secretary was on the phone demanding an answer did Redford capitulate. 'The reason I finally decided to do it,' the actor explains, 'is that I had faith that Pollack would make something more out of the character than was in the original script. Had I not had faith in Sydney and myself and David Rayfiel and Alvin Sargent working together to create some kind of depth to the character, I wouldn't have taken the role. As it was written, he was shallow and one-dimensional. Not very real, more a figment of someone's imagination, of what Prince Charming should be like.'

So the rewrites began and, according to Redford, a darker side to the golden boy began to emerge. This was in line with his self-image as a flawed American hero, outwardly perfect but inwardly aware of feet of clay. He also demanded a show-down between Hubbell and Katie. 'In the original, the character was passive all the way through, he was just there for her to love as an object. She loved him and loved him and loved him and then they fell apart. There wasn't any cataclysmic moment. So we created a massive argument scene in Union Station to give the character a point of view. And that was that if she were a person of causes, he was a people-person, people were more important than

Ripe for romance as Hubbell Gardiner, the ultimate 'Wasp' in *The Way We Were* (1973).

causes. They were both valid points of view, but Hubbell's wasn't in the original script.'

It is not difficult to see Redford's influence on some of the lines that now came Hubbell's way. 'Like the country he lived in, everything came easy to him. But at least he knew it,' the thirties student wrote at the start of his college essay. 'Are you still a nice gentile boy?' Katie enquires after his adultery. 'No,' he snaps, 'and I never was.'

In the final analysis, the changes amounted to little more than window-dressing. The finished Hubbell remains an ordinary man temporarily linked to an extraordinary woman. His acceptance of the *status quo* is shared by most of the people, most of the time. He believes that putting yourself on the line for your beliefs is stupid, and dangerous, and ineffective. Studio hacks can rape his novel as part of the commercialisation process and he'll go along with it, content to save what he can. He deludes himself into believing that if he knows he's selling out, his integrity can't be touched. As he sees it, there is no free speech in America, nor is there ever likely to be, so what is the point of courting trouble by speaking out? Political activism doesn't change things but the kind of commitment it demands ruins relationships. Which is the more important, unattainable idealism or true love? His and Katie's answers will never be the same.

The shooting of *The Way We Were* was a nightmare on many levels. The script was being reworked as the cameras turned and Columbia, lumbered with an expensive picture they had little faith in, were not amused by the soaring budget. The timing was bad because they hadn't had a hit for years, a decline they were trying to reverse by changing management. As a result, Ray Stark monitored the picture obsessively, irritating both Pollack and Redford. 'Bob felt he was made to work in a straitjacket,' Pollack comments, and Redford was equally disgusted with the studio's treatment of the director. 'Toward the end of the picture, Sydney began wandering around the sound stage – being on that set was like doing overtime at Dachau.'

Then there was Barbra Streisand herself, as neurotic in real life as Katie is in the movie. An intellectual tyrant quite capable of calling the shots, she prefers to discuss each scene exhaustively before getting down to doing it. Redford knew all about this approach from his work with Paul Newman, but time hadn't changed his attitude towards it. 'She'd talk and talk and talk and talk and drive me nuts,' he says of Barbra. 'And the amusing thing was that after she'd talk and talk and talk and talk, we'd get down to doing it and she'd do just what she was going to do from the beginning.'

For Pollack, the balancing act was delicate. Every evening he'd get an hour-long call from the actress to discuss the next day's schedule. Come the morning, they'd forgather to mull it over some more. Redford would show up late and resentful at not being able to get down to work straight away. Barbra felt he was rushing her, he felt he was frittering away his performance in rehearsal, and both were right because Streisand did find more through repetition and Redford did hit a peak, then flag thereafter. To be fair to both was impossible. 'I was like a jockey trying to figure out when to roll the camera and get them to coincide,' said Pollack wearily.

'There comes a point,' said Redford, 'when you're ready to go and then you're better off expending your energies in front of the camera trying things. Films are made up of pieces and you might get something usable. But you learn too much in rehearsals. Things start to get pat and film is a medium of behaviour and spontaneity.'

There was also the vexed question of profile. Both actors preferred to be photographed with the left side of their face towards the camera, an impossibility in any movie, let alone a relationship movie which requires a lot of mutual gazing into each other's eyes. In Redford's case, the reason is the three prominent moles on the right side of his face: he does indeed look better from the left. There is no obvious cause for Streisand's preference: her nose is equally intrusive no matter which way you approach it. However Redford, whether gallantly or *faute de mieux*, gave best to Barbra on this point. In *The Way We Were*, the moles show.

Inevitably there was intense competition between these two strong-willed actors to come out on top. Streisand had been close both to Sharif and O'Neal which may have smoothed matters when it was time to work, but Redford, with or without moles, didn't intend to be trampled under her tiny feet. 'I'm not interested in my performance. I want good performances all around me,' she had said by way of justification for her bossiness, but her reaction to Redford's insistence on the rounding out of Hubbell Gardiner hardly suggests she meant it. 'Where are my close-ups?' she demanded angrily. 'I had close-ups in every scene in *Funny Girl*.'

Streisand's nightly calls to Pollack included laments over Redford's excellence in the rushes. 'How does he do it?' she would ask enviously. Redford didn't go so far as to call his friend but he too believed that he was lousy and she was wonderful. When they weren't trying to impose their will on one another, they spent a lot of the time joking together. Streisand was particularly amused by Redford's attempts to say anything Jewish, a running joke that worked its way into the Californian beach scene when Katie cracks up as Hubbell tries to learn some Yiddish words. 'I liked her a lot,' says Redford. 'I found her very talented, intelligent, insecure and untrusting. Untrusting because she's been told too many lies, she's been hustled, misled, used and jounced by too many hangers-on and hucksters.'

Gardiner's choice is Barbra Streisand, but the marriage is too
fraught to last.

When the film opened in America in October, 1973, no critical
doubts could keep the public from queuing round the block, much to
the astonishment of the protagonists. One of the first in line was Lola
Redford. She'd heard plenty of moans about how bad it was from her
husband but, when she returned to the Fifth Avenue apartment, she
proved to be a very accurate barometer of the nation's taste. 'It's a very
moving picture, Bob,' she summed up, 'and your work is terrific in it.'
'You're kidding,' he replied, but she wasn't.

Redford himself was more in tune with the critics who found the
artificial marriage between romantic love and politics hard to handle. 'I
think it was trying to bring in too much,' he comments. 'It was an
interesting device, but it was neither here nor there. It was just a device
to break up their marriage. I think the movie could have been achieved
without it.' Predictably Streisand took a more personal view. 'I'm tired
of seeing them take the best scenes out of my movies and turning them
into nothing much,' she has said of *The Way We Were*.

Redford's friend and neighbour, Richard Schickel, more than cor-
roborated the actor's point of view in *Time*. 'If this ill-written, wretch-
edly performed and tediously directed film may be said to have a central

flaw, it probably lies in its reckless violation of a bit of conventional theatrical wisdom: when you call a lot of attention to a gun on the wall in Act One, it had better go off – loudly – by the end of the evening. The weapon everyone is pointing at, here, is politics, specifically left-wing popular front politics in the 1940s.' That's just for openers. He goes on to say that 'no one, least of all director Pollack, seems to have the faintest idea of the way we really were, spiritually and intellectually, in a testing, fascinating time of transition. The ideas and issues, and above all the human passions that arose out of them, are quite simply missing from this slick, cold and gutless work.'

Esquire described the screenplay as 'sheer, piddling hokum' but, as so often happens, Pauline Kael came closest: '*The Way We Were* is a fluke – a torpedoed ship full of gaping holes which comes snugly into port.' After listing the gaping holes which range from ugly cinematography, a whining title ballad, an excruciating score and a number of dishonest plot devices, she admits that it is enjoyable and puts her finger on the reason why. 'It stays afloat because of the chemistry between Barbra Streisand and Robert Redford. The movie is about two people who are wrong for each other, and Streisand and Redford are an ideal match to play this mismatch . . . We can see what draws them to each other: she's attracted to the fairy tale prince in him, and he can't tear himself away from her emotionality, from her wistfulness and drive.'

And stay afloat it did, earning thirty-four million dollars in its first three months at the box office and holding its place as one of Columbia's all-time big three earners until overtaken by inflation in the eighties. In the days before the Academicians put the hex on her for what they see as her tyrannical ways, Streisand's performance won her an Oscar nomination for Best Actress. However she'd already picked up a statuette for her first film, *Funny Girl*, in 1970 and had to give best this time to Glenda Jackson in *A Touch of Class*. Redford had his supporters for *The Way We Were*, but found himself nominated – for the first and only time as an actor – for *The Sting* instead.

More significantly in so far as his personal life was concerned, he was named *World Film Favourite* jointly with Streisand by the *Hollywood Foreign Press Association*. And the world agreed, proclaiming him the number one sex symbol. Before *The Way We Were*, he'd controlled his remarkable looks to create an image of the thinking man's troubled hero; after it, he was the lusting woman's crumpet. This is partly because *The Way We Were* is a woman's film in that it fulfils female fantasies: Barbra Streisand is no beauty, yet through sheer personality she gets this gorgeous man not only to go to bed with her, but to marry her. If she can do it, there's hope for all of us.

This was not what the film makers had in mind, but lust will be lust, as Gavin Miller noted in the *Listener* when the film opened in London in February, 1974. 'We are meant to believe that his is the greater loss, that character and beliefs are not only insuperable despite love, but that in the long run they count for more. We are meant to believe that that's what the film is telling us. But all the while it is really telling us: don't believe it. He may be hopeless but he's wonderful. So he doesn't care about the Hollywood Ten. Never mind. His smile is magic.' Alexander Walker, writing in the *Evening Standard*, was even more certain as to where the film's true attraction lay. 'Redford, with a tummy so flat you could use it as an occasional table for a wine glass (as he does) and hair so blond you could turn it into cereal and eat it for breakfast, is just lovely,' he drooled.

Redford too noted his dangerous change of status. It was after *The Way We Were* that two middle-aged women spotted him as he waited for the lights to change at the corner of Fifth Avenue and 82nd Street just a few blocks down from his New York apartment. As he was on the way to the dentist, he was in an introspective mood but even so he couldn't fail to notice that they were transformed into giggling adolescents. When the traffic slowed, one dashed across the street and demanded, 'Are you Robert Redford?' 'Only when I'm alone,' he replied.

'Yeah,' he says world wearily. 'It did make a difference. I noticed it first in print. I was being labelled a romantic symbol and in many ways it cut into my ability to be persuasive in other types of roles. I think it's hurt the acting part of my career. And a lot of these articles paint this unreal picture of me as some kind of god. I'm a human being with the same problems and bad aspects as everyone else. I don't like to think about it and I don't pay too much attention to it. One thing it has unquestionably done is create great problems of privacy.'

Hollywood being Hollywood, there was always going to be money in the bank for a second collaboration between Redford, Newman and George Roy Hill. Redford had already accepted Hill's proposal that he should play *The Great Waldo Pepper* but, as the film had to be made during the summer months, both men had a gap to fill when the cameras stopped turning on *The Way We Were*. Meanwhile Hill had received a script called *The Sting* from one David S. Ward. Initially he didn't think much of it beyond the fact that there was an obvious role in it for Redford. True to form, the actor had already read it and turned it down, mostly because he believed at the time that Ward was set to direct it. As he had reservations about the over complex plot, he didn't want to put himself in the hands of a first-timer but as soon as he was told the writer had been replaced by Hill, he agreed to go ahead.

The Sting, as originally written, was the story of the kid and the slob, respectively Johnny Hooker and Henry Gondorff, two mini-league con artists working out of Chicago in 1936. They meet in a brothel after

Hooker's first partner, Luther Coleman, is killed by rival gangsters. By way of avenging his death, they set up an elaborate hustle involving a one-million dollar bet on a horse-race and engineer their own 'deaths' to avoid future pursuit.

Hill's problem was that Hooker and Gondorff were not parts of equal size and weight. Hooker was very much the lead role, while Gondorff was the side-kick, and a 'burly oafish' side-kick at that. Hill believed there was no way Paul Newman, the senior partner in *Butch Cassidy*, was going to accept that. When the two men met over lunch in New York and Newman complained that the director was making a film with Redford but with no role in it for him, Hill told him so, adding 'read it if you want and see for yourself'.

Newman didn't like what he saw but Hill, inspired by the spirit of devilry that underpinned his relationship with the actor, decided to needle him. 'I started telling him it was a great part for him and why didn't he do it. I was probably trying to gain points with him later so I could say, "Look, you turned down that great part in *The Sting*."' No one was more surprised than he when Newman called back to say he'd decided to accept Gondorff. Disguising his embarrassment as best he could, Hill called an outraged Redford to arrange a three-way meeting. Newman spent most of it going through actors who would be more suitable than him and it was Hill who finally broke the stalemate. 'What the hell are we thinking about?' he asked. 'The part can be played as a river-boat gambler. This isn't a classic. We enjoy working together. Let's just do it.'

So they did. Hill lined up a high-class supporting cast: James Earl Jones shared the early scenes with Redford as the con man on the brink of retirement; Robert Shaw added his considerable weight and talent to Doyle Lonnegan, the major-league gangster who gets his come-uppance at the hands of Hooker and Gondorff; and the excellent and estimable Charles Durning plays Lonnegan's tame bent cop. Women were even more conspicuous by their absence this time around. Those who do appear have a purely ornamental function: the men use and discard them as readily as a glass of bourbon, boosting their own image as slick operators and tough guys in the process. This was the bra-burning era, but the increasing awareness of women's lib certainly didn't rub off on *The Sting*.

Filming went ahead in the spirit of light-hearted fun that had characterised *Butch Cassidy*, with the crucial difference that Redford's new status put him on a nearly equal footing with Newman. Five years earlier, it had been a case of Newman first and the rest nowhere as the journalist Ivor Davis recalls. 'I'd come to Cuernavaca to talk to Paul Newman on the set of his new film when a pudgy Hollywood publicist sidled up to me at breakfast and whispered, "Look, you'd do me a great favour if you'd have a word with Newman's partner. You don't have to write anything." I sat down under an olive tree and chatted with a handsome young actor in sweat-stained Western garb with several days of beard growth and we made pleasant conversation for half an hour or so.'

By the time *The Sting* came around, interviewers were queuing up for both actors and the financial gap had narrowed to the point at which Newman received a 500,000 dollar fee plus a percentage of the gross while Redford received a straight 500,000 dollars. This gave him a better licence to complain which he seems to have used freely but amicably. The chief bone of contention was that he had to carry the plot, a necessary task as its labyrinthine complexity meant that it had to be constantly explained. Redford was required to say things like, 'you meet me at the corner of Ninth and Fifth and I'll telephone the guy at Eighth and Sixth and then we'll cross the street and the bell will ring four times . . .' and so on. 'It's not acting,' he yelled. 'Every time I come on there's a five minute pause while I tell the audience what the hell is going on.' Meanwhile Newman, with no burden of explanation to carry, sat around looking smug.

Conmen don't come much cockier than Johnny Hooker in *The Sting* (1973).

Redford did it because he believes that Hill is a great storyteller. 'If he has a good story, his work is inclined to be better. He doesn't go in as much for character study as other directors, like Pollack. He's very demanding, a tremendous disciplinarian and a taskmaster. That becomes stimulating in itself, working for someone who's constantly challenging you to do the job as well as it can be done. The implication with George is that it can always be done better. He runs a very professional set. As a matter of fact, it's like being in a bomber squadron.'

Given the zany nature of the on-screen activities, it is hardly surprising that the practical jokes continued off it. The best-known of the extra-curricular *Sting* hustles was set up by Redford. When he spotted a wrecked Porsche lying by the roadside, he bought it and had it delivered to his co-star. Newman returned the compliment by having it compacted and delivering the metal block to the Redford home, ingeniously circumnavigating the security system along the way. 'Although he appreciated it,' he wrote, 'Mr. Newman is returning this gift to you because he cannot get the mother-fucker started.' Redford turned the tables again by swearing his family to secrecy and refusing to admit that he'd received the compacted car.

During shooting, those connected with *The Sting* believed they were making a filler, a caper comedy with a colander plot that would appeal, if at all, to men who'd never grown up. When it was finished, they learned they had something more: a multiple Oscar winner – *The Sting* took Best Picture, Best Director and five other awards – and a box-office hit. Redford quite liked *The Sting*, but doubted that he should have been nominated as Best Actor when Newman wasn't. Nor did he rate the Oscar ceremonies very highly at that stage in his career, so giving best to Jack Lemmon in *Save the Tiger* didn't faze him too much.

'It seemed like an awful lot of extravagance for nothing. And the awards were always being won by people who had done better work before or did better work later. The Oscars just reflect the opinion of Academy members. The guy who wins an award for a foot-race gets it because he was the fastest guy on that track on that day. That's the only kind of race I have any respect for. To a certain extent, I was honoured because I realise there are people who do care about the awards. But when I didn't win, I was relieved. I just didn't deserve it.'

The success of *The Sting* was remarkable because Hill aspired to nothing more than repeating the *Butch Cassidy* formula of getting the audience to support two lovable criminals. The film is designed to appeal to emotionally retarded males of all ages as sure as *The Way We Were* is designed to appeal to the fantasies of women of all ages. It panders shamelessly to the notion that men may need women to cook and sew and screw, but they are at their happiest and their most dynamic with other men. In other words, it encourages all men to be as Neanderthal as most of them would like to be.

Newman and Redford represent male pair-bonding at its most seductive. Their only genuinely sympathetic quality is their loyalty to each other but they win friends and influence people by bucking authority, a fashionable thing to do in the aftermath of the freewheeling sixties. They feed off one another by tricking their adversaries and treating women like dirt. On paper, they are reprehensible; on celluloid, no red-blooded male can fail to wish he was out there with them. And that includes Redford himself, a thirty-five-year-old 'little boy' at heart. 'Once you lose that, you might as well wrap it up,' he said at the time. 'I enjoy being with children. I get mad at them but they're so much fun. Adulthood has never appealed to me much. Growing up is losing your freedom.'

The reviewers were quick to finger *The Sting* as male bait. 'This isn't a movie, it's a recipe,' wrote *Time*'s Jay Cocks. 'The people who put *The Sting* together followed the instructions on the *Butch Cassidy* package: one Paul Newman, one Robert Redford, a dash of caper. Stir in the same director, if available. He was. *Butch Cassidy* may not have been very good, but it made a bundle, so what difference does it make? Newman and Redford pass a few facial expressions between them and try to cool each other out. If there ever was much of a script, it can be said to have gone to waste.'

In fact, there wasn't, as Vincent Canby noted in the *New York Times*. '*The Sting* looks and sounds like a musical comedy from which the songs have been removed, leaving only a background score of old-fashioned, toe-tapping piano rags that as easily evoke the pre-World War I teens as the 1930s.' Faulty history or not, he allowed himself to be seduced as did most of his colleagues with the exception of the perceptive Mr. Cocks. '*The Sting*,' he continued, 'was not made to be taken seriously, but many people may find it difficult even to enjoy the movie casually. It lacks the elements that could give it a true drive: a sense of an urban underworld, or of the Depression that sucked so many people into it; an understanding of the con man's pathology that goes beyond surface style and patter; a story that depends not on plot twists but on characters. The movie ends up with a lot of expensive sets and a screenful of blue eyes.'

Perhaps Redford can be excused his juvenile *joie de vivre* over *The Sting* on the grounds of entertainment, but it is much harder to understand why he made *The Great Waldo Pepper*. Again it reunited three *Butch Cassidy* majors: Redford himself, writer William Goldman and director George Roy Hill. This was something of a pet project for Hill. As a dedicated amateur pilot, he had long been fascinated by the barn-stormers of the twenties who scraped a precarious living out of giving dare-devil aerobatic displays.

Waldo Pepper is such a man. Unlike Johnny Hooker, who is little more than a charming cipher, he has lots of character, most of it bad. He has two major ambitions: to perform the 'outside loop' and to outfly Ernst Kessler, a German ace from World War I. He is duplicitous, competitive and thoroughly amoral. When he finds opposition on what he sees as his patch, he sabotages his rival's plane, then steals the money he has ostensibly collected for his medical fund. On the positive side, he is kind to small boys who are hooked on flying. It is not enough.

The Great Waldo Pepper is not a buddy-buddy movie, but it is male-bait nonetheless. It fits in the genre of noble confrontation with xenophobic overtones: the cream of America versus the cream of Germany, and may the best man win. It is the kind of movie in which the adversaries respect each other, a gladiatorial contest between opponents who are worthy of each other's steel. There can, of course, be only one winner – Waldo, the American hero – but the loser gets to keep his dignity. When the battle is over, he salutes the victor in the traditional way and is saluted in his turn. In common with most Redford characters, Waldo speaks out dogmatically against authority in the belief that he is too special to submit to it. 'Are you going to license the clouds?' he demands angrily when he is told to get a permit.

Redford says he made *The Great Waldo Pepper* for fun. 'It has no message. It should be very entertaining and have a sense of style, adventure and romance,' he commented, but the reality of being flown around in small aeroplanes was less amusing than he'd imagined. Hill had taken him up in his own plane before the picture started and performed every aerobatic stunt he knew with Redford cheering him on. 'He was really freaked on it,' the director remarked. However, getting the stunts and the climactic Pepper–Kessler dogfight in the can posed all sorts of problems.

As Redford was no flyer, the planes he had to be seen to be in control of had to be flown by licensed pilots. To keep them out of shot, they were tucked under the machine-guns which meant they were flying blind. Meanwhile Redford sat tall in the rear cockpit, apparently lord of the Texan skies. 'I knew pretty well what the limits were,' Hill explained, 'and we went right up to the limits of being safe. I didn't ask anyone to do anything I wouldn't have done myself. I did go out on the wing of the plane and stand up in the back cockpit, not so much to prove that it could be done, but to prove that the camera angle would work and that the angles were right.'

In fact he went over the limits on at least two occasions: one pilot was injured in a crash and the veteran Frank Tallman, the air sequences supervisor, was fortunate to survive when his plane flew into high-

The Great Waldo Pepper (1975) at work.

tension cables. Redford himself was luckier. He walked on the wing of a plane flying at 3,000 feet above the ground and emerged unscathed and something of a real-life hero in the media. 'I felt incredible freedom but then I thought, what am I doing here?' Tallman, who'd worked with the greats of derring-do, was impressed. 'He's the gutsiest guy I've ever worked with. Not even Doug Fairbanks walked the wing of a plane in flight!'

Hill said the walk was necessary on grounds of realism, but that he cut to a stuntman as soon as Redford was established on the wing so as not to push his luck. On another occasion, when the actor appears to stand on the edge of the wing to transfer to another plane, Redford is standing in the back cockpit. The camera angle did the rest. Redford has said that he was 'cosmically terrified' but Hill's view is that he was uneasy rather than nervous, and that because he knew he couldn't get the plane down if anything happened to the pilot. 'This feeling of helplessness kind of spooked him because he always likes to be in control. Mind you, I could have made an entire movie if I'd counted the number of minutes it used to take for him to get from his dressing-room to the plane. He'd conduct business, pick out a scarf, try on four pairs of gloves, using every device possible to avoid the moment when he had to get into the airplane. But he did it, and my hat's off to him for it.'

Off set he made sure he had a good time by using his motel room in San Marcos, Texas, as an office and spending his nights on a private ranch outside the town. 'I wouldn't stay in a motel,' he comments. 'I'd rather sleep in a tent. Making one movie after another is bad. Your ass is dragging at night, you can't read, you don't meet people, you don't get into what's happening in the world. You begin to get dumb and dull because there's no real input. So I try, when I'm filming at least, to get a piece of the place I'm in. I like being here in this raw country meeting real people – that's meaningful – instead of being shut up with the company in an incestuous existence.'

Only Richard Schickel of the major American critics has anything positive to say about *The Great Waldo Pepper*. He enjoyed its flamboyance and found it 'eminently satisfying as a spectacle'. He also admired Hill's dedication to authenticity. Meanwhile Pauline Kael

In discussion with director George Roy Hill for *The Great Waldo Pepper*.

continued with her anti-Redford campaign. 'I can't tell if Americans will like this movie, but I think Hitler would have drunk a toast to it. It's a paean to purification through heroism, with the heroes fighting for the love of fighting and to determine who is the better man. Waldo and Kessler salute each other like lovers, and ram each other's plane.' She went on to describe the fruits of Waldo's victory as a 'choice bit of homoeroticism', which allegedly resulted in a sharp rebuke from Hill beginning, 'Listen, you bitch . . .' Ms. Kael was not amused.

Variety concluded that Hill had 'laboured mightily to produce a comparative mouse', and it was left to Liz Smith, always one of Redford's most ardent fans, to put the female point of view in *Cosmopolitan*. 'He is almost too blond, too beautiful, too good to be true. Sure, this movie is gossamer, romantic fluff for those of us who admire Redford's considerable acting talents. Meantime, *Waldo Pepper* gives you an evening of Redford. What's not to like?' The public found plenty and stayed at home.

9

A Doomed Romance

When times are bad, it is only natural to search through the archives for the glorious past as an antidote to the dismal present. By 1970, American morale was beginning to buckle under the twin swords of Vietnam and Richard Nixon, making the time more than ripe for a good wallow in nostalgia. And what could be more nostalgic than the glittering lifestyle of Long Island millionaires at the height of the Jazz Age in the early twenties. This was the world captured by F. Scott Fitzgerald in *The Great Gatsby*, a novel about top echelon class distinctions in an era noted for conspicuous consumption. No matter that Fitzgerald was no plot maker, no matter that his glamour was illusory, a thin veil that does little to conceal his despair at the human condition: America loved him and Hollywood had always had its eye on him.

The Great Gatsby, with its scope for exotic visuals, was potentially a particularly succulent plum. Experience however had suggested otherwise: two films made from it had been failures and, by 1971, it was generally regarded as unfilmable. The silent version had come out in 1926, shortly after the book was published, with Lois Wilson as Daisy Buchanan and Warner Baxter as Gatsby. Shot in a Long Island mansion during a July heatwave in four to five weeks with Fitzgerald in attendance on occasion, it bombed. The only print in existence today is in the archives in Moscow. The film was made by the Famous Players-Lasky Corporation which changed its name to Paramount Publix Corporation in 1930 and to Paramount Pictures Corporation in 1936.

It was Paramount who tried again in 1949. This time they made a black and white talkie, with Alan Ladd in the title role and Betty Field as Daisy. 'Rather bland and uninteresting attempt to accommodate a unique author to a formula star,' was Leslie Halliwell's assessment, and the audiences agreed with him. Twice bitten, once shy might have been their reaction to a third bite of the plum had it not been for Ali

MacGraw, an indifferent actress who'd made a huge impact as the mortally ill heroine of *Love Story*. More importantly, she was a Scott Fitzgerald freak and she was married to Robert Evans, the head of production at Paramount. She laboured under the huge illusion that she was born to play Daisy Buchanan and Paramount, fat on the back of two blockbusters, *Love Story* (84 million dollars) and *The Godfather* (145 million dollars) could afford to pick up the tab.

Bob Evans is in the record books as saying, 'The making of a blockbuster is the newest art form of the twentieth century,' and he certainly set out to prove it with *Gatsby*, which he saw as the third leg of a personal Triple Crown. His initial move was to ask Broadway producer David Merrick to re-acquire the film rights his company had let slip through its fingers after the 1949 fiasco. 'I want to do this picture for Ali,' said Evans in 1970, 'and I think you have the class to do it properly. And, of course, you're a friend of Scottie's.'

This was relevant because the rights to the book had reverted to Fitzgerald's only daughter, Scottie Smith. She was willing to deal but competition from, among others, Robert Redford and Ray Stark had already been alerted by the time Merrick got to her. It took him eighteen months and 350,000 dollars plus a generous percentage of the gross (instead of the 130,000 dollars he'd planned) to pin her down. It was the beginning of an uphill struggle on every front: financial, artistic, even meteorological.

The next step was to adapt the novel for the screen, a job that initially went to Truman Capote. He certainly brought a personal perspective to it by making Nick Carraway and Jordan Baker homosexual. When Paramount rejected this interpretation, he sued them, eventually settling out of court for 110,000 dollars. The studio then turned to Francis Ford Coppola, their golden boy in the aftermath of *The Godfather*, and he delivered a faithful, even reverential dramatisation in three weeks. The price tag was 150,000 dollars.

By this time Merrick, producing his second film following acclaim for the Broadway musicals, *Fanny*, *Gypsy* and *Hello Dolly*, was beginning to find out what he'd got himself into. Initially his problems centred around the deeply unpopular Ali MacGraw. Peter Bogdanovich, Arthur Penn and Mike Nichols, all hot tickets at the time, refused to direct the film if MacGraw played Daisy, forcing Evans to look across the Atlantic for an alternative. His choice was the Englishman, Jack Clayton, who'd made five well-respected films including *The Pumpkin Eater*, *The Innocents* and *Room At The Top*. However he hadn't worked for seven years and there were always doubts as to whether a foreigner could capture Gatsby's quintessentially American spirit. Nevertheless Clayton was signed for 315,000 dollars, given casting approval, and promised a free hand.

Paramount's first choice for the lead was Warren Beatty who had considered producing Gatsby himself five years earlier. Ironically he'd offered Evans, then an actor, the title role. Now he turned it down himself unless Ali MacGraw was prepared to take the smaller part of Jordan Baker. Jack Nicholson made a similar proviso but Evans was adamant. 'There was no equivocating,' he stated later. 'My wife was going to play Daisy.'

In any case, he believed he knew where to look next: ex-Godfather Marlon Brando was as bankable as ever. What matter that he was approaching fifty when Gatsby was thirty-one. Fortunately the actor, still smarting over what he saw as an inadequate percentage for *The Godfather*, demanded an exorbitant fee plus percentage deal this time. 'Marlon wanted the moon and the stars,' Evans recalls. 'I told him we didn't have that kind of budget and he said, "Well, take a slice of *Godfather*".'

Redford was the next actor approached and the hunt stopped there. He had committed supporters in David Merrick and Jack Clayton who considered him perfect casting after a brief meeting at Heathrow Airport. 'He is absolutely ideal for the part,' he commented. 'He has the right characteristics. Gatsby just happens to be set in the twenties. The true substance of the story concerns a brave strong man with enormous charm and energy who, unfortunately, directs all his talents

A grimly determined Jay Gatsby on the road with Nick Carraway (Sam Waterston).

towards one woman. Gatsby falls for Daisy, but she belongs to one class, a class he could never, ever belong to himself.'

Evans alone had his doubts. 'What about Steve McQueen?' he asked Merrick and Clayton at one point. In a climate of wild rumours about the MacGraw–McQueen romance even then gathering momentum on the Texan location for *The Getaway*, the two men could only stand and stare. It fell to Clayton to break the embarrassed silence. 'No, McQueen cannot speak the language,' he said firmly. 'I guess the easiest man to con is a con man,' Evans admitted later. 'I didn't believe the rumours.'

He didn't have to wait long for confirmation. The next development came from McQueen himself: he wouldn't allow MacGraw to play Daisy unless he played Gatsby. When the answer was no, the third Mrs. Robert Evans filed for divorce. *The Great Gatsby* went on the back burner in May, 1972, earning Jack Clayton a further 100,000 dollars for the delay. After two months of negotiation, Paramount paid MacGraw a $1 release fee and the hunt for the new Daisy was on. Actresses who were normally too grand to test queued for the privilege, among them Candice Bergen, Katharine Ross and Faye Dunaway who spent four hours with her own make-up man and hairdresser preparing for the brief ordeal. The only actress to turn down the opportunity was Tuesday Weld but heads were still being scratched all round when a cable came from London. Addressed to Evans, it read, 'Dear Bob, may I be your Daisy?'

Clayton tested Mia Farrow in London with the results that satisfied everyone concerned. 'She brought a mystical quality, a kind of spoiled arrogance, which made her especially interesting,' said Evans. Merrick approved of her 'aristocratic look', and Clayton found her appropriately 'vulnerable and fragile'. Charles Bluhdorn, the President of Gulf + Western who owned Paramount, provided a minor hiatus by asking, 'Farrow, Farrow, what has she done before?' It was hardly an edifying question as the actress had helped the studio to its current prosperity by her performance in *Rosemary's Baby* in 1968.

Once Bluhdorn was overruled and Farrow was signed for 100,000 dollars the rest of the cast fell into place quite quickly. Bruce Dern was paid 75,000 dollars to play Tom Buchanan, the rich, philandering husband Daisy chose above Gatsby during World War I. Sam Waterston took on the narrator Nick Carraway, with Lois Chiles as Jordan Baker, Karen Black as Buchanan's mistress, Myrtle Wilson, Scott Wilson as her cuckolded husband, and Howard da Silva, who'd played Wilson in the 1949 film, as Gatsby's mysterious business partner, 'the man who fixed the 1919 World Series'.

Redford, signed before *The Way We Were* and *The Sting* had established him as a major box-office star, received 250,000 dollars for Gatsby. From the start he had his doubts about the studio's attitude to the project – 'The fact that they approached Marlon really makes you wonder. Didn't anyone at Paramount read the novel?' – but he wanted Gatsby so badly that he was prepared to overrule them. 'He is not fleshed out in the book, and the implied parts of his character are fascinating. It was a chance to elude a stereotyped image,' he explained. But he recognised the problems too. Fitzgerald wrote that Gatsby 'simply didn't talk like a real person'. Redford saw this as a challenge but he knew that if the film went wrong, it would be his neck in the noose.

Given the turbulence surrounding the pre-production on Gatsby, it wasn't surprising that things failed to run smoothly when the cameras began to turn in June, 1973. The events in the novel take place in East and West Egg, twin peninsulas facing each other across Long Island Sound. East Egg housed old money in opulent mansions with lawns sweeping down to private docks on the water's edge, while the *nouveaux riches* spent their summers in rented cottages on West Egg. The social gulf is unbridgable and those who dare are doomed: the millionaire Gatsby just as surely as Myrtle Wilson, married to a garage mechanic but upwardly mobile thanks to her affair with Tom Buchanan. In this corner of Fitzgerald's world, only the privileged survive.

Paramount's location scouts started their search in Long Island, but discovered that the pockets of exclusivity such as the Guggenheim's Falaise estate were surrounded by creeping suburbia on the land and oil rigs in the Sound. Moving north to Rhode Island, they found everything they wanted for the exteriors but failed to note that the weather is reliably wet throughout June and July. So it came about that *The Great Gatsby*, ostensibly set in a long hot summer of discontent, was lashed day and night by Cape Cod rain and filmed by a crew wearing rubberised khaki macs from Japan.

Key members of the production including Clayton, Redford, Farrow and Dern, got themselves a taste of old money by renting cottages on the nearby Hammersmith Farm estate owned by the celebrated Auchincloss family, the mother and stepfather of Jackie Onassis. The crew was housed in Newport at the Sheraton Hotel or the Viking, universally nicknamed 'The Viper's'. Redford brought his family in for the summer vacation and spent much of his spare time walking around with blonde three-year-old Amy on his shoulders. 'Daughter hell,' said one journalist, embittered at being denied an audience. 'He got that kid from rent-a-child to keep the press off his back.'

Such comments were typical of the acrimony which marked the making of *Gatsby*. Much of it stemmed from Paramount's decision to protect its six-million dollar investment by mounting an unprecedented worldwide publicity campaign. It all began when the Japanese designer, Kenzo Takada, revealed '*le style tennis*' at the Paris Collections in 1972. His flannel pants and sweaters with striped borders were seen by

Frank Yablans, the thrusting Paramount president, as the perfect peg on which to hang the 'Gatsbyisation' of America. There was nothing that Yablans, the son of a Brooklyn taxi driver who'd first gone to work as a chicken plucker at the age of twelve, didn't know about hype and he gave *The Great Gatsby* his best shot.

Stage one was persuading *Women's Wear Daily*, America's fashion bible, to change '*le style tennis*' into 'The Gatsby Look', in order to inspire a rash of fashion shows and imitators in stores across the country. Stage two involved product tie-ins, valued at six million dollars, the same as the film cost to make. The plan was to put *Gatsby* in every Main Street, but at someone else's expense. 'I figured we could get twenty million dollars in paid publicity from someone else's budgets,' was how Yablans put it.

There was no shortage of manufacturers wanting to be 'Gatsbyised', but only those who reached an acceptable level of taste and, more importantly, could put their money where their mouths were, got the go ahead. In the end four out of well over a dozen applicants were accepted: '21' Brands, the makers of Ballantine Scotch and the only firm recruited directly by Paramount; Glemby International which had a chain of five hundred hairdressers; a men's sportswear manufacturer called Robert Bruce; and E. I. Du Pont for their classic white Teflon cookware 'in the tradition of *The Great Gatsby*'. 'I think Daddy would have loved being a Teflon pan more than anything else,' joked Scottie Smith, but not entirely without bitterness.

The manufacturers were paid off as cheaply as possible. Though Gatsby's showcase kitchen is stocked with gleaming copper pans rather than Teflon, the film gives it a good deal more exposure than might seem warranted in a story about the super rich. '21' Brands were allowed to mount a 350,000-dollar advertising campaign promoting the notion of Ballantines as the 'in' drink at Gatsby's parties – illegally of course as these took place during Prohibition. Robert Bruce might have guessed they'd be knocking their heads against a brick wall when they asked Redford to model their 'Gatsby's Times' range, but it didn't stop them trying. 'Drape me in a suit like a *Vogue* model? No way!' was the indignant response.

However, the company was allowed to shoot the advertisements in the Newport locations. In return, it gave tickets to the movie as prizes in the 'Gatsby Man' contests it sponsored in its 400 department store outlets. Glemby, too, had little luck with the stars: Farrow's blonde marcelled wig hardly puts hairdressing in a good light. However, they ran 'Gatsby cut' promotions in all their salons and Du Pont, with displays of the book, the record and the film about the making of the film, did the rest. By the time Gatsby hit the screens, there was no one who didn't know about it.

An automatic corollary of these proceedings was that every journalist in the world was asked to come onto the Gatsby set. Most were refused but some resorted to disguises to get through the security, and, one way and another, it was a hassle all the way. 'It was like being in a strait-jacket for eighteen weeks,' was Redford's exasperated comment on these proceedings.

In most respects, the filming went pretty smoothly though there were occasional flare-ups between Merrick, who liked to offer suggestions, and Clayton, who certainly didn't want to hear them. There was also the surprise announcement that Farrow, then married to conductor André Previn, was pregnant, a problem for the hard-pressed wardrobe department which had to add concealing frills as the weeks passed. The gutter press created a feud between Redford and Farrow. 'How do you kiss a man you can't stand? Every time a love scene came up, I had to bite my tongue. He thinks he's the greatest actor in the world, that he knows everything and anyone else is inferior,' she was reported as saying in the *Sun*. The paper also suggested that Redford was upset by her pregnancy and that he didn't bother to conceal the fact that he thought she was 'a lousy actress'. Farrow won a libel action against the *Sun* for these inventions, collecting her legal costs and an undisclosed sum in damages.

Redford dyed his hair brown for Gatsby, the only time he has ever wavered from his spectacular natural colouring. 'I wasn't happy about it, but in retrospect I think it was a good idea because it helped me feel slightly awkward, and an important part of Gatsby's character, it seems to me, was his awkwardness – and the attempts he made to conceal it.'

The film's most opulent scenes, the elaborate parties in the Gatsby mansion, take place at night which meant forgathering every evening as darkness fell and working through till dawn. Rosecliffe, an elegant white-pillared house built in shameless imitation of the Petit Trianon at Versailles for the Oelrich family in 1900, was chosen for these revelries. The extras were recruited from the plutocratic ranks of the summer residents through ads in the local paper: between 250 and 500 worked for twenty dollars a night, but most would have gladly done it for nothing. Farrow and Chiles, wearing Twenties jewels hired from Cartier and insured for 89,000 dollars, were comprehensively matched by 'guests' with 'old money' who raided their own safes for the occasion. 'Must be forty billion dollar's worth of extras working on the set tonight,' David Merrick remarked. 'Absolutely not,' said one of the locals. 'I doubt if there's more than twenty-five billion dollars at the most!'

As the loss of a night's shooting would have cost Paramount 53,000 dollars, the cameras turned no matter how wet it was. The Gatsby banquets were supplied by Rex Galvin, a local restaurateur who was instructed to create a 'sumptuous feast', no expense spared. He took his instructions literally by using 200 pounds of beef, 400 pounds of fish, unlimited lobsters and oysters, suckling pigs, roast turkeys, succulent hambone and legs of lamb, all of it glazed and garnished in an elaborate display of bad taste. The food was sprayed each night to keep the insects away but by the end of the week, the smell was noxious. Anyone standing downwind was apt to demand 'What died? What died?' while burying his nose in his handkerchief.

Everything else was on the same scale. Out of a total wardrobe of 1900 outfits, Farrow had thirty costumes and Redford twenty. The cars, hired through advertisements in papers across the country, were worth a fortune in their own right. Gatsby's is yellow, Jordan Baker's cherry red, but they were all driven by their owners who preferred to dress up as chauffeurs rather than allow strangers behind the wheels of their most treasured possessions. When shooting finished in Rhode Island, the cast and crew shipped over to Britain to do the interiors at Pinewood, a trip that saved an estimated 1,500,000 dollars thanks both to lower costs and a favourable exchange rate.

Redford has never been particularly at home in England. He did hitch-hike round the country as part of his grand European tour, ending up in prison for the night after winning a yard-of-ale contest in a pub in

The domestic Gatsby winding up his gramophone and surfeiting on shirts.

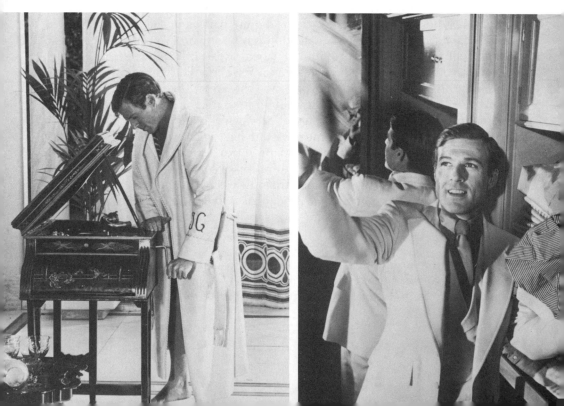

Berwick-on-Tweed, but the country has never impressed him as much as Spain, Italy, France and Greece have done. At Pinewood, he kept himself aloof from the natives, even refusing to use a British stand-in, and he is not remembered with any warmth by fellow workers who found him stand-offish and unco-operative.

So too did Paramount: when the hype reached a climax as *The Great Gatsby* opened in New York in March, 1974, Redford was notable by his absence. The première was followed by a benefit dinner-dance at the Waldorf Hotel for The Boys Club of New York attended by 950 guests, many of them Manhattan socialites, dressed in Twenties *haute couture*. Peter Duchin's orchestra piped Twenties tunes and the Waldorf displayed its best goldplate tableware, last used when Queen Elizabeth visited the city a decade earlier. Champagne, caviare, breast of pheasant and hot apple charlotte were served to the guests by waiters in tail coats and white gloves.

It was a slightly nerve-racking occasion for the principals, especially David Merrick and Robert Evans whose mutual admiration hadn't survived the *Gatsby* vicissitudes. In years to come, Merrick would sue Paramount for the 7,500,000 dollars he claimed the studio owed him as his percentage of the film's gross. Now he contented himself with glaring at his adversary across a barrier of white roses as they sat at adjoining tables. Meanwhile Charles Bluhdorn and Frank Yablans made merry at the top one. The bill for this lavish bash was picked up by Paramount. 'Take the Waldorf bill, pay it, don't say anything about it. I don't want to hear another thing about it,' said Gordon Weaver, the studio's Vice-President, in charge of publicity. 'Well worth it', was his verdict when the press notices came in.

Jack Clayton, Francis Ford Coppola, Sam Waterston, Karen Black, Bruce Dern and Scott Wilson attended, but Redford and Farrow did not, further angering David Merrick. Stars who refused to make personal appearances on behalf of their pictures should be penalised, he said the next day, adding, 'They should forfeit their percentages. Such provisions should be in their contracts.'

With *Gatsby*, that was hardly necessary because they never got any percentages. By the time the film opened, the Gatsbyisation programme had resulted in 18.6 million dollars in advance bookings, so ensuring that it was profitable before anyone saw it. This comprehensively justified Paramount's opulent campaign: without it, *The Great Gatsby* would have been a financial disaster. As it was, it was widely judged to be an artistic one by critics who may have been embittered by the massive publicity.

'The film is faithful to the letter of F. Scott Fitzgerald's novel but entirely misses its spirit,' wrote Jay Cocks in *Time*. 'Much of Fitzgerald's prose has been preserved, especially in Nick Carraway's narration, but it only gives the film a stilted, stuffy tone that is reinforced by the dialogue. Fitzgerald wrote dialogue to be read, not said: and the Coppola screenplay (much rejuggled by director Clayton) treats Fitzgerald's lines with untoward reverence.' He goes on to criticise the film for its length, its lavish clumsiness and for its failure to capture the novel's tough-minded, hard-edged social insights.

He reserves his harshest words for Mia Farrow – 'a catastrophe' – and some of his kinder ones for her co-star. 'Redford does not have the mystery or the rough edge required for the role, but he is surprisingly good at conveying Gatsby's uneasiness. The social graces are not natural to him. He has a tenuous poise, a mask that falls away when he is introduced to Daisy's small daughter or when Nick pays him a sincere compliment which makes him, for the first time, smile genuinely. Redford also has a sense of Gatsby's obsession. His look of longing, fulfilment and hopelessness when he sees Daisy for the first time has, momentarily, the depth of passion that the movie never achieves again.'

In Britain, the major critics disagreed with each other over Redford and most other aspects of *The Great Gatsby*. David Robinson of *The Times* thought that the casting saved the film. 'Robert Redford has the presence, the solidity and the dexterity to hold the character together pretty well, to convey the romantic doomed optimism of his passion for Daisy, to give credibility to his appreciation of Nick's outburst, "You're worth the whole damn bunch put together", above all to give full weight to Gatsby's strange, equivocal summing up of the mess, "In any case, it was just personal."'

The *Guardian*'s Derek Malcolm took a diametrically opposite view of a film he considered to be 'an intelligent but whopping failure'. 'Curiously inept casting has Redford as Gatsby seeming about as mysterious and fascinating as a handsome clothes-peg. When Carraway, obviously Fitzgerald himself, talks of the man's "extraordinary gift for hope – a romantic readiness such as I've never found in any other person", it is a distinct surprise. The actor suggests only an optimism that is at best ambiguous and at worst more than a little vacuous.'

Though Redford rarely liked his own work, he resented criticism of Gatsby which he considered to be ill-informed at best, malicious at worst. 'I think a lot of the knocks I took were because of the image. Critics said, "Redford was too good-looking, Redford was awkward with the language." Fitzgerald never said Gatsby wasn't good-looking. He said Gatsby was a fine figure of a man, an elegant young rough-neck. He said Gatsby's language was awkward, bordering on the absurd. That was a key to the character. That was a quality I worked for. I mean, didn't they read the book?'

Disappointed he certainly was, but some good came out of *The Great Gatsby*. Concluding that the experience had been 'like robbing a bank and discovering you took the wrong bag', Redford decided to go back to controlling his own films, something he hadn't done since *The Candidate*. To this end, he bought the film rights of the upcoming book, *All The President's Men*, from Bob Woodward and Carl Bernstein for 450,000 dollars. As he was getting in on the project before the book was written, he was able to encourage the Watergate journalists to shape their story in a way that would be suitable for the cinema.

It was while he was dividing his energy and enthusiasm pretty evenly between this and the enlargement of Sundance that he got involved in *Three Days of the Condor*, a fourth Sydney Pollack–Robert Redford collaboration that came about more or less by chance. It is a *genre* thriller, the kind in which an innocent man becomes the target for professional assassins without having any idea why they should want to kill him. The situation is made more interesting because the man, Joseph Turner, is a scholarly, bespectacled researcher, more at home in a library than with a gun. He works as a reader at the American Literary Historical Society in Manhattan, a research organisation set up to analyse popular fiction as part of the CIA's intelligence gathering.

One ordinary lunch break, the mild-mannered Turner returns with sandwiches for his colleagues, academics like himself, to find that they've all been murdered. At this point, he wisely goes on the run himself, but without ever looking likely to survive the attentions of such highly-trained killers as Max Von Sydow. Unable to trust people he believed to be his friends, he enlists the help of a female photographer who specialises in emptiness – unoccupied park benches and bare winter treescapes – and sets about righting wrongs. Having taken over her apartment and her car and tied her to the lavatory, he also finds time to make love to her, a wise, if improbable, decision as she is played by Faye Dunaway.

This plot was based on *Six Days of the Condor*, a novel by James Grady which Redford liked for its speed over the ground. 'Wait a minute, Pollack,' he told his friend as they were mulling over their separate futures. 'I just read something the other day. It's absolutely ready to go. It's bullshit but it's the kind of picture we've always talked about wanting to do, where you don't have to worry about the meaning of this and the meaning of that. It's a popcorn movie, a thriller. You'll see when you read it, it goes like the wind.'

Pollack agreed. He and Redford knew their way around one another so well by now that they had a kind of shorthand which made working together relatively simple. 'Sometimes I literally don't say a word and he knows exactly what I mean,' says Pollack. 'Sometimes he'll do a take and I'll see him catch the corner of my eye and he'll see a little hesitation and he'll say, "Okay, once more."'

'I used to think it was better to work with as many directors as you could for variety and educational reasons,' Redford commented. 'Now I think you can do better working with someone who knows your work as an actor, especially if you tend to be on the subtle side. Sydney understands me as well as any director and is able to bring out certain things in me as an actor that don't have to be talked about. It really has a lot to do with familiarity.'

In the event, *Three Days of the Condor* was to test the complacency these remarks suggest rather more than either could have anticipated. One problem was that Redford's mind wasn't totally on the job when the cameras turned in New York in October, 1974. By now he was working on the script of *All The President's Men* with his old friend, William Goldman, and he was making political speeches on behalf of Wayne Owens, a Utah Democrat campaigning for a seat in the Senate. Rumour had it that Pollack was pretty pissed off.

' "Pissed off" isn't exactly the way to describe it,' Pollack explains. 'It's one thing to be angry at somebody and not sympathetic. Redford's too good a friend for that. It's another to be selfishly angry but totally understand, which I did. I'd tell him, "Look, Redford, what are you doing?" But I was telling him as much for him as for me. His attention was being split. He was constantly on the phone. Everybody wanted a piece of him. The fact is that it took a lot more work for me to get the work done with him. It frustrated me trying to get his attention. I'd say, "I'm trying to talk to you", that sort of thing. But once he starts acting, he does what he has to do and he's good at it.'

Another cause for concern was the role of the photographer. The script was being re-written even as the film was shooting, mostly to flesh out a character that was quite undeveloped in the novel. The love scene, too, posed problems. 'There's the old theory that you stop the action with a relationship in a thriller and you risk losing the audience,' Redford commented. 'It's a very tricky thing to pull off, but I think it worked in this film. I think the re-writing turned it from a very good thriller into a very classy thriller.'

As so often with female co-stars, Redford found Dunaway extremely difficult to work with. 'I liked her enormously but she's troubled, she's somewhere else. I was asked my opinion of her by a reporter and it was a question I found hard to answer. I was trying to think of something that would get across my regard for her as a person and not get into critical analysis of the work. So I thought and thought and thought and I could sum up what I thought in two words. She has woman weight. It's an abstraction but that's the way it is. She has tremendous weight on the screen, good female weight. She's a real woman and she projects that and I think that's a virtue.

'Well, I said that and I was told, "Jesus, you can't say that! Woman weight? It sounds like she's fat." and I said, "No, that's not what I mean.

If no one gets it, too bad." Well, I was talked out of it in favour of something innocuous like "real pro, fun to work with", shit like that. I'm not sure people ever really say what they mean.'

Before it was released, *Three Days of the Condor* benefited from an accident of timing: the CIA, under the direction of Richard Helms, was making headline news as details of undercover operations including political assassination and illegal surveillance were revealed to an eagerly-waiting world. This raised interest in a film which was expected to dramatise these events in a significant way. *Three Days of the Condor* had never been designed to fulfil such expectations but the publicity did it no harm, not least by giving some slight credibility to the incredible things that happen in it. The pacing did the rest, as Redford had anticipated from the start: no one thought it was a masterpiece, but a lot of people enjoyed it a great deal.

'There is a chilling sense of reality about it all,' wrote Kathleen Carroll in the *New York Daily News*, 'and Sydney Pollack creates such an atmosphere of dread and danger that his film remains convincing enough to support our worst fears about CIA activity. Interestingly, Redford has never seemed better. One often feels that his approach to acting is too intellectual – he seems so remote and cold on the screen – but here, looking haggard and tense (and thoroughly deglamorised), he brings an awful loneliness, even a vulnerability, to the role.'

On the run in *Three Days of The Condor* (1975).

Jay Cocks, caustic as always, put it less amiably. 'A piece of dotty, slightly paranoid intrigue, *Three Days of the Condor* promises little, and keeps its word. It is hard to be indignant about it or enthusiastic either. There is no clear compliment the movie can be paid without an immediate qualification: it is smooth but forgettable, bearable but brainless. The film has nothing novel to say and nothing to offer except Robert Redford. But the way things work in Hollywood these days, Redford is enough.'

So endeth Redford's most conspicuous cashing-in period. In six years, he'd made twelve movies and a ton of money. He'd established himself as a major star and discovered, usefully, that he appealed to almost everyone. As a flawed lover, he was irresistible to women of all ages. As an action man and especially as half of a wise-cracking action man pair-bond, he brought a certain validity to his particular brand of conservative rebellion. By glorifying the past at the expense of the corrupt present – and there was no present more corrupt than America's in the mid-seventies – he told young men what they wanted to hear. Bucking the system would not result in dangerous change, only in a rewarding illusion of freedom.

It was also the message Redford himself most wanted to believe. As he approached his fortieth birthday in the late seventies, he began to analyse his rather too easy success with a view to shaping the rest of his life. From here on in, his game plan was to buck the system, especially the Hollywood system, but always without seriously rocking the boat.

10

Home Sweet Homes

Although his marriage has fallen apart in the eighties, there can be no doubt that Robert Redford was both perceptive and extremely lucky in his choice of wife. Lola is as dutiful and earnest as her Mormon background suggests. She supported him financially and emotionally through the early years of struggle, submerged her ambitions to his during the middle years of triumph and backed him all the way when he wanted to break out of the acting straitjacket to do his own thing. The younger Redford was, at best, a haphazard financier as he recognised when he said, 'If they depend on my business sense out in Utah, we'll all go broke', and it was Lola who habitually consulted with the family's bank over details of major and minor expenditure. In 1974, she made economic sense out of her husband's wish to double the size of the Sundance empire.

The opportunity to do this occurred when 3,000 acres of ranching country at an altitude of 1,500 feet came up for sale. This block fitted in with a fifty-six-acre farm fifteen miles down Provo Canyon which the Redfords already owned. It had the remnants of an old ranch on it with some barns and a run-down indoor-riding area. Redford intended to farm this land until he realised he could establish the Double R horse ranch he'd always wanted by incorporating it into the larger block.

For Redford, riding is the second great escape after skiing. He and Lola had taken horses into the mountains since they first arrived in Sundance in 1963, often with their tiny children perched on the saddle pommels in front of them. For Redford, the ranch was the culmination of a liking for horses that began in early childhood. 'There are two things I do when I need to get my head straight,' he says. 'They're skiing and taking off across the open country on horseback. I've been interested in horses all my life. I remember as a little kid in Santa Monica, California, where I was born, riding a pony in the ring and thinking, "I wish there weren't any railings around this thing to keep me inside. I'd take this horse and go where I wanted." I did that once and it really excited the guy who led you around on the pony. I decided right then that some day I'd have my own horse.'

Once he'd bought the land, he hired Noel Skinner, born and raised in the saddle in the wilds of Wyoming, to set up and run the ranch. The two men discussed the kind of horses they wanted to breed, the strong-boned quarter horses of the American West with the endurance for cross-country rides over hundreds of miles. Skinner, an expert in blood lines, was given a limited budget and left to get on with it pretty much as he wished. His first purchases were a yearling stallion called Tuff Joe Jet, and two fillies, a two-year-old and a yearling, from a Texan ranch that was noted for its fine stock. As the Double R developed, Skinner showed the horses in-hand in quarter-horse formation classes and later, when they were old enough to be ridden, in cutting competitions.

'I leave the showing up to Noel,' Redford comments. 'I really don't have the time to do more than go down to the ranch and work the horses occasionally. In summer, we keep eight horses for the family to ride up at our place in the mountains. We have an arena where we work them and then we take them out on the mountain trails. Noel tunes them up in the valley at the horse ranch in the late spring, and then we bring them up in the mountains to our place. Our whole family enjoys riding. We ride every day during the summer, often ten-hour rides through the wilderness country and we cover a lot of ground in a short amount of time. Of course we do a lot of hiking too, and enjoy the wild life and the scenery. There's just nothing greater than that for your head.'

Although his leg has never really recovered from the shattered knee cap and severed tendon it suffered just before *Downhill Racer*, Redford, the skier, showed no signs of slowing down as he got older. Even in his fifties, he goes at it hard and fast, skiing all day without stopping for lunch. 'If I'm going to ski, I ski until the flames start coming out of the thighs. I like the edgier side of sport rather than the safer side. It's not because I'm courageous – I'm just as chicken as anybody else – I just enjoy it because the exhilaration is a little bit greater on the other side. I like to ski with people who are good at the sport and love it. I don't like hot dogs who are more interested in singling themselves out than in just enjoying the sport. I'm not a professional skier, and I didn't learn until late in my life, but what absolutely turns me on is downhill skiing in powder snow.'

Indeed powder snow is a cult at Sundance where Brent Beck keeps the public off untracked slopes until the proprietor – or a lucky guest like myself – is ready to make that first magical descent. Redford compares the experience to being 'scared breathless', so shocked that all your breath is gone. 'Just imagine that shock to be pleasure. I always feel that I don't want to breathe until I get to the bottom: it's a way of capturing the moment. There's a tremendous expression of mental and physical freedom combined in powder skiing. Very few sports can do that. To ski powder in rarefied air is about as good an experience as I can think of.

'When you're racing downhill, going over a jump, there's a little of the unknown, rather like riding a wave on a surfboard. It's a little more fun because you don't quite know everything about it. Leaving a little mystery is very important to me. I'm very good at powder skiing. I just plough right through it. I scream, yell, laugh and sometimes cry when I'm skiing badly. I catch my edges, miss my weight change, get mad as hell and fall a lot, but I love it.'

When he's burned out on the slopes, Redford relaxes by watching Charlie Chaplin movies on television. For the most part the Redfords lived simply, with Lola, the virtuous Mormon bride, doing her own cooking in both New York and Sundance. 'Up in Utah, they have no living-in staff at all,' Paul Newman told David Lewin of the *Daily Mail*. 'Bob likes to enjoy luxury, but he decided early on he wouldn't get sucked into the culture of luxury. So when you stay with them either you make the breakfast, or Lola does, or he does. There isn't anyone else – except outside to clear the path of snow in winter. Part of this is for the sake of the children. It's too easy in California to let luxury take over the children. If it does, then it is disaster.'

Redford concurs. 'One of the things I don't want is my family paying a price for my fame. That's one of the major reasons I insist on a lot of privacy. If I go out to dinner with my family and lots of people start crowding around the table it confuses the kids. They know I'm famous. We've talked about it, but still it's strange and often upsetting for them. I want them to grow up as normal as they possibly can, not unhappy like so many children of famous parents. They go to regular schools and are treated just like their classmates. I don't spoil them either. If they want to go skiing, nobody chauffeurs them around. If they want extra money, they get part-time jobs.'

The boundaries of normal family life extended as far as Provo, a town of some 60,000 inhabitants dominated by the Mormon university, Brigham Young. No one bugs the Redfords as they wander down its broad main street. Redford is well known in the local shops, especially the men's store where he buys essential items such as socks. When he asks for them, the man behind the counter suggests a tie and everybody laughs. For the known tie-hater, it is a running joke. Other shopping expeditions take place in Orem where Redford buys most of his clothes, including an endless supply of Levi 501s, in Wolfe's Sporting Goods. Not designer jeans, he insists, just the regular model bought off the peg same as everyone else does.

For many years the Redfords enjoyed a marriage of the kind that had gone out of fashion in the free-wheeling sixties and the liberated seventies. Redford always claimed that he was faithful to his wife: in return, she was expected to let him call the shots. All this had been mapped out in his mind from the beginning, so much so that when Lola turned down his first long-distance proposal, he'd already written to her father, Frank Von Wagenen, to ask formally for her hand.

It was, by Von Wagenen's account, a remarkable statement of intent. 'We'd met him, of course,' he recalls, 'and he seemed a pleasant enough young man. But in the letter he wrote, "Your daughter will not have to go without life's necessities." He even outlined at that early stage his future: he would become an art director. He went even further. My daughter has light-coloured hair. Bob's hair has red in it. But in the letter he promised that one of their children's hair will not be red. It was a remarkable thing to write but he kept that promise too. The first two children had red hair but when his youngest child, Amy, was born, she was a blonde. It was Lola who stopped Bob drinking. She's a Mormon who practises her faith. She doesn't drink, so neither did Bob.'

This may be the proud father talking because Robert Shaw, Redford's co-star in *The Sting*, had another more likely explanation for the cutback. 'He told me he'd decided to knock it off when he was holed up with Lola in Spain because it would stop him getting to the top. He decided to get back to America where he would go right to the top.' In Shaw's opinion, that was 'the essential Redford'.

However, there are others who take the Van Wagenen line, among them a friend in New York who wishes to remain anonymous: 'Lola saved Bob. Without her, I think he would have continued to go right down. He loves her, respects her and above all admires her. The key to understanding Bob is Lola. She is sexy, strong and vital and intelligent. And she does things, rather than just sitting at home waiting for Bob to come in.'

One of the things that Lola did not do was hang about on film sets with a view to protecting her gorgeous husband's chastity. Yet no hint of scandal, or even of a minor fling, besmirched the Redford name and the actor has always been outspoken on the question of marital fidelity.

'There are lots of women I'm attracted to but I'm a very happily-married guy,' he said in 1976. 'I know what I want and I've got it. It's that simple. I've no regrets. I don't feel that I might have missed something. I did all my fooling around as a teenager. I ran around with my share of the girls, bummed around the world, got it all out of my system. I enjoy feminine, independent and smart women. Girls who don't come on like Supergirl. The type that's vulnerable. I find vulnerability very attractive.'

Although Lola was extremely young and inexperienced when she married, she stood up for herself from the start and the Redford rows were fairly legendary. 'There are times,' Redford has admitted, 'when I feel threatened by her, when I feel she's asserting herself in our relationship a bit more than I'm ready to handle. I tell her to back off. We argue and eventually work things out. Most often it's my fear of having my manhood taken away from me.' According to Frank Van Wagenen, one of the tenets of the Mormon faith is that rows have to be sorted out before the protagonists go to sleep. Thanks to Lola, the Redfords' rows were settled, at least for the first twenty years. One advantage of Bob being an insomniac is that it didn't matter how long the sort-out took.

On a more positive note, Redford appreciated the sacrifice his wife had made. 'Lola could have had a career of her own as a singer. She has a great voice. Or she could have acted in some of my movies like other actors' wives. But as far as I'm concerned, she chose the hardest road because she had to sacrifice her own interests to mine. At the beginning of my career, when we lived in cold-water flats in New York's West Side, she didn't even know whether I would amount to anything.

'In the beginning we lived by our wits. Lola made Carnation milk from powder and dishes we could eat all week. There wasn't a thought in those days about "I'm doing this for you" or "You're doing that for me". It just was, and we did it because it felt right. The couple that struggles together usually stays together. The bond between Lola and me is too strong for any other human being to fracture.'

Although these words were not prophetic, there is no doubt that the actor believed them at the time. He also credited the Mormons with having the right attitude to marriage. 'The ideals and aims of the women are more directed to the family than other women's are. They do not look upon managing a household as beneath them, or taking care of children as drudgery. Mormon women are not averse to having large families. The men used to have more than one wife, too, although monogamy has been the trend for the past few decades. That aspect might appeal to a lot of men, but not to me.'

As a non-practising Mormon, Lola Redford could drink alcohol but she doesn't, because she doesn't like it. However, she does have one bad habit: she is an addicted smoker, a source of continuing irritation to her husband. 'I took a puff or two in my younger days, but not any more. Lola enjoys cigarettes but avoids smoking in my presence. Every now and then I've gone into the bathroom after she's come out, only to find it full of smoke. Smoking is her privilege. This is a democracy. But in my heart, I know I didn't build that house high up in the clear air of Utah away from the pollution of the cities to get smoked out, even by my adorable wife.'

The Redfords shared their paradise with a constant stream of

Hollywood guests, invited at their peril and challenged to play with Redford's expensive dangerous toys. 'The casualty list is endless,' says Richard Schickel, 'and if you're Redford's friend you learn to accept the inevitability of a certain amount of pain and humiliation. It is never really his fault. He surrounds himself with all this terrific stuff – skis and water skis, motor-cycles and Ski-Doos, horses and racing cars, and he is so competent with all of them, so obviously has fun with them and so obviously wants you to share his pleasures that you just have to try. He is, of course, the soul of sympathy after disaster strikes, instantly turning accident into anecdote in which victim becomes hero. A comic hero, of course, but centre stage for all that, and esteemed for avoiding the only truly reprehensible crime in Redford's book – "taking the pip".'

Though these designer games were still seductive in 1974, Redford was developing more serious interests in Utah as his and Lola's preoccupation with ecology grew. Although it is he who is renowned for his interest in the subject, it was Lola who first introduced it way back in 1969. The trigger was a frantic telephone call from a New York neighbour and friend, Ilene Goldman, the wife of William Goldman who wrote *Butch Cassidy and The Sundance Kid*. Ilene told Lola how her five-year-old daughter Suzanna had come back from school and rushed through their Manhattan apartment, banging shut the windows as she went. 'Don't let the air come in,' she wept. 'It's going to poison us.'

The upshot of this incident was that Lola and Ilene founded a pressure group called Consumer Action Now (CAN). With twenty friends, they published a newsletter for New Yorkers. Each issue dealt with a different topic: food, chemical additives, cleaning products, drugs, water, energy. 'We started at a time when people didn't know how to pronounce ecology, let alone understand it,' Lola remembers. 'We were a group of women disenchanted by life in New York City who decided to do something about it.' Five years later, CAN had grown into a full-scale, national consumer public interest operation. Lola went to Washington roughly once a month and spent two days beating on doors on Capitol Hill.

'We didn't know how accessible people were when we first started lobbying. That's the thing that surprised me the most. We knew nothing about lobbying when we began – and we learned to listen, as well as talk. We started with people already on our side. They told us the important aspects of the legislation, the things that couldn't be cut, as well as the compromises they were willing to make. We had no idea how to lobby a swing-vote. We learned what arguments we would hear and how to counter them. Sometimes we heard arguments that we couldn't answer, so then we'd go back to our side and ask.'

Lola's first venture into lobbying was on an amendment to the Food and Drug Act to prohibit the allegedly carcinogenic hormone DES from being used to stimulate growth in cattle. Tom van der Voort, legislative aide to Senator William Proxmire, a Democrat from Wisconsin, was clearly impressed by their first meeting. 'She and a gal named Goldman came in. They said they didn't know much about lobbying, and who to talk to, but they were really interested in the bill and in doing whatever they could to help. One interesting thing. She never mentioned her husband, not once. There was none of this business, "I'm Robert Redford's wife". She just wanted to know how she could help. And she was pretty determined.'

Lola claims that there were advantages and disadvantages to being Mrs. Robert Redford. On the debit side, the media always wanted to talk to her about her husband rather than her own work. However, she appreciated her access to show business patrons who helped her out, financially and practically. As for Redford, he was always 'tremendously supportive'. Not only did he make *The Great Waldo Pepper* available as a benefit for CAN, but he broke his own rules by attending its première in New York in March, 1975, and the fund-raising picnic and auction that followed it.

Lola practises what she preaches by using safe cosmetics. Her beauty routine includes mayonnaise to condition her hair and egg whites to erase wrinkles, temporarily at least. She washed in rain-water and cleans her skin with witch-hazel and rosewater. She rubs Albolene, a pure petroleum jelly, all over her body and favours Clearasil for 'an occasional pimple'.

Redford's increasing awareness centred more on Utah than New York. His interest in politics came into the public consciousness for the first time when he travelled to Washington in May, 1974, to attend a campaign fund-raising event for his friend, Representative Wayne Owens, the Democratic candidate for Utah in the Senate race. The party took place in the gardens of an elegant house in Georgetown, the home of the former Governor of New York, Averell Harriman and his wife, Pamela.

A few weeks earlier, Redford had been tieless when he'd met Carl Bernstein and Bob Woodward in the Montpelier restaurant of the Madison Hotel – the *maître d'* had refused to admit him until he borrowed a string bow-tie from one of the waiters. On this occasion, he was correctly turned out in a black suit, a black and white striped shirt and a polka-dot tie. Only the fact that he chewed gum throughout the evening marred the overall effect. This was a cause for regret for at least one fellow guest. 'Has he got rid of his gum?' she asked. 'No, I don't think so. Why?' her companion replied. 'Because I want to keep it,' was the answer.

'I'm not used to this,' Redford mumbled as he climbed out of a long

A gala occasion for Lola and Bob Redford.

black limousine. 'I'm doing it because of Wayne. He's the only person I would campaign for. I think what is needed is an effective Congress, and I think Wayne is an example of a man of great honesty and integrity, qualities badly needed in government. He is also a man who has established a rapport with people.' Redford spent the next two hours chewing his gum on a receiving-line, greeting the 300 people who'd paid 100 dollars a head to support Wayne Owens. Fortified only by an occasional sip of beer, he smiled and charmed with the best of them: the perfect *Candidate* revisited.

Although Redford is a registered Democrat, he has always insisted that he is not to be taken for granted politically any more than in any other area of interest. 'I'm not as political as people might think. I support people I really believe in, but I support the person, not the party. I'm not a slavish, knee-jerk Democrat. I have as much criticism of Democratic party politics as I do of Republican politics. I have supported Republicans round the country because of their stands on certain issues and if I saw a Republican candidate I thought was terrific, I'd probably go out and stump for him.'

Back in Utah, his efforts were less formal than in Washington, but by no means simpler. From the outset, he was ambivalent about what he wanted to achieve. 'Utah seemed to be the place that I wanted to build a life away from the work I had to do, and I always viewed the work somewhat like missions behind enemy lines – you go in, drop the bombs and get out – you don't linger or you'll get caught by strafing or counterfire. But this is where I chose to make my life so I want it to be quiet and private. That's on the one hand. On the other hand, something you care deeply about, you speak for it; you try to do something. I have a true love of the state, and my concerns about it led me sometimes to speak out against things that I felt were genuinely wrong.

'That's where it gets screwy,' he continued, 'because suddenly when you speak out, you're an outsider. When you shut up, they love you: "We're so glad you're here; you're doing so much for the state", and as soon as you speak out about your concerns, suddenly, "Who the hell are you?"'

One of the first things Redford spoke out about, the proposed coal-fired generating plant on the Kaiparowits Plateau some 250 miles south of Sundance, involved him in a great deal of controversy leading to considerable animosity. As there was a basic clash of interests, it is easy to see how it came about. On the one hand, any dedicated conservationist would protest against the building of such a plant in an area surrounded by magnificent national parkland; on the other, the local town, Kanab, had unemployment running at twenty-seven per cent and the plant would bring in 5,000 jobs, rising to 13,000 in future years.

Redford went so far as to appear on television to plead his case against the plant. 'If we let them build one, they'll want to build another,' he said. 'What it stands for is a symbol of what we're going to be doing to our land and some of the valuable parts of our heritage. I worry about so many decisions that affect the quality of our lives being made by technocrats who seem to have no blood in their veins.' Easily said, of course, by a major landowner who could be accused of vested self-interest and by a major star who would certainly never have to worry about putting groceries on his own table. Small wonder that when the Redford campaign was successful, the citizens of Kanab held a mock funeral for the loss of their fifteen-year fight. An empty coffin stood in

135

the place where the power station would have been and a gallows was erected near the courthouse: from it hung a life-size effigy of Robert Redford.

This incident would seem to establish Redford as campaigner who tends to put ideals above people, but he is vehement in his denial. He claims he raised 25,000 dollars for a study programme, then considered the issues from all sides before he put his weight behind the veto faction. 'What emerged were facts that were so alarming that I had no choice in my own conscience but to speak out, because what I saw coming was not going to be an advantage to the local people, was certainly not going to help the state; it was a "no win" deal that no one had analysed properly: the real cost of that plant from a sociological, economic and environmental position. All that got lost somehow in place of just Redford, the actor, speaking out about something he didn't know anything about, in an area where he didn't live.'

Redford also fought battles in his own back yard. Some of them he didn't win, most notably the one over the building of a rival ski resort, Park City, a large, modern development with hotels and superior ski slopes just forty-five minutes away from Sundance by car. Some of them he did, like the one with the Utah Highway Department over the proposed six lane road through Provo Canyon. In addition, he supplemented his activities at the sewer commission by setting up a Water Conservancy District with a view to saving the water running off the side of the mountain for use in the summer droughts.

'The reason I did it is that nobody wanted to be sewer commissioner, but a lot of people thought it was the only justified job I ever got. There was a lot of humour about it but I had some strong feelings about the sewage situation and water use. I think that there's very poor water planning in Utah and, for that matter, in most of the west. I was looking to the future when there would be development all around the area and there was no water plan, no master plan for water use. There was just indiscriminate use of water so I felt we needed to develop advance sewerage that would take into consideration the environment and pollution.'

It was in the mid-seventies that Redford's liking for the west turned into the obsession which triggered a brief subsidiary career as a journalist and author. While he was stuck in Washington making *All The President's Men*, he found himself thinking more and more about the 'Old West'. 'I was full of myths and stories but I didn't know all that much. I kept thinking about what I'd seen and heard was being lost, desecrated out there.' Gradually his thoughts focused on the Outlaw Trail until it became a symbol for the general desecration. In the late nineteenth and early twentieth centuries, it had provided outlaws on the run with an almost foolproof escape route from Canada to Mexico via Montana, Wyoming and Utah.

Redford heard of it first when someone pointed out the remains of some old wood cabins near one of the *Jeremiah Johnson* locations. As one particularly dilapidated structure had allegedly been built by Butch Cassidy, it was inevitable that his interest should be stirred. Uncared for and unguarded, this nugget of American western history was weathering away. 'Just like the Outlaw Trail,' said Redford. 'It's in danger of total obliteration because so few people know about it. There's no hope unless someone tries to identify it and some kind of heritage trust is arranged.'

When he was in Washington, home of many such trusts, Redford decided that he was the person best equipped to spotlight the problem. His first stop was the *National Geographic* magazine, chosen because of its moderate political and moral stance, and because it has the best pictures. What did they think about a story on the dangers facing the west? 'I made a rather impassioned plea, emphasising the richness and romance of its history. Well, they got so fired up, they said, "Why don't you write it?"'

Redford hadn't quite expected that, but he could see the logic in it. But what exactly was he to write about? After all, he'd never ridden the Outlaw Trail. No problem: he got together a nine-man safari party made up of men who loved the 'Old West' and wanted to preserve it, among them the novelist and naturalist, Edward Abbey, the historian, Kerry Ross Boren, and Terry Minger, the town manager of Vail. As soon as shooting stopped on *All The President's Men*, this party assembled in Canada for the start of their adventure.

For the next three weeks, they journeyed south for the most part on horseback, but occasionally by van or on foot. The highways – 'the second rape of the west', says Redford, 'the first was the railroad' – had obliterated sections of the Trail so it was no longer possible to make the whole trip in the traditional manner. 'Our goal was to open up completely to the experience. We got history from Kerry Ross Boren. Along the trail, we made deals with ranchers for their horses, just the way the outlaws did. There were fifth generation ranchers we ran into. Some remembered men who'd sold horses to Butch Cassidy and the Hole-in-the-Wall gang. It was rich and full especially when we were alone on horseback along the trail, and we looked up to see ourselves juxtaposed against the future rush of jet trails in the sky.'

The *National Geographic* sent along a photographer, then waited for Redford's prose. They expected between 5,000 and 10,000 words which they planned to edit to 4,000 so they were astonished to receive 35,000. 'I went from beginning to end. It just flowed,' said Redford, making authorship sound enviably simple. The magazine edited the magnum opus as best they could and ran it in November, 1976. Publishers were quick to spot the potential coup in the Redford name combined with contemporary and archive pictures, but the actor was vehement in his refusal until he was approached by Grosset and Dunlap.

They baited their trap in a way that would appeal to any writer's vanity. Surely, they suggested, there was more to the story than the *National Geographic* had printed? It was what Redford wanted to hear and he began to waver. 'I know there are people who'll come out to see what you look like, but I don't think they'd care if I just philosophised in print,' he commented, but he allowed himself to be persuaded that he was wrong.

In fact, he had more than enough research material for a book. During his journey, he'd regularly taped conversations and his own reflections. 'There were a number of stories too salty to be included in the magazine article,' he remembers. He also had a number of his own drawings to offer the eager publishers. 'Because I was an artist, I can recall things by sketching them. Sometimes there was no time to write down impressions about attitude and character so I'd sketch how a rancher was sitting, and that would remind me.'

Writing in longhand because he can't type, Redford reduced this mass of information to 60,000 words, concentrating in particular on what might be saved through restoration and, in extreme cases, relocation. He regretted massive water projects like the one that flooded the pioneer settlements in Wyoming and the general neglect of old buildings left to rot through lack of interest. It was inevitable too that oral history would become less and less available as the people who remembered the west, as it had been, died off.

'Soon there'll be nothing left to preserve and we'll enter that dangerous area of distortion of fact,' the actor insisted. 'We'll have to take the historians' word for what existed instead of seeing it for ourselves. At the start, I was flat out against what was happening there; against the coal boom and the impact it was having on the countryside and on families. Coming up against economics and ideals and the very complicated Western personality was like cold water in the face. It gave me a more balanced view of development and of what can, and should, be preserved.'

As the book proceeded, it became clear to Grosset and Dunlap that their star author was as bad at keeping deadlines as he was at keeping dates, but they knew better than to protest. 'They levelled me with guilt because they were so decent,' said Redford. 'I didn't have it finished, but they didn't bug me.'

When *The Outlaw Trail: A Journey Through Time* was finally published in 1978, he quite fancied his new career and made tentative plans to extend his 'philosophising' to cover American politics, or the raising of children, or the feelings of old people. Or even to write fiction.

'When I was young, I escaped into fantasy and I grew up with fiction. Four of the most meaningful words I know are "Once upon a time",' he said, but as yet he hasn't got around to writing them down.

11

More Than Just A Pretty Face

If Redford's career contained half a dozen films of the calibre of *All The President's Men*, it is unlikely that he would have to live with the stigma of being the golden boy of the wide silver screen. Whether you like it or not – and most people did like it a lot – it is a fine example of purposeful film making. It is exciting, relevant, well cast, well acted and well directed. It says things that needed to be said and it made a lot of money. How many Hollywood films achieve even a part of that?

For all this the credit goes to Robert Redford, executive producer rather than to Robert Redford, star. That's not to say that *All The President's Men* wouldn't have been made if he hadn't become involved. The unequal fight for the soul of America – David versus Goliath, Bob Woodward and Carl Bernstein versus Nixon and aides – is such a good story that it was always going to be filmed. But Redford's input covered every stage of production, starting even before the journalists wrote their book. It would be churlish to deny that this is his film.

That Redford became interested in the Watergate burglaries while he was promoting *The Candidate* was thanks to timing that was anything but accidental. The purpose of the five-man break-in at the Democratic National Headquarters in the Watergate Complex in Washington DC was part of a strategy designed to take Nixon to the White House for a second term. The publicity campaign for *The Candidate* included a 'whistle stop' tour of Florida in June 1972 – some four weeks after the burglary – and was designed to tie in with the Presidential election later that year. As Redford was accompanied on his trip by a number of newsmen, it was inevitable that they should discuss the scandal as, little by little, it began to emerge.

'There had been a big splash when it happened,' Redford told Melvyn Bragg in *New Review*, 'and then it went underground. It went dry, and I couldn't figure it out. The reporters said it would probably stay underground and I said, "What do you mean by that?" and they said, "Well . . ." and there were a lot of sidelong glances, and snickering and so forth. They were very cynical about the prospects of the truth ever coming out and I was very depressed by their attitude. They said, or implied, that Nixon was going to be re-elected and that the power of his administration, and the people who worked for him, was so great that people were afraid; and the idea that Washington, the entire city of Washington, and our whole congressional leadership could be frightened of something, particularly of one man, really fascinated me.'

As the man was Richard Nixon, it also horrified him. This was the hollow man of his childhood, the Senator from California whose handshake had chilled him when he gave him an athletic award aged thirteen, the man he'd never been able to connect with telling the truth. 'As a kid with no real knowledge of politics, I felt such a strong vibration of insincerity even when I saw him on TV, I couldn't understand why other people, especially the press, couldn't feel it. So when I heard a lot of political press talking about the fact that Watergate could be tied to Nixon, I not only believed it, I wanted to believe it. And when nothing was happening, I got angry. I was half angry for my own feelings and half for the system, for justice.'

At this stage, Redford hadn't heard of Woodward and Bernstein so he set off for his summer holidays at Sundance resolved only to monitor the story when, and if, it broke. By the time he returned to New York in September, the revelations were coming thick and fast as the reporters began to link the dirty tricks campaign, the sabotage tactics and the slush fund to the White House. In November, the United States went to the polls, with Nixon winning a landslide victory over Eugene McCarthy. It was then that Redford first tried to contact the *Washington Post* reporters. The investigation, he discovered, had been given not to the paper's stars, but to two of the lowest men on its staff. 'One [Woodward] was a police beat reporter covering rat droppings in restaurants, the other was lazy, covering the legislature for a local county seat, and about to be fired from his job.' Clearly the *Washington Post* had no premonition of the glory that Watergate was to bring it.

Redford's first approaches to Woodward and Bernstein were met with waves of depression and self-pity. 'They were at their lowest,' he recalls. 'They'd bottomed out, and everyone felt that they were wrong and they were getting castigated, not only by the administration, but also by the public. That interested me. Up to that point, I had been mostly interested as a private citizen, but then I became interested from the standpoint of it being possible film material because of the difference in the two characters. They were such contrasting characters.'

When he eventually got through to a disbelieving Woodward, the reaction was distinctly negative. 'Look,' said Redford firmly, astutely diagnosing fear on the other end of the line, 'I don't want to go through this back and forth. I sense you don't trust me and you don't know who I am. Let me come to Washington and in ten minutes I'll tell you what I have in mind.' So he did, a piece of decisive action that won him Woodward's cautious co-operation. Three months later, the actor-producer faced his quarries across a table and said, 'This is what I'm interested in doing. If you say yes, fine. If not, fine.' They said yes.

What Redford proposed was an amalgam of all his most successful work, a 'how to do it' film with buddy-buddy undertones – *Downhill Racer* or *The Candidate* lightly touched by *Butch Cassidy* or *The Sting*. 'If you can inform people and entertain them at the same time, that to me is the best kind of movie.' He told Woodward and Bernstein that he wanted to focus on the period when they were working in the dark, when no one believed what they were doing, let alone expected them to succeed.

At this point, with Nixon's resignation two years ahead, they'd been planning a book about the burglaries but they agreed to go with Redford's vision by concentrating on their own roles as investigative reporters. If they'd resisted both the charismatic actor and the chance for personal glory, they would hardly have been human. 'The material was so bizarre and complicated,' Woodward summed up, 'that it needed

Washington Post journalist Bob Woodward (left) with his *alter ego* in *All The President's Men* (1976).

a story line, and the reporters could give it that story line. Redford was a factor in getting us to write the kind of book we wrote.'

'I didn't buy the option until a year later,' Redford remembers, 'when all the lawyers, agents, legal people, parasites, had their hands on it.' But all along he knew the kind of film that he wanted to see made. It was to be hard-edged with a lot of design to it, but above all it was to be real. Redford never saw Woodward and Bernstein as knights in shining armour. Why should he when he'd had a running war with journalists for years?

'I'd always been on the other side. It was a double-edged sword for me. I'd seen myself criticised unfairly, misquoted, accused of things that weren't true and at times downright slandered by the press. I'm only human. I react. I get stung. I get hurt when someone writes something unnecessarily cruel about me. I find predisposition in the press inexcusable. On the other hand, I'd often been unduly praised and blown up to gigantic proportions, equally unjustified. So I was fascinated by this monster. I wanted to find out what caused such inaccuracy and lack of perception by something that was supposed to be in the accuracy and perception business. I have a lot of ambivalence about the press, and I wanted that in the film.'

Although it was natural for the rest of the press to present the famous duo as crusaders after truth, heroes who had dared to call on one of the world's two strongest governments to account for its actions to the people, Redford's view was, 'that's all bullshit'. He believed that Woodward and Bernstein were onto a good story, something they desperately needed to give credibility to their largely unsuccessful careers. They'd stumbled onto part of the story, and then employed methods that were borderline in terms of ethics in order to get at the facts. In many cases, their tactics were as dodgy as those used by the people they were trying to catch. 'The truth did not come easy or clean,' he said. 'Let's put it that way and hopefully the film will show that, yes, we should be grateful, yes, they are heroes of a sort, but not pure and clean.'

Whether or not the film rights seemed expensive at the time they looked cheap enough at 450,000 dollars once the book came out early in 1974. On publication it climbed sharply to the number one spot in bestseller lists nationwide. By this time, Redford had commissioned his old colleague, William Goldman, to reduce the 300-page book to a 115-page screenplay 'without losing impact, without losing relevance and without losing the pieces of the puzzle'. In other words, Redford wanted a detective story and a thriller which Goldman provided. Less satisfactorily, he used the two men against the world structure he'd been given as a peg on which to hang another exercise in male camaraderie, with Woodward and Bernstein as wisecracking allies in adversity.

'Butch and Sundance Bring Down the Government', as a wit at the *Washington Post* had it.

His superiors were not amused, especially Ben Bradlee, the newspaper's formidable executive editor, who threatened to cut off all co-operation if it weren't revised. 'Just keep this in mind, pal,' he told Redford. 'Whatever you put up there on the screen stays. Whatever I am on that screen is for ever in the minds of people when they hear the name Ben Bradlee. You can always ride off into the sunset in a western or jump in the sack with some good-looking girl in your next film but I'm forever an asshole.' Redford agreed that Bradlee was right to be worried, and reassured him by telling Goldman to re-work the screenplay in semi-documentary fashion with as much input from the *Washington Post* staff as possible. Goldman, the Oscar-winning professional, made no waves as he set about eliminating the offending camaraderie. 'Movies are a collaborative art. If you can't accept that, you don't belong in the business.'

Redford had less sympathy with Bernstein who converted his objections to the first Goldman script into a screenplay of his own, written with assistance from his girlfriend, Norah Ephron, who later became his wife. 'It was outrageous,' the actor recalls. 'It showed Bernstein as the great lover hopping in and out of bed and made Woodward appear dull and grey. I had to tell Carl that Errol Flynn is dead.'

From the start, it was Bob Woodward who appealed more to Redford and who supported him more resolutely in return. Woodward had the reputation of being the plodder of the pair, the one who pursued the quest with minute attention to detail but in a rather less than inspired manner. Bernstein was the better writer, but slow, lazy and given to jumping to conclusions without putting in the necessary groundwork. 'I'm kind of boring, very undramatic,' Woodward is on record as saying. 'True, absolutely true,' Redford concurs, then adds, 'The truth is, he's not boring, he's fascinating. He would like you to think he's boring; that suits him very well for his work, because there's a kind of anonymity to him, a facelessness about him as he goes about doing his job. But the truth is Woodward is a very layered person and as you get to know him, he becomes more and more fascinating. He wears very well. I like him a lot.'

And it was reciprocated. 'It's entirely accurate even down to the mistakes we made,' Woodward would say of the finished film. 'Redford looked at our original notebooks which no one else has done. He's also a nice guy. We got on well.'

Though it was not what he had originally planned, Redford found that he had to play Woodward in order to get the film financed. 'The role is certainly not illustrious or revelatory or scintillating. It's a kind of dogged, concentrated character. But I wanted to do the project and playing the role was a sacrificial thing to get it going.' And sacrificial it turned out to be, because Redford had to turn down the role that won Jack Nicholson an Oscar in *One Flew Over The Cuckoo's Nest* because of his commitment to *All The President's Men*.

The next step was to find an actor to play Bernstein, a task greatly simplified by the fact that Dustin Hoffman had offered 400,000 dollars for the film rights to the Watergate book shortly after it was published. He was looking for a 'good' Jew, a complete character reversal after a 'bad' one – the tortured Lenny Bruce. He believed he'd found him in Carl Bernstein, 'a nice Jewish boy who, (almost) single-handedly, unmasks the political scandal of the century', as his biographer, Patrick Agan, puts it. He also found, of course, that Redford's Wildwood Enterprise was two years ahead of him.'

'We came from similar backgrounds although we didn't really know one another before *All The President's Men*,' Hoffman comments. 'We were born in the same month in the same year. We went to New York at the same time. But I didn't put my first money into land as he did, never thought you could if you didn't have money. I don't think Bob had money either at the time – but he got it.' Perhaps there was some kind of feeling of inferiority on this score, and on being outwitted over the book, because Hoffman claims he wouldn't go to Redford and ask for Bernstein. 'I wanted it and I waited so long, read about so many other names being considered, I thought I'd never get it. Then finally he phoned me and I said, "What took you so long?"'

In fact Redford could think of no better actor than Dustin Hoffman for the extroverted Bernstein, so much so that he gave him top billing. Given Dustin's enthusiasm, the gesture of goodwill probably wasn't necessary but it expressed Redford's admiration for his contemporary. 'He is a fantastic actor. Working with him is like working with a stream of pure electricity. He's so intense and fluid you can't help but react.' An added bonus was that Hoffman, with shaggy shoulder length hair and casual journalists' clothes, looked very much like Bernstein.

On the debit side, potentially, was his ego which had been known to make strong men quail. Recognising the need for a firm director, Redford chose Alan Pakula, the producer he'd worked for on *Inside Daisy Clover*, above Elia Kazan, Arthur Penn and Joseph Mankiewicz. Pakula's record as a director included *The Sterile Cuckoo*, the movie which put Liza Minelli's name in lights in 1969, and *The Parallax View*, a critically acclaimed political thriller, made in 1974, starring Warren Beatty.

A man who could control Beatty and Minelli would have a chance with Hoffman, but the crucial factor was Pakula's handling of *Klute*, the thriller that won Jane Fonda an Oscar for her portrayal of a call-girl stalked by a killer. Redford had not been impressed by the screenplay, but the fear and menace in the finished film was exactly what he wanted for the dark underbelly of Watergate. As the audience had lived through the ending of *All The President's Men*, creating the necessary suspense would be doubly difficult. *Klute* convinced Redford that Pakula was the man for the job. Hoffman, himself a long-time admirer of Pakula, concurred.

During pre-production for *All The President's Men*, authenticity was a prime consideration. Redford spent several months in the offices of the *Washington Post* watching Woodward and his colleagues at work. He wanted to use little details of the reporter's behaviour as keys to his character. He studied him as he dialled a number, noted what he did while the other person was talking and how he kept people on the phone when they wanted to get off. He saw him handle rude people and people in the midst of tragedy. He watched him type because he didn't know how to, and he went with him on assignments. Of course he had to stop short of actually meeting his leads – it would take a quite exceptional interviewee to concentrate on a story with Robert Redford around – but he waited outside to question Woodward afterwards.

Although he never expected to say it of a journalist, Redford admits that Woodward emerged as 'quite an honourable newspaper man. Very often he wouldn't tell me a lot of what had happened, which I liked. That impressed me. What I wanted most was to know how he behaved. I guess I'm fairly arrogant about actors' perceptions. I would trust an actor's perceptions on behaviour and attitudes, human attitudes, more than a reporter's. And so, I obviously feel that I have perceptions about people's behaviour. So I was watching his behaviour and it was going to give me clues to his profession, rather than taking it from the external point inward.'

Hoffman, too, haunted the offices of the *Washington Post*, homing in on the habits of Carl Bernstein. He was particularly struck by the long and difficult hours reporters put in to meet their deadlines, and by the unrelenting nature of their work. 'I couldn't get over the fact that the paper really does get out every day. Except for a few flurries of activity, it's as quiet as an insurance company. But it's also the pleasantest environment I've ever spent any time in.'

Equal care was taken with the *Washington Post* newsroom. Redford had originally hoped to shoot it for real, but his study of the workings of the paper convinced him that putting a film unit in for several weeks would bring publication to a standstill. Instead the newsroom was meticulously reconstructed in Warner Brothers' Burbank studios. The 33,000 square foot open-plan office took up two sound stages and set-designer George Jenkins was entrusted with making it exact down to the last detail.

Each desk, each fluorescent lighting tube was measured and precisely placed. Several tons of *Washington Post* rubbish were shipped out to California so that set-decorators could place authentic bent paper clips and empty cigarette packs in strategic positions. The *Post* reprinted the relevant front pages from its 1972 editions so that the appropriate copies could be left lying about for whatever day was being filmed. When Redford dialled out, the telephone he used had Woodward's extension number on it.

The price tag was between 450,000 and 500,000 dollars and when it was finished, Redford and Hoffman were so enthusiastic that they hosted a journalistic bonanza. On July 2, 1975, a hundred or so reporters, photographers and impostors were taken on guided tours through the huge sound stages by the actors. 'The movie doesn't have so much to do with what Watergate was, as with what it represents symbolically,' Hoffman told them. 'I just resist the symbol of the picture of Watergate because it's more about the newspaper business and how it functions and how it operates.'

American heavyweights were hired to fill the senior positions on the *Washington Post*: Jason Robards was executive editor, Benjamin C. Bradlee, Jack Warden was metropolitan editor, Harry Rosenfeld, and Martin Balsam was managing editor, Howard Simon. The excellent Jane Alexander was cast as the bookkeeper at CREEP (Committee to Re-elect the President), who broke silence to reveal that her organisation had paid the Watergate intruders. Finally, Hal Holbrook was hired to meet Woodward in an underground garage, as the shadowy anonymous informer, 'Deep Throat'.

Of the names immortalised by the long-running scandal, former Attorney-General John Mitchell, Attorney-General Kleindienst and Secretary of Commerce Maurice Stans were in but Erlichman, Haldeman, Magruder and many others were out. 'We depicted the people who, I think, had the greatest impact on events at that time,' Redford explained. 'Finally we just had to hone it down and make a choice: this character stays because he represents the syndrome. John Mitchell was doing a lot of things which controlled our lives. And Maurice Stans was guilty of a lot of corrupt behaviour while he had the public office of going around and stumping for the President. I think all that stuff should come out.'

Shooting took place over ninety-six days in the autumn of 1975, partly at Burbank, and partly on location in Washington. No matter where the camera turned, both Redford and Hoffman were constantly on the hot line to the *Post* to check details. This didn't always find favour with the paper's publisher, Katharine Graham, who had expressed doubts about the project from the beginning. In the belief that Hollywood was invading her patch, she discouraged her employees from talking to the actors. Many indeed refused but Woodward,

Advice from editor Ben Bradlee (Jason Robards) for the Watergate investigators, Bob Woodward (Redford) and Carl Bernstein (Dustin Hoffman).

Bernstein and Bradlee stayed with the belief that their immortalisation should be as accurate as possible.

Three-way consultations between Redford, Hoffman and Pakula invariably ended in a call to one of the principals. Can you dial the White House direct? Can you remember what you said on such and such an occasion? What did he reply? What did you do next? Would it be right if we did so and so? Two of Redford's key questions were, 'What did the editors do about Deep Throat? What was their attitude?' Although Woodward has never revealed the identity of his key source – there were, and are, those who are not convinced that he even exists – he had to be treated in the film, albeit indirectly through the eyes of Woodward's superiors.

Redford asked both Bradlee and Woodward about their discussions over Deep Throat and received conflicting answers. Woodward said Bradlee had broached the matter at the water-cooler in the office corridor; Bradlee claimed he'd taken Woodward to the park to avoid the risk of being overheard. When Redford taxed Woodward with this, the reporter agreed that it was indeed a park and recalled exactly how their conversation went. 'What can you tell me about Deep Throat?' Bradlee asked. 'What do you need to know?' Woodward replied. 'I don't want to know who he is,' said Bradlee, 'but I want to know who he is because you see I can't do the reporting for my reporters, which means I have to trust them, and I hate that. I hate having to trust anybody.'

'It was a great line,' said Redford, 'a terrific line for Bradlee, a key to his character, so we put it in the film. A lot of time was spent on that kind of thing.' And a lot of time was spent and, in Redford's opinion, wasted, in discussing character interpretation. Hoffman, like Newman and Streisand before him, was a cerebral actor with a liking for analysing a scene through and through before he performed in front of the cameras, while Pakula demanded as many takes as possible to give himself the necessary choices in the cutting-room. Meanwhile Redford fretted, as an actor and a producer, as time and money and spontaneity slipped away. 'Dustin is very much like Barbra. He likes to talk everything to death. I'd always be thinking, "Let's get it over with."'

Hoffman was also given to letting off steam when the pressure got too great. When co-operation flagged at the *Washington Post*, he demanded that the name of the paper in the film should be changed, only reluctantly allowing Redford and Pakula to talk him out of it. However, there were times when their relationship hit a lighter note. Redford, greatly daring, played a practical joke on Hoffman by telling the Warner security-guards that a scruffy, long haired weirdo had been bugging members of his staff. 'When Dustin turned up, they wouldn't let him in,' he recalls. Hoffman was amused both by this and by working with Redford. 'He is wonderful fun to play against. Fast and very daring. If you stubbed your toe or dropped a pencil, he picked up on it right away and made it a part of the scene.'

By November, 300,000 feet of film had been shot at a cost of 8.5 million dollars, 3.5 million over budget and thirty-five days over schedule. 'Part of me had to be the responsible producer,' said Redford, 'and part of me wanted to be creatively indulgent as an actor. These parts were always at war. I was very uncomfortable being in the production category on this and also acting in it because part of me wanted to see the director have all the freedom in the world and the other part got very upset when I thought he was wasting time or just had the wrong approach, or was indecisive. All bothersome. I should have been able to separate the two, but sometimes it was hard.' Small wonder that Redford was described by a crew member as 'the wasp of all time', while Hoffman, with much smaller responsibilities, picked up the perhaps undeserved accolade, 'He is a delight and very co-operative with everyone'.

When shooting stopped in November, Pakula set about reducing the footage to the 12,240 feet required for a two-hour-twenty-minute movie. Redford was constantly involved, sleeping just four hours a night as work went on around the clock to get the film ready to be released in the spring. Everyone agreed that his idea of typewriter keys hitting a piece of paper, backed by an explosion of sound for the opening sequence was a good one. It is followed by the arrest of the five Watergate burglars after they fail to crack open a safe at the Democratic National Committee offices. When the papers are alerted to the judicial hearing, Woodward and Bernstein are put on the job, and the stage is set for their painstaking search for the truths that will topple the President.

As the film came together, it was the ending that posed the only real dilemma. Should it be archive footage of Nixon leaving the White House in a helicopter or should it, as Redford wished, be a repeat of the typewriter keys? 'This film is not about Nixon. We could have screwed Nixon lots of times if we'd wanted to. It is about how two reporters get a story and how a newspaper works. It's a "now" film,' he commented, but the Nixon ending stayed until *All The President's Men* was previewed in San Diego in front of an invited audience. When assorted movie moguls and their nearest and dearest assembled on the tarmac at Burbank for this expedition, jangling nerves were soothed with sandwiches and Scotch on the rocks as they waited for Redford. Inevitably he was late, causing a delay in the departure of the Boeing 727 the studio had rented for the occasion.

On arrival in San Diego, Redford, thinly disguised in a hat and dark glasses, was driven to the cinema in the back of a van and smuggled into the back row just after the credits rolled. He left again before the lights came up, but by that time a lot of his worries were over. The audience had cheered Woodward and Bernstein and had booed Nixon and Mitchell, they'd laughed in the right places and stayed to the end. Only the final helicopter sequence had been greeted without enthusiasm, leaving the way open for Redford's preferred ending.

As the release date approached, the question in everyone's mind was did the public want to rake through Watergate or did they want to forget it? After the critical and commercial disappointment of *The Great Gatsby*, it was an especially worrying time for Redford. Although *All The President's Men* wasn't deliberately hyped in the *Gatsby* manner, it had received more than its share of publicity on account of its stars, its subject matter and its representation of the reporter as hero. Warner Brothers decided to go for blanket coverage by booking it into more than 500 cinemas nationwide, a strategy developed by Joseph Levine for a bummer called *Hercules* in 1957.

This take-the-money-and-run approach relied on the notion that if the film were widely available, enough people would see it before news of its true quality – or lack of it – leaked out. It had worked with *The Great Gatsby*. Later it would work, but in a rather different way, with *Superman* which proved so popular that hundreds of cinemas were needed to cope with the crowds. Which category would *All The President's Men* fall into? Anxious connections didn't have long to wait:

on April 8, 1976, the film opened to almost unanimous enthusiasm. It grossed seven million dollars in seven days, a figure that comprehensively beat *The Godfather* over the same period, and thirty million dollars in six months.

The major critics loved the film, the direction and the acting. '*All The President's Men* is a lot of things all at once,' wrote Vincent Canby in the *New York Times*. 'It is a spellbinding detective story about the work of. the two *Washington Post* reporters who helped to break the Watergate scandal, a breathless adventure which recalls the triumphs of Frank and Joe Hardy in that long-ago series of boys' books, and a vivid footnote to some contemporary American history that still boggles the mind. The film is an unequivocal smash hit – the thinking-man's *Jaws*.' And he added words of praise for the actors. 'Mr. Redford and Mr. Hoffman play their roles with a low-keyed understated efficiency required since they are, in effect, the straight men to the people and the events they are pursuing.'

Rex Reed commented on the craftsmanship of the writing and the cinematic brilliance of Alan Pakula before he got down to what he saw as the nitty gritty. 'Best of all, however, are Robert Redford and Dustin Hoffman, as the glue holding all the bits of paper together, and somehow they manage the impossible task of submerging their own superstar images literally to become the reporters they are playing. Redford's well-bred, Ivy League charm is used to good advantage as Woodward, while Hoffman's eager, rumpled, chain-smoking Bernstein is a perfect counterpart. As different as they are, they merge into one molecular structure in a powerful scene that gave me goose-bumps.'

John Simon summed up the consensus among his peers when he wrote, '*All The President's Men* is worth seeing twice: once for everything about it and again, just for the acting.' However, some of the minor reviewers had complaints to make. John Barbour of *Los Angeles Magazine* requested the Nixon ending that now lay on the cutting-room floor. *New West*'s Stephen Farber went much further: '*All The President's Men* is tedious and literal minded; it diminishes the most dramatic story of the decade.' Nor did he have much sympathy for the portrayal of the reporters: 'sanitised and emasculated, the characters never come alive,' he concluded.

Hoffman, too, allowed himself a little gripe about the film's semi-documentary style. 'I told Bob he was drying the picture out. I said he should add a scene where Woodward and Bernstein were really having it out. But he didn't. I would have fought more, but by the time I saw the film, it was too late to make the radical changes I wanted. In my opinion, the film is a little too smooth. I would have left a few hairs on the lens. It really is a landmark in as much as it's the first movie that really said anything even half-assedly true about the press. Bob deserves this success. Not to take anything away from Alan Pakula, who directed it, but this was Redford's project all the way. He may be the hardest-working actor I've ever known.'

At this time, Hoffman was no friend of the Academy Awards which he considered to be demeaningly political. As he had described the Oscar ceremonies as 'ugly and grotesque' on CBS networked television during the summer of 1975, it wasn't surprising that his name was absent from the nominations when *All The President's Men* came up for judgment. Redford's omission might seem more surprising until you remember that there is a right-wing bias among the Academicians, which makes it unlikely they would honour the men who overturned a Republican President, even at second-hand. The film did receive nominations in eight lesser categories, with William Goldman collecting for his much maligned and changed script and Jason Robards for his portrayal of the gruff Ben Bradlee.

If Redford were hurt, he didn't show it and he was well satisfied with his financial bonanza and his artistic success. He countered Hoffman's view with a more positive one of his own. 'Story and atmosphere were the important things here. Character and relationships were less important. We decided that right at the beginning, and we stuck to our guns. I never worked on a picture that so much thought went into. A lot of it was preventative thought, not so much do this as don't do that. Don't make it a movie about Nixon or Watergate. Don't take a partisan position. Don't set out to celebrate the press. Don't be too impressed with the history involved. Don't fall in love with the *Washington Post*. Do make a movie about the press, about two reporters who did a difficult job of reporting and did it well.'

By laying down his own ground rules in this way, he earned the right to be pleased when he kept to them and, on this rare occasion, he admitted that he was: 'To an extent that surprised me, the movie I wanted to make is right up there on the screen: a movie about the truth, and how close we came to losing the right to know it.'

Redford's own chance to take the money and run came when he received a call from Richard Attenborough offering him two million dollars for three weeks' work on *A Bridge Too Far*. After four years involvement and two years non-stop commitment to *All The President's Men*, he'd decided to take a break for at least a year. 'I'm not concerned with momentum, I do enough movies. I need some time to cool out and re-charge,' he'd said, but the 'knee-buckling' figure changed his mind, especially as he could do the movie and be free through the summer of 1976. 'It's so much money I'd be nuts to turn it down,' was his verdict and Lola, with the books to balance at Sundance, hastened to agree.

A Bridge Too Far was based on Cornelius Ryan's account of Field Marshal Montgomery's over-ambitious scheme to cut short World War

Two in the autumn of 1944. The aim of Operation Market Garden, as the offensive was known, was to parachute 35,000 British and American troops into Holland to capture six crucial bridges. Once the paratroopers had accomplished this task, they were to be joined by infantry for the invasion of Germany and the long march to Berlin. As Montgomery and his staff had underestimated the narrowness of the roads and the strength of the German forces in the area, the reality was rather different, more especially because fog in England prevented effective air support and the paratroopers were hampered by radio failure. These accumulated errors and mishaps came to a head in the one-sided aerial Battle of Arnhem, where powerless Allied troops floated gently down into a barrage of German artillery.

From the start, *A Bridge Too Far* was almost as ill-conceived as the events which inspired it. Producer Joseph Levine and director Richard Attenborough recognised the sprawling nature of a plot that required brief appearances by a number of faceless soldiers. Their solution was to hire superstars to play them so that audiences would find instant points of identification. 'They must have immediate impact,' said Attenborough. 'There isn't enough time for long, layered searches for character.'

So it came about that most of the twenty-two million dollar budget – a record scheduled film cost at the time – was earmarked for actors'

Richard Attenborough explains the situation to Redford as Major
Julian Cook in *A Bridge Too Far* (1977).

salaries. Much of the rest went on authentic detail, as ordained by Attenborough. 'A number of my colleagues and acquaintances died here,' he said. 'It would be intolerable if we were sloppy.' Redford was joined in this galaxy by Dirk Bogarde, James Caan, Michael Caine, Sean Connery, Edward Fox, Elliott Gould, Gene Hackman, Anthony Hopkins, Laurence Olivier, Ryan O'Neal, Maximilian Schell and Liv Ullmann. Owing to the size of his role, Redford's name comes some way down this list but it was definitely at the top where it counted: in the money stakes. Levine, who reckoned that making flat payments would be cheaper in the long term than handing out percentages, believed that Redford was a snip at the price. 'I'm cheatin' him,' he boasted.

The actor later claimed reasons other than avarice for saying yes. 'I wanted to do *A Bridge Too Far* because it gave me a chance to turn down *Superman*,' he explained flippantly. 'I don't look good in a cape and I don't like to do my own flying.' On another occasion, he tried a more serious approach by invoking the uncle who'd died on a bridge outside Luxembourg a few months after the Battle of Arnhem. 'Such a large part of war is waste – waste of manpower, waste of courage – that I was interested in the project. This battle is probably the best example of the blend of courage and waste with games played by a few generals of anything I can think of. And it makes one wonder about all the other wars that are history, and how many battles were fought with the same futile end, battles that we didn't even hear about.'

One way or another, Redford flew into Deventer, a Dutch town some twenty-five miles outside Arnhem, in late September, 1976, to play Major Julian Cook, a hero who lost most of his men during a rash Waal River crossing. Attenborough described the sequence as the most dangerous in the film and Redford insisted on doing it all himself, paddling his inflatable boat across the water with the butt of his M-1 rifle just as it actually happened. During the crossing, the soldiers join their officer in reciting the Hail Mary. Redford, who is of the undoubtedly correct opinion that war is inevitable though not, of course, desirable, drew on his knowledge of the customs of the old west to endorse this as an authentic response to stress.

'I'm interested in people's behaviour under duress and I think that a lot of courage is absolute panic and fear being manifested in some sort of action,' was his somewhat pompous verdict. 'They do say that when Indians used to attack the cavalry and covered wagons in a circle, when they would start to yell and chant on their attack, a lot of people for years felt that was an attack cry. In truth it was expressing fear . . . and I think a lot of what happened during the crossing of the boats was just that. They keep talking about the crossing being the most courageous, heroic event in the war. I think there was no choice.'

A Bridge Too Far opened to yawning critics and an indifferent public in June, 1977. The completed film went four million dollars over budget and ran for 175, largely turgid, minutes. As Redford was on screen for perhaps twenty of them, the glum reception was of absolutely no importance to him. The reviewers stuck the knife into Ryan O'Neal and Elliott Gould, leaving Redford stranded on the middle ground of being a recognisably handsome face in a motley, anonymous crowd. 'This is an old dinosaur of a movie that may be the last of its size and scope,' Andrew Sarris summed up in *Village Voice*.

As he faced up to moderate box-office returns, Joseph Levine came to recognise the huge extent of his miscalculation: the stars' percentages of the film's profits would have been derisory compared to the fat fees they received. Redford shed no crocodile tears over the fate of his fellow producer. That would have been hypocritical from a man who was laughing all the way to the bank.

12

Marking Time

Putting the perils of the River Waal behind him, Redford retired to Sundance before Christmas, 1976, and this time his retreat was for real. Two years would pass before he allowed a thoroughbred horse, a suit of lights and Jane Fonda to tempt him back into the movies. Meanwhile he had a lot of thinking to do. The official reason for his semi-retirement was the unbearable distortion of his life. Since the *Butch Cassidy* watershed, he'd worked more or less non-stop. The time was ripe for reassessment.

'I was frightened by the size of the image emerging at the time,' he explained. 'My name would pop up on Hollywood Squares. My face appeared in comic strips. It was always slightly distorted, larger than life. The columns carried items lacking any basis in fact. I began to feel like a cartoon-celebrity figure. This was happening despite the fact that I gave almost no interviews and did not appear on talk shows. It seemed to be self-generating. This wasn't the first time I took a recess from acting. But it was the first time I really felt I had no choice.'

Redford has always believed he's paid too high a price for fame but there is evidence to suggest that actors get the amount of attention they want. There are millions of dark-haired Jews who look more or less like Dustin Hoffman and millions of blond, freckled Californian surfies who look much like Robert Redford. Yet Hoffman has always been able to stroll in the street and Redford can't. Is it because Hoffman, supremely talented actor that he is, is better able to play anonymous? Or is it because he sincerely wants to be overlooked? Of course Redford is a heart-throb and a sex symbol, but the fact remains that there are some 280 million Americans. Would you expect the man standing next to you to be Robert Redford rather than someone who looked quite like him?

Derek Malcolm, the *Guardian* film critic, remembers an incident in the early seventies which illustrates this point. When he interviewed Redford, the actor said he would like a game of tennis so Malcolm invited him to play singles at his club. Redford accepted cautiously, not because of his tennis – he assured Derek that he would have reached Wimbledon standard if he'd chosen to concentrate on the game – but because of the mobbing he imagined was in store. However, no one recognised him through two hard-fought sets. 'How about a drink?' Malcolm asked when the score was one set all. 'Oh, I don't know . . .' Redford replied, but he agreed to go into the clubhouse. After he'd left, a fellow member asked Derek whom he'd been playing against. 'Robert Redford,' he answered. 'Oh, go on. Don't give me that. Who was it really?' was the reply.

This suggests that if Redford had chosen to live in Europe, as he liked to do when he was young, he could have had a relatively normal existence while continuing with a lucrative international film career. Instead he became increasingly interested in all things American, and particularly western American. By 1976, his Fifth Avenue apartment was filled with elaborate spotlighted collections of Kachina dolls and tubs filled with Rocky Mountain plants. Only the sagebrush failed to survive this drastic change in circumstances.

Of course, attitudes towards him had altered since the days when he walked to work down Broadway in his pyjamas and sat for an hour in a trash-can on 57th Street just to see what would happen. The answer was nothing much: very few people even noticed. Post-Cassidy, Redford was often spotted in Manhattan, but usually in a rough and ready way he could live with. On one occasion, he hit a photographer who bugged him, in the street, but more often he lets recognition go with an easy smile. 'It's a tough, honest, dirty city that doesn't pretend to be anything else,' he explains. 'It's a place where cops or cabbies say, "Hey, Rahbert!" and then leave you alone. People don't goon out the way they do in some cities.'

Redford has said that if he'd been raised in Omaha or Atlanta or London or even New York, he might have been better able to play the star game. Familiarity with 'the tiny, ugly, little street' that is Hollywood, bred a contempt that spilled over to cover the whole town. 'Hollywood is a state of mind more than anything else,' he told Melvin Bragg. 'Los Angeles holds no fascination for me because it has no roots. The roots that I ever felt as a kid growing up there are gone, they've long since been gone. Also Los Angeles to me was a place that you left to go somewhere else because everything was too perfect. The sun was always shining, no one seemed to be starving, everyone seemed mildly happy, everyone looked well. It was sort of suffocating.'

As the years passed, the nature of Redford's disaffection with his home town increased in direct proportion to his developing obsession with the destruction of the environment. 'It's red alert,' he insisted. 'Smog, sulphur content, people coughing and wheezing and going into air-conditioned rooms to lie down. Hollywood hasn't changed though. It only changes for one reason – fear. The whole town is built on fear.'

Although Redford hadn't spent much time in Los Angeles, he'd lived with this Hollywood mentality non-stop since he'd become a producer eight years earlier. He'd met regularly with the new style moguls who had taken over from the traditionalists at the end of the sixties, the corporate giants like General Foods who knew nothing about making movies. 'They assumed you could run an art form like a business, with a computerised, businesslike approach. But then a lot of multi-million-dollar films, with big, big budgets, went right on their ass. There's something very natural about the film business which makes it impossible to calculate entirely. I heard somebody say, "Hey, guys, I think we have a chance here to make an Academy Award film," and I had to leave the room. I couldn't take that. So the corporate guys went under, and there was a new wave – agents, say, as heads of studios. And we saw what kind of corruption that led to.'

Irritatingly, everyone expected Redford to be grateful for his good fortune, so his complaints about his lack of privacy never met with much sympathy. 'It's like saying I'm so unhappy I'm so rich, and expecting people to feel sorry for you. What frightens me more than anything is the shrinking. The environment shrinks on you. People begin to treat you more and more like an object, and the danger is that you begin to feel more and more like an object and the chances are that you begin to be more and more like one.'

Although the Sundance Institute and the Institute for Research Management were still some years ahead, Redford spent a lot of his double sabbatical formulating the ideas that would underpin them. As he approached his fortieth birthday in August, 1977, he was at his most active politically. If he was in a city, it was usually Washington where he lobbied in the corridors of power for the causes he believed in. The line between being taken for a nutty radical and a pompous ass is a fine one, as he soon discovered, and he certainly wouldn't claim to have always walked it successfully.

'It's very easy to take someone whose profession is in one area, but who's doing work in another and make light of them,' he told Daniel Geery of the *Los Angeles Herald Examiner*. 'When actors, in particular, get involved in civic or national affairs that are unrelated to acting, they become pretty good targets of ridicule. Their credibility is usually attacked. I like to think that I'm a little more thoughtful and probably more moderate than a lot of people might think. I really resist labels of any kind. I'm concerned about the quality of life that we're leading now and that we're going to lead – however it is that you label that.'

Arousing interest in environmental issues was, he was soon to learn, a decidedly tricky business. Only when decisions directly affected them did citizens stand up to be counted on such topics as industrial development, pollution and population control. Outside their own little orbits, they didn't give a damn. 'We must face the fact that we're going to have to change our life styles whether we like it or not,' Redford insists. 'And history has shown that Americans don't like changing the way they live. Usually we fight, kick and scream about changing. And we're going to have to get over this idea of the "last frontier". The truth is that the frontiers are gone. In the United States, they've been gone for a long time.

'Population control ties in with the fact that we have diminishing resources, diminishing space and diminishing quality of air,' he continues. 'We have a responsibility to keep things in a kind of balance – human life, resources, industrial development and so forth. That's my overriding theme in just about everything – create a balance. So if I appear to be a radical on the environment, it's because care for the environment needs to be brought into balance with the accelerated increase of industrial development.'

With the Democrat Jimmy Carter in the White House, Redford had reasonable grounds for believing that his ideas would find favour – and in theory they did. Carter's energy programme was, as Redford admitted, very well intentioned and solar energy, his own particular baby, had a part to play in it. The trouble, as with so much of Carter's ineffectual administration, was that it never really got off the ground. This was partly because the oil and gas companies defended their vested interests with an intelligent pre-emptive strike. With so much to lose if there were major government investment in solar energy, they were willing to spend a fortune on bending the public mind to their way of thinking. They took full page advertisements in prominent newspapers to announce their own sympathy for solar energy. 'In fact, we're taking a leadership role in researching it,' they stated. 'But we've got a problem now. Solar energy isn't going to be here for a long time and we don't know if it's ever going to satisfy our needs.' In essence, it was don't call us and ask for it, we'll call you when – and if – it's ready.

Redford blamed Carter's Energy Secretary, James R. Schlesinger, for the fact that this bluff was never called. After withholding his reactions until the newcomer had had a fair chance to show his paces, the actor came out with the following indictment: 'After a period of time in office, I've pretty well settled on the fact that he is not good. He is pro-nuclear power. I've met with the man twice. He doesn't know anything about solar energy. He talked about getting the energy conservation message across to the people, and then proceeded to do nothing about it. So I have to conclude that he wasn't really sincere about it. He's a politician. He is a man who has spent most of his professional life not in the public interest, but in administrative positions and in government cabinet positions.'

While Congress, where many of the members had oil-company contracts, systematically savaged Carter's programme, Redford retired to his mountain to enjoy the fruits of his workaholic's progress through the previous decade. 'I use whatever position I've gained to do something I want to do,' he explains. 'It's kind of selfish but it's what I think is important. I'm concerned, obviously, with bringing children into this world. I feel an obligation, a responsibility to do something about the life my family will be leading. I don't want to be responsible for bringing them into the world, then creating an atmosphere impossible for them to live in – that's a form of genocide.'

So be it. If he couldn't make his views stick on a national stage, he would implement them at Sundance where his power was absolute. The house that he and Lola had built fifteen years earlier was pulled down and replaced with an eight-bedroom solar home. The huge two-storey living-room has a south-facing glass wall, the better to collect the sun's rays, and a spectacular view over the ski slopes. The children's bedrooms, each with a raised sleeping area and a bathroom, also face south. Downstairs a patio leads to gardens with ornamental waterfalls and a three-acre grass area with a tennis court, a bathhouse and a solar-heated pool efficient enough to allow the Redfords to swim at 8,000 feet from May to November.

The foreman and his family live in a second solar home in the grounds. Redford drew the line at showing his own place to would-be imitators, but allowed his employee's house to be used as a model, a double standard as far as privacy is concerned. On the agricultural side, he expanded his farming operation with crops that would complement the horse-breeding programme, mainly barley, oats and alfalfa. As the greenhouse makes the most basic use of solar energy, he also went into vegetables and added further to his self-sufficiency by building a trout pond.

There were other instances of double standards in Redford's life at this time. The one that got the most publicity was his illegal helicopter skiing expedition onto the slopes of Mount Timpanogos. Sundance may have been developed along impeccable ecologically conscious lines, but Redford's passion for powder skiing tempted him into landing a chopper in a National Park. After he and Brent Beck made a gloriously isolated 4,000-foot descent through virgin snow, they were met by outraged authorities. 'Mr. Redford,' they said, 'we're sure sorry about this but you're operating a motorised vehicle on government property without a permit.'

'Aw, Jesus,' the actor replied, 'I could take this a lot easier if the Forest Service stopped taking a double standard on what it regulates.

You're making an issue of this, and on the other side of the mountain you have this massive development that is going to rip apart the whole Wasatch front, and is a total boondoggle.' One irony in all this was that if Redford had jumped the last few feet, the trip would have been perfectly legal: it was the landing, not the skiing, which had infringed the law. The other more poignant irony from his point of view was that he'd been trying to drum up publicity for an eight-minute film on solar energy he'd helped to make, but without success. 'I'm not much on publicity, but this was one thing I wanted to attract attention to. So we had a series of press conferences and there was hardly any coverage. I get more coverage trying to sneak in and out of a restaurant,' he said bitterly.

As absolute power is rarely popular with those who live in its shadow, there was a certain amount of feuding between the laird of all he surveyed, and the few unlucky citizens who came under his gaze. Among them were Jack and Phil Ekins, brothers from neighbouring Provo and long-time friends of Lola Redford's father, Frank Von Wagenen. Even before the Redfords had built their first home, the Ekins had bought two plots in Timphaven with a view to putting up two houses at some unspecified future date. When Redford bought up the surrounding land, their plots became islands to which they had to request access. Redford agreed and put up a barrier on his own land, securing it with a padlock to which he gave the Ekins a key. Later he changed his mind, and with it the padlock, refusing to give the brothers the new key.

When they took him to court, he said that allowing people to cross his land would make it easier for thieves, vandals and would-be kidnappers to get at him. When a Utah judge ruled in favour of the Ekins, Redford appealed, possibly in the hope that lack of funds with which to feed the voracious American legal system would force his adversaries to quit. 'It has cost us a lot of money,' Jack Ekins commented, 'and it is still going on. It's funny in a way because I have known Redford's father-in-law for years. We grew up together and I can remember him telling me that his daughter Lola was involved with some crazy actor fellow in Hollywood and was going to marry him. We were all pleased for her. I never dreamed that one day we would be fighting each other in court.'

Redford shrugs off what seems to be unreasonably bad behaviour on his part. Everyone's happy with actors so long as they remain on the screen, he complains, but let them join the real world and resentment sets in. The implication is that he doesn't see why he should have to behave any better than anyone else. On this occasion, it's clear that he didn't; rather worse in fact since the Ekins, though no doubt prosperous, would be greatly disadvantaged in any legal battle with him. This is the kind of incident that confirms the widely held view that Redford, a man whose best friends admit they daren't come close to him, cares more about issues than individuals. As a blueprint for happiness, it has serious limitations, as the actor who had almost everything would one day learn.

Meanwhile he emerged occasionally from his retreat to bask in a little passing adulation. In 1977, watched by one of the old enemies, Spiro T. Agnew, he accepted an honorary degree in human letters from Williams College, Williamstown, a début in cap and gown for the habitual academic drop-out. He also narrated *The Predators*, a documentary about American wild life shot in twenty-five states over three-and-a-half years and aired on NBC on May 9, 1977. 'There are no good guys and no bad guys in the wild,' he intoned. 'There is no security for any creature that the greatest predator of all – man – declines to let live in peace.' It is easy to believe that it was an assignment he enjoyed.

By 1978, Redford was beginning to feel that if he didn't act again soon, he never would. The lay-off had aroused all his old doubts about the validity of his profession. On the one hand, he found some pleasure in giving people a temporary escape, on the other he wondered if acting really were a suitable job for a grown-up. Was his privacy really his top priority, he asked himself, or was he secretly pining for the limelight? Apparently he could never make up his mind.

'I really do miss being able to go through life a little less noticed,' he told Michael Rogers of *Rolling Stone*. 'It would be horseshit to say I don't respond to flattery and attention. Clearly there's something in the psyche that makes you want to be an actor in the first place. But I feel a sense of loss at not being able to enjoy the give and take of life a little more. I guess I don't like the fact that my life is becoming less and less my own – the prevailing attitude that you have an obligation to deliver yourself to the public. Actually, you're delivered to the public whether you like it or not. I guess if you don't like it, you should stop doing what provokes it. In my case, that's acting.'

Having mulled over this dilemma and decided against permanent retirement, he called Sydney Pollack to discuss their next project. Their first choice was *A Place To Come To*, based on a novel by Robert Penn Warren about the struggles of a poor, white southerner to establish himself in the prosperous north-east over forty years starting in the late twenties. The role would have required Redford to age from eighteen to sixty, but he and Pollack pulled the plug on the assembled crew when the script didn't match up to their expectations. Another possibility was the tale of Tom Horn, a bounty hunter who roamed Wyoming in the 1880s, but it fell through when Redford learned that Steve McQueen had a rival version in the pipe-line. A third proposition was a European climbing film based on Gary Hemming's Alpine exploits during the sixties.

In the end, Redford opted to stay with what he was coming to know best: the American west. When he'd received the outline of *The Electric Horseman* from writer Shelly Burton, in 1976, he'd recognised points of identification between himself and Sonny Steele, an ex-rodeo champ who has been dehumanised by corporate greed. The sinners are Ampco, the multi-national giant which hires him to promote Ranch Cereal by wearing a suit of electric lights and riding a twelve million dollar champion racehorse called Rising Star at supermarket openings and sales conferences.

Both Sonny and Rising Star need help to get through these ordeals. Sonny's crutch is alcohol, taken voluntarily in anaesthetising quantities. Sometimes he doesn't show up for his well-paid public engagements and a stand-in takes his place: Ampco is just beginning to realise that no one notices the difference. Rising Star is on drugs and steroids, the first to prevent lameness from a damaged tendon and to subdue him in cheering crowds, the second to keep him looking good. When the horse-loving Sonny's protests fall on deaf corporate ears, he rides Rising Star straight through a Las Vegas floor show and out into the wide black yonder.

For the most part, *The Electric Horseman* is a two-hander, with the second hand belonging to an upwardly mobile and very ambitious television journalist called Hallie Martin. She teeters after Sonny in high-heeled boots in pursuit of a scoop. Initially she is scornful of his drunken unpunctuality and lawless ways, but soon she is won over by his integrity and his deeply sincere rejection of new-fangled capitalism. Not that this prevents her from trying to sell him down the river to further her own career but ultimately nearly everyone wins: the stallion gets his freedom, Ampco gets a thirty per cent increase in cereal sales, Hallie gets her story and a night of passion under the stars. Sonny gets immunity from prosecution but, unlike Rising Star, he has to return to the real world with its tawdry values – and without Hallie. Can this be the first movie in which it is the horse, now running free with others of his kind in a verdant mountain paradise, who gets the girl?

Small wonder that Redford, having decided to forgo his own mountain paradise for the bright Hollywood lights, believed that *The Electric Horseman* was a suitable case for treatment. In the event, the scriptwriters' fifty-five-page treatment of Shelly Burton's story fell substantially short of what was required. It didn't reflect Pollack and Redford's vision of recapturing the optimism and the patriotism of the thirties and forties as expressed in Frank Capra movies such as *Mr. Deeds Goes to Town* and *It Happened One Night.* 'We wanted to make a fable or a morality play,' Pollack comments. 'The good and evil are clear-cut and virtue triumphs. From talking to our kids about this, and from listening to our own sensibilities, we realised that something innocent and marvellous had been lost. We wondered why not make a picture like that now, full of fantasy and optimism and good feelings.'

So they did, but they had to write it themselves as they went along, with the actors contributing lines on scraps of paper even as the cameras were ready to turn. From the start, Pollack had known that only a 'genuine fourteen-carat movie star' would be able to match Redford in the key role of Hallie. Both men had worked with Jane Fonda before, Pollack on *They Shoot Horses, Don't They?* and Redford on *Barefoot in the Park*, and both had admired her talent and intelligence. However, the intervening decade had turned her from a privileged sixties swinger into a left-wing political animal and Redford, in particular, had suffered in the metamorphosis. 'I've known two Robert Redfords,' she stated in her characteristically forthright way, 'when we made *Barefoot in the Park*, he was a young man full of interests, sensitive to the problems of his time, politically and socially involved. But now he's perfectly integrated and an instrument of the star system. I think he was bluffing before. There was a time in Hollywood where you had to look like a progressive. But he is, and remains, a bourgeois in the worst sense of the word.'

Reunited with the delectable Jane Fonda in *The Electric Horseman* (1979).

These unkind words appeared in *Village Voice* on March 3, 1977 which suggests either that Redford didn't read the radical paper and didn't know anyone who did, or that he has a fairly large capacity for forgiveness. Either way Fonda was signed to play Hallie for one million dollars, the same fee Redford commanded, and they got on well together throughout, perhaps because *The Electric Horseman* covers the middle ground on which they were able to reach agreement. 'People are frightened of Jane,' Redford told Jilly Cooper in the famous *Sunday Times* interview of March, 1980, 'but she's like the lion in *The Wizard of Oz* – all roar, but frightened herself underneath, and full of heart. People think Jane and I relate politically but actually we relate on a human level.' Cooper suggested that this was meaningless waffle, but the reality is that the two actors liked each other enough to submerge political differences in a long-term friendship. On set they kept their distance, perhaps because Sonny and Hallie spend more time as antagonists than friends, but, throughout the eighties, Fonda habitually took her husband, Tom Hayden, and her children to stay at Sundance over Christmas and New Year. 'He's changed and so have I,' she admits. 'I was too abrasive then.'

The early razzmatazz part of *The Electric Horseman* was shot in Las Vegas, with Caesar's Palace, hardly a natural habitat for either of them, as the unit base. 'It's a place built on greed, representing the absolute worst in our culture,' said Fonda didactically. 'The ethic that built this city is horrendous.' Redford too found a personal axe to grind. 'It's amusing to me. A sign in the hotel room says, "Turn off the lights when you leave. Help us to conserve energy." Then take a look at the Strip, all that all-night incredible energy-consuming neon!'

Las Vegas didn't return these insults, but basked in the glory of the superstars' presence. Redford came in for particular attention in a place designed to attract trivial, star-struck, autograph-hunting women. It was a situation in which everyone wanted to know his magic secrets but, although he responded with unusual amiability, he made sure he didn't have any answers. 'I don't believe in analysing something that is going well for me. If it were the other way around, if a lot of people found me loathsome, I'd probably try to figure why. I don't understand the popularity, but I don't analyse it. If I'm a sex symbol to some people, it's because I made love to a woman in a picture that was successful. If I'd made love to Barbra Streisand in a movie that flopped, I would not be considered a sex symbol.'

A six-month search for the perfect horse to play Rising Star ended when veteran movie wrangler, Kenny Lee, visited a dressage school in the San Fernando Valley. Let's Merge, a five-year-old bay thorough-bred, was owned by classical guitarist, Christopher Parkening. He'd kept him on his ranch in Montana as a saddle-horse and family pet

before sending him off for further training. Lee and Redford appreciated his conformation and his turn of foot but it was his gentle
disposition that got him the assignment. It would hardly do if the lead in
a film about a drug-abused horse had to be sedated before the cameras
rolled.

Both Redford and Let's Merge were fitted with 'light-up suits'. The
horse's saddle and bridle were studded with miniature light-bulbs as
was the actor's outfit. His purple satin tunic and trousers were deco-
rated with green and gold *fleur de lys* and punctured by hundreds of
tiny holes. Each contained a bulb soldered to a wire leading to a central
wiring system that connected with a battery pack in the horse's saddle.
The suit was lined so that the wiring didn't scratch Redford, but during
preliminary tests to establish the most effective voltage, the system
short-circuited and sent a shock down his left leg. 'Now I know what
they mean by hot pants,' he joked. Once the 35,000 dollar costume was
complete, Pollack warned him most vehemently not to spill anything on
it because there was no way it could be cleaned.

Both Redford and Let's Merge had doubles and Kenny Lee imagined
that it would be the stuntman rather than the star who would ride down
the Vegas strip in the middle of rush hour traffic. Predictably he was
wrong. 'Like most smart horses, Let's Merge is very sensitive to his
rider's mood and ability,' he said with the pride of temporary owner-
ship. 'He'll obey an experienced rider – he was beautiful with Redford –
but put a novice on his back and he's apt to horse around. No pun
intended. We thought the strip scene would be hard to get, but we were
through in three days.'

This was only one day more than the 280,000-dollar 'kiss' between
Redford and Fonda. They did it forty-eight times, starting at nine a.m.
on a Tuesday and finishing at six p.m. the next day. Out of the 7,500
feet of film that covered it from every angle, fifty feet were used for the
twenty-second sequence in the final film. It would indeed have been
cheaper if, as one cost-conscious accountant suggested, Redford had
kissed the horse.

When *The Electric Horseman* was ready to hit the cinemas, Columbia
and Universal, its joint backers, thought up some pretty tacky ways of
promoting it. At one stage, they dared to suggest sending Let's Merge
on a publicity tour. 'Gentlemen, you don't know what you're saying.
That is exactly what the movie condemns,' was Pollack's retort. Even
when he'd talked the studio representatives out of that piece of mis-
placed zeal, he still had to live with advertising that emphasised the
word 'electric' in reference to Redford and Fonda. 'It's not dirty or
anything, but it seems cheap to me. And the TV ads seem cheap and
corny. They embarrass me. The marketing of anything is full of
exploitation and lies and hype. On the other hand, am I to forgo film

making because I don't like the promotion? That pure I'm not. I'm corrupt enough to want my pictures to be successful.'

He certainly got his wish with *The Electric Horseman* which pulled in a handsome forty million dollars during its first few months of release. On the whole, the critics preferred life with Robert Redford to life without him. *New York*'s David Denby mentioned his own pleasure, and the palpable pleasure of those around him, at seeing the actor as Sonny Steele before delivering the nitty gritty. 'Robert Redford has always been a natural, intuitive, unemphatic movie actor who drew us close with his extraordinary good looks and his sweet candour and then shut us out by never revealing much of himself. Redford has considerably less identity than, say, Burt Reynolds or Jack Nicholson. He's trying to stretch himself a little in this movie, but the screenwriters have written a largely synthetic role for him, and the director, Sydney Pollack, doesn't pull much out of him.' He also complained about Redford and Fonda who had, he claimed, generated more heat in *Barefoot in the Park*. 'It's almost as if they were too big now – world powers, almost – to sully themselves with sex or anger. Redford may get drunk on screen – it's a macho prerogative – but he's not going to make a pass at a girl (too undignified), so the romance takes for ever to get under way.'

Although *Time*'s Richard Schickel correctly stressed the improbability of the plot, and especially of a well-staged, but basically impossible, horse and car chase, he was more generous with the actors. Having praised Fonda's 'winning grace', he saved the best for his old friend: 'Redford, making his first major appearance in four years, is in top form. He's a knothead, trying to disguise his essentially moral nature and his native shrewdness with a lot of "good-ole-boy aw shucks-ing". There is tension, good observation, and fine comic-timing in his work. It's obvious that both stars saw this film as a vehicle to advocate causes they care about, but they are good-natured about it.'

Redford himself pulled out all the stops to make sure his comeback didn't go unnoticed. He may have calmed his nerves by eating two boxes of unbuttered popcorn when he took his family to see the film in Provo, but he later made a rare journey to London on Concorde to talk to journalists about it.

Jet-lagged over a late dinner in his hotel, he told Jilly Cooper that the supersonic plane made him feel like Jonah in a very narrow whale, but not how he managed to reconcile its fuel consumption figures with his conscience. Warned not to mention ecology by the publicist, she was mortified when her nerves got the better of her and she blurted out a question which elicited a twenty-minute lecture on pollution and solar energy. It was a bad beginning from which neither she, nor Redford, ever really recovered. As the courses came and went, the actor's string of platitudes failed to satisfy the inquisitive and sexy journalist. 'He was terribly nice, but I never got near him,' she concluded sadly. Presumably her evasive quarry felt equally pressurised because he drank four lagers and five glasses of red wine over the two-and-a-half-hour meeting, not bad going for a man widely believed to be virtually teetotal.

Once the interview had appeared in *The Sunday Times*, Cooper assuaged her disappointment by subjecting Redford to the Dinner Date Test in the *Daily Mail* and making the following judgments. Humour: good for a laugh, but not at himself (5 out of 10). Manners: tired towards the end and looked at his watch, but managed not to yawn too much (8). Grooming: fine for a man who'd just come off the plane (9). Clothes: jeans too big on the hips (8). Fulfilment of image: not as sexy in the flesh as on the screen; she didn't fancy him and didn't think he fancied her (5). Intelligence and conversation: six 'O' levels and perhaps one 'A' level; superficially meaningful but essentially meaningless as a conversationalist (6). Figure: the tops; you'd definitely crick your neck in the street (10). Overall assessment: laid-back and not her type. Superficially amiable but basically detached. Definitely no vibes (7).

At least she saw the date through to the end which was more than could be said of another London-based journalist who received the call to interview Redford. A thorough man, he had made notes of his first impressions of the actor when he saw him in *Barefoot in the Park* on Broadway back in 1964. 'Newcomer Redford clearly fancies himself a great deal,' he'd written on a small card, 'and he wasn't that good. I don't think he will go on . . .' After discussing *The Electric Horseman*, the journalist produced the card and showed it to the star in 'an egg on my face' spirit of self-deprecation. The next thing he knew, he was walking towards the lifts: Redford had flung him out of his hotel room. Yes, Jilly, you are perfectly right, Mr. Redford does not laugh at himself. The score for humour should have been 2 out of 10.

More than a year before he failed to arouse Ms. Cooper, the Golden Loner (as she described him) had made *Brubaker*, a prison-reform drama which started shooting five days after *The Electric Horseman* wrapped. This didn't matter to Redford who was already well versed in the ramifications of a character he'd agreed to play long before Sonny Steele slipped into his suit of lights. His briefing came from the reality behind *Brubaker*, one Thomas O. Murton, a prison reformer who had been put in charge of two Arkansas prison farms by the newly-elected governor, Winthrop Rockefeller, in 1967.

An articulate, intelligent man some years ahead of his time, at least so far as the 'Deep South' was concerned, Murton put his head into a noose from the start. 'No one sends an Olympic swimming-team to practise in the Sahara,' he told the *Guardian*'s Tom Tickell, 'but most countries do something just as stupid. They take people who have made bad decisions, stick them in jail for five or six years, without allowing them to make one single decision for that time, and are then surprised and angry that they do not come out as model citizens.'

Armed only with this liberal viewpoint, Murton arrived as a 'prisoner' at Tucker Farm in 1968 to find a multiple nightmare. The prison was run by trusties, a group of privileged gangsters who organised crimes behind bars as adeptly and as ruthlessly as any Mafioso band. In this they were comprehensively backed by the state of Arkansas which allowed them to carry guns, divert and sell prison supplies to create profits with which to buy freezers and colour television sets and rip off, or brutalise, the rankmen, depending on their financial status. 'You could get a room or a better job in the jail, or women or liquor, provided that you had enough cash to make the trustie interested,' Murton explained. 'What happened otherwise? You survived as well as you could. But God help you if you were young and attractive. We had a lot of fourteen and ten-year-old boys in the jail and they were sometimes subjected to a homosexual gang-bang.' Those who were unwise enough to complain were beaten or subjected to the Tucker telephone, an old-fashioned crank instrument which was connected to an electrode strapped to a man's penis or big toe. Turn the handle and electricity went through the victim's body, sometimes to the point of unconsciousness.

Corruption within was mirrored by corruption without. Those who had influence with the governor or the trusties regularly received stolen prison materials and convict labour for the price of a kickback to the providers. In this way, crops were harvested, logs sawn and swimming-pools built for a fraction of their true cost. 'The origins of the system probably go back to the Civil War,' said Murton. 'They may have abolished slavery, but the landowners still needed people to pick their cotton. What happened was that convict labour replaced slave labour.'

State officials habitually turned a blind eye to these illegalities in the belief that prisons should be as invisible and profitable as possible. At Tucker, a 5,000-acre farm, five paid staff ran 300 men. This ratio was only possible if some of the prisoners were appointed as overseers in the fields, a service that was rewarded with the freedom to exploit the men who worked under them. According to Murton, the jail generated a one million dollar surplus which made the state very proud. 'People used to boast that Arkansas was the only state in the world to have a prison system which paid for itself. I only discovered later that two million dollars were slipping through the system.'

Murton began his counter-attack with speed and commitment. He ended all physical punishment and brought in better food and new clothes to raise morale. He allowed journalists into the prison to see conditions for themselves, so getting the newspapers on his side and putting the frighteners on the authorities. He tried to break the power of the trusties, not immediately but gradually by trading concessions. When he burned down their shacks, he balanced it out by giving them some extra home leave and he told them that in the short-term, he had no plans to end drinking or gambling.

So far, so good but when Murton took over Cummins prison farm as well, he went too far. He knew that the prison system could be blamed for some 200 murders in Arkansas. He knew that trusties who shot runaways were rewarded with extra parole. He knew that this practice gave them a licence to murder awkward prisoners and bury them near the boundary walls so it would look as if they'd been trying to escape. At Cummins, he learned from the prisoner who made the coffins where to dig for the bodies and he dug, regardless of instructions to the contrary from the governor. Inevitably he was fired after just eleven months on the job.

'A grand jury considered indicting me for grave robbing,' he recalled. 'They were more interested in why the men were dug up than why they were buried. Whenever a true reformer comes in, he's going to be opposed by those who have a stake in the old order. Eventually he will push too hard and they'll get rid of him. I'm not the first – or the last. The sad thing is that I have harmed my cause. Now they have seen what I mean by reform, they will never let it happen again.'

Sitting tall in the saddle as the reforming prison governor in *Brubaker* (1980).

Murton spent the two years before he got another job – as Professor of Criminology at the University of Minnesota – immortalising his experiences in a book called *Accomplices to the Crime* (with Joe Hyams). Producers Ron Silverman and Ted Mann were quick to spot its movie-potential but, for eight years, the studios refused to finance it. Paramount agreed to do it, then backed out and two attempts to make it as a television movie failed. When Twentieth Century-Fox finally committed to it, they signed Redford for three million dollars to play Brubaker and Murton for 10,000 dollars to advise him on how to do it. 'Redford's too pretty,' was the ex-prison reformer's verdict, 'but he's a straight enough guy. He takes things seriously.'

W. D. Richter's factually accurate dramatisation begins with Brubaker posing as a newly-arrived prisoner at the Wakefield State Penitentiary, just as Murton did. After a half-hour horror-revealing tour of the prevailing conditions, he breaks up a fight to the death between two inmates and announces that he is the new warden. This brief endurance test may have equipped him to know what is wrong but it certainly hasn't taught him much about putting it right. As compromise is the dirtiest word in his book, it is inevitable that he will eventually be asked to make one and that he will refuse.

Once he has established himself as the rankman's pal, Brubaker sets about his murder hunt with blinkered integrity in the Murton manner. The governor's special assistant, Lillian Grey, tries to persuade him to help the living by studying the system and changing it from within rather than investigating the dead to the embarrassment of all and the advantage of none. She is backed up by a senator who offers Brubaker the means to make his reforms stick if only he will quit grave-digging. A stronger man would have toughed it out for the greater good; Brubaker, a stubborn saint, walks away alone. He is presented as the only force for good in a world he is obliged to share with people corrupted beyond recall. Vicious or well intentioned, prisoners, politicians or liberal do-gooders, they can't hope to match Brubaker's purity. 'He came to redeem us,' wrote Pauline Kael scornfully, 'but we were beyond redemption, so he failed.' Small wonder she thought that the film didn't have a single believable minute in it.

As Redford had made at least half a career out of walking away alone, he had a gut feeling for Brubaker, a man in a movie which would probably never have got off the ground without someone of his pulling power to play the title role. 'He is a controversial figure,' he stated, 'not your hero type, although he has heroic proportions of a different order. He fails on one hand, due to his black and white sensibilities, but he wins a moral victory. Brubaker is a complex character with complex relationships. I wouldn't have taken the picture if it had been just another prison film.'

The *Brubaker* set was built in an abandoned state prison in Columbus, Ohio, a grim institutional building which became the production headquarters for the three-month duration. After ten days' shooting, Bob Rafelson, a quirky director who might have tempered the black and white characterisation with redeeming shades of grey, succumbed to 'creative differences'. He was replaced by Stuart Rosenberg, chosen for two wrong reasons: he was immediately available and his reputation rested on another prison drama, *Cool Hand Luke*, made some twelve years earlier. What if it wasn't very good? In Hollywood's eyes, its very existence was qualification enough.

Jane Alexander plays Lillian Grey, the liberal special assistant who gets Brubaker the job but fails to persuade him to hold it down. The part was written for a man and Ms. Alexander had to forgo her customary period of research in order to pick up on it at very short notice. As the only woman in the cast, she was regularly pestered with questions as to what it was like to work with Redford, more especially as she'd once said that she always fell in love with her leading men. Since then she had married but journalists have long memories and the inferences kept coming.

'Of course Bob Redford's wonderful,' she countered. 'He is very good-looking. He has an extremely strong sense of values – stronger than many actors I can think of. He reminds me, in a way, of Clark Gable, although they don't look alike. But Gable, like Redford, had a sort of nonchalance. Like Gable, part of Redford's charm is that, although he's very good-looking, he does not pamper himself. He doesn't seem conscious of his good looks, and all the hullabaloo doesn't appear to affect him. I suppose I've matured since I said I fall in love with all my leading men. It was truer several years ago than it is today. My husband is just dynamite and it's hard for me to feel a deep attraction to anyone else.'

Brubaker was met with critical pessimism when it premièred in Columbus in June 1980 in the presence of 1,000 local people who'd worked on it. Thomas Murton was among them. He thought the characters were 'humourless and one-dimensional' but praised the 'ninety per cent accuracy' and the fact that it made 'a powerful statement without clichés'. What he appreciated most was that it could have been so much worse. 'I looked at nine or ten scripts and those creative folks must have been smoking pot or something because some of those other scripts were rather bizarre,' he concluded.

This time it was David Denby who stressed the plot's lack of credibility – would the golden loner really have been able to spend a week among killers and armed robbers without being raped or hassled? – before sticking the knife into the actor. 'Redford obviously believes in this man, but he can't play him. Life-time reformers like Brubaker are usually flaky, full of tics; in *Norma Rae*, for instance, Ron Leibman managed to suggest some of the irritating obsessiveness of the type. But Redford is so eager to avoid any trace of grandstanding that he's painfully straight and dull. An actor like Gene Hackman carries the weight of authenticity in his slouch and heavy gut, but Redford with his fighting trim and gleaming locks appears to be a fairy-tale prince visiting the commoners. For a while we enjoy seeing the hip idealist racking up points. But the movie turns sanctimonious in the end.'

Redford, already editing *Ordinary People* by the time *Brubaker* opened and with his three million dollars safely in the bank, allowed himself the luxury of doubt. Was June the right time of year to release *Brubaker*? Would press intimations of failure pull it down? Was the studio strategy of opening small and building on word of mouth, sound? In the event, box-office receipts of thirteen million dollars over the first seventeen days, escalating steadily as the months went by, proved him wrong. 'I was surprised. I had been dubious as to how it would work as a summer film. But I've had more feed-back from the general audience on this picture than with most films. It may have something to do with audiences wanting stuff of substance – who knows? The film business runs through cycles, and maybe this cycle was the end of the disaster-horror cycle. Audiences are tiring of that and want something else. Anyway, I was very happy when they responded.'

So it happened that, by mid-1980, Redford was right back where he belonged as an actor and a star. However scornful he'd been of Hollywood during his lay-off, two hits were two hits, and the money he needed to finance his plans for the new decade was his for the asking. Though he was by no means certain of it at the time, Redford would act after *Brubaker* but he would never be just an actor again. By 1980, he knew what he had to do: he was ready to start on the rest of his life.

13

Getting It Right

As an artist manqué, it was logical that Robert Redford would make his own movie. If there was one thing he was consistently vain about all through his formative years, it was painting, yet this vanity was always underpinned by nagging doubts. These worked both ways, depending on where his Irish moods were taking him at the time. In his manic phases, he was confident that he could have made a decent living as a painter, though he has never been so arrogant as to suggest he could have been a master. At such moments, he wondered if he'd made the right decision when he swapped art, which he has always believed he loved, for acting, 'a girl's job' he'd always believed he despised. In his depressive phases, he recognised that the swap was inevitable: he was a better actor than he ever would be a painter. Only when he was on a high did he allow himself the luxury of retrospective optimism.

The relevance of all this lies in the fact that glad or sad, his priority was painting: could he have? Should he have? From here it is a small step to see film making as an extension of the painter's art, a visual medium through which he would be able to give expression to the things he'd never got down on canvas, or anyway not to his teacher's satisfaction. As the subjects of his paintings had always been people at their most tormented, it followed that his first film as a director would reflect this essential *angst*. And so it turned out to be.

It was in 1976 that Redford received the galleys of *Ordinary People*, a novel by Judith Guest. Raised exclusively on American adventure stories, his taste in fiction was still restricted to native writers. 'I guess I'm a chauvinist, really. I'm not interested in foreign work, but I sure am interested in what's going on in, say, the streets of Chicago. That's why I like Texas writers. They have a real love-hate relationship with their own soil. Almost all of them leave Texas to write, then end up writing about Texas. I like that. It's very American. They can't not write about Texas.'

His preference was for John Irving and Joan Didion, Edward Abbey and Rudy Wurlitzer, Sam Shepard and Tom McGuane. To this exclusive list he now added a Minneapolis housewife in her late thirties who'd written her first book while her sons were at school and her computer executive husband was out at work. With no agent and no knowledge of the business, she'd had considerable difficulty in finding a publisher. When she did, the timing was right because Redford had decided he was ready to direct while working as a producer and actor on *All The President's Men*. 'The little details would drive me crazy,' he told James Spada on the set, 'but I'd let someone handle those. What I would enjoy is visualising a movie and seeing it turn out that way on the screen. That's when it's really fun.' Accordingly he bought the film rights to Guest's book, another example of sound commercial judgment because it rose rapidly in the charts to become a bestseller later in the year.

Redford's liking for *Ordinary People* stemmed from his identification with the teenage lead, Conrad Jarrett, the deeply disturbed son of upper-middle-class parents from Lake Forest, a privileged Chicago suburb. His father, Calvin, is a tax lawyer; his mother, Beth, is obsessed with golf and appearances and immaculate arrangements in the home. These do not include a much loved son, Buck, who has died in a sailing accident, or an unloved one, Conrad, who not only failed to save him, but slit his wrists in remorse. 'She'll never forgive me,' he tells his psychiatrist, 'for spilling blood on the bathroom floor.'

Redford found some rather contrived parallels between the cocoon of wealth in Lake Forest and the sun-soaked beaches in the falsely glamorous shadow of Hollywood where he was raised. Like Conrad, he wanted to get away from what others envied. 'There was such a heavy emphasis on joining – putting your best foot forward, having a shine on your shoes, putting in a presentable appearance. All of which was pretty uncomfortable and oppressive for me. That's why I identify so much with Conrad Jarrett . . . it's the loneliness of being the outsider and of not being heard. And being young enough not to know better than to think you're crazy. If I knew at seventeen what I'd learned by the time I was twenty-five, I would have had a much happier childhood.'

Whether Redford would have been able to finance *Ordinary People* if the book hadn't taken off, must be open to doubt. In the late seventies, seventy-five per cent of moviegoers were aged sixteen to twenty-four and their preference was for *Star Wars* and *Smokey and The Bandit* and their attendant satellites and spin-offs. They definitely didn't want to see small intense films about miserable people. Hollywood would have been more than happy to supply Redford with a blockbuster to direct, something full of car chases and commercial gimmicks, but it was beneath his dignity to accept. 'I saw no virtue in that kind of thing,' he explained. 'I thought it best to start with something which might be difficult, but which was tied to elements I felt about strongly.' In 1979, he persuaded Paramount, with whom he had had an on-going love-hate relationship since he walked out on *Blue*, to see it his way.

Guest's – and Redford's – *Ordinary People* may be ordinary in so far as they can't cope with life, but there are serious doubts as to whether they are people or merely excuses on which to hang an excursion into the psyche. Certainly Calvin Jarrett, a punch bag for a woman whose values are up the creek, barely exists in his own right. 'He is a blob created to be tyrannised by Beth', as Pauline Kael has it, and he is so ineffectual that it is hard to imagine him as a successful lawyer, let alone as the provider of the Jarrett family home, an American Gothic palace on the shores of Lake Michigan. Beth, on the other hand, is everything you ever feared in a repressed personality. She is illogical, tense, socially insecure, proud and irredeemably cold. There is absolutely nothing to like about her. When Calvin turns to her in their bed at night, it is the most passive passion you have ever seen. Only Conrad has any kind of range, as if the novelist is telling us that people, ordinary or not, may be sensitive when they are extremely young, but after that, they're either all hard or all soft.

The success of *Ordinary People* as a film rests partly on an adept adaptation by Alvin Sargent who'd done such a fine job with *Julia*, and partly on Redford's decision to cast against stereotype, a device that diluted the novel's banality. Donald Sutherland, with his pale, manic eyes and his long, narrow bones, has a presence that lends itself to the oddball, the malevolent and the comic. As Calvin Jarrett, he had to suppress it totally. It was a challenge he claims he enjoyed. 'Redford thought it would be a daring, off-the-wall piece of casting. I certainly didn't look like a tax lawyer. I had an immediate affinity for the character after I read it. I felt sympathy toward him and after I saw the finished film, I found things in it that reminded me of both my marriages.'

For Beth, Redford selected Mary Tyler Moore, the archetypal sitcom queen, in the certainty that he could explore a side of her personality that few people imagined existed. Beth Jarrett would have the same plastic features and the same relentless smile as the sunny, resourceful Mary Richards, the darling of *The Mary Tyler Moore Show*'s millions of fans, but this time they would conceal an unfeeling WASP witch. By taking alcohol cures at the Betty Ford clinic, Mary Tyler Moore has revealed that she is less invincible than she seemed in 1979. To his credit, Redford was the first to suspect and use her negative characteristics. 'The courage and rhythm she has as an actress has always appealed to me,' he revealed. 'I thought of her the minute I read the book because

En route for an Oscar at his first attempt, Redford directs Timothy
Hutton in *Ordinary People* (1980).

I've always been intrigued by what I imagined was her dark side. Would
she be willing to expose it? I have odd impulses, I guess.'

In the days before the 'Brat Pack', it was never going to be easy to find
an actor who was young enough and good enough to convince as Conrad
Jarrett. One who ran into Redford at his worst was Michael J. Fox, now
a tiny, perfectly formed Hollywood golden boy himself. In those days,
however, he was less well known. 'It was a nightmare,' he says of his
meeting with Redford. 'I'd hardly had any sleep and was maybe five
minutes late for the audition. He took one look at me and obviously
hated me on sight. When I explained I'd been working on another film
until the early hours, he said gruffly, "So what? Everyone in Hollywood
is always up all night." Then he just sat there flossing his teeth and
looking bored throughout my audition.' When Fox had to go up before
Paul Newman on a subsequent occasion, he felt more than a twinge of
fear that he would be like his screen buddy. 'Paul was so friendly, I
couldn't believe it,' he commented, adding that Redford was the
'rudest' film boss he'd ever met.

After searching nationwide, Redford went for heredity rather than
experience by choosing Timothy Hutton, the nineteen-year-old son of
actor, Jim Hutton. He'd never been in a film before but he matched
Mary Tyler Moore physically and Redford believed he would project
the combination of vulnerability and rage Conrad needed. The other

177

major parts, Conrad's psychiatrist and his girlfriend, went to Judd Hirsch from television's *Taxi*, and Elizabeth McGovern, another Redford discovery.

The Electric Horseman and *Brubaker* had overrun by a total of sixteen weeks, leaving Redford with four days to finalise his preparations for *Ordinary People* before principal photography started in the autumn of 1979. As he wanted to remain true to the reality he thought he saw in the novel, the shooting was mostly done in Lake Forest itself. Some of the interiors were built in an abandoned laundry-room on a nearby army base, others in the Paramount studio in Hollywood where the production wrapped on January 3, 1980. Chartered in 1861, Lake Forest lies some thirty miles to the north of Chicago. In the early eighties, its 15,500 residents earned an average of 30,000 dollars a year, a figure that would have been higher but for a black minority and a rather larger number of academics who staffed the town's two colleges and three private schools.

Movie makers had been this way before, and recently too. Robert Altman had found the smug family he needed for *A Wedding* in Lake Forest and Brian de Palma had chosen it for part of *The Fury*. Less respectably, one of the local colleges doubled for the ivy-covered academy in *Omen II*. From Redford's point of view, the affluent community was an excellent location. Many of the residents were well accustomed to celebrities; others were sophisticated enough to leave them alone. When an *Ordinary People* assistant scouted the Lake Forest college campus for students to participate in swimming scenes with Timothy Hutton, several thought movie making too trivial to bother to apply.

As more than a third of *Ordinary People*'s six-million-dollar budget was spent in the locality, the authorities were happy to provide extra police to control the crowds. Better still, interest waned steadily once the initial scenes outside Marshall Field's department store in Market Square were completed, leaving a relatively peaceful working environment. Redford, who'd been mobbed by Columbus' unruly masses on *Brubaker*, found that the greatest danger he faced from the Lake Foresters was a liking for practical jokes. On one occasion, the director's chair with his name emblazoned on its leather back, was stolen by girl students holding it hostage in return for roles as extras in the film; on another, his rimless glasses, which he now needed to counteract short sight, disappeared. Predictably he didn't find these pranks nearly as amusing as the practical jokes he set up himself. 'I suppose it's part of the price of success in this business,' he sighed, 'but I'll never get used to it. I'd like to live like a human being.'

When he left Lake Forest after a two-month stay, on Christmas Eve, 1979, Redford made peace with the natives by taking out a newspaper advertisement apologising for any inconveniences. 'The impact of a visiting film company can be complicated at least and sometimes unsettling,' he wrote. 'We hope that our stay did not in any way disrupt the natural rhythms of the community. I, personally, am grateful that I didn't get as many traffic tickets as I probably deserved.'

Later he elaborated on his reasons for taking this fairly unusual step. 'In making every film there's somebody who is out of joint, who thinks you've violated his life. I like to think that the films I do are real, but that also carries a special responsibility when it comes to real people. So I was very careful about shooting in Lake Forest. These days, you can't even shoot a western in the west – too many power lines. You've got to go to Spain to shoot Texas. So Lake Forest was a find – like finding the elements for a Norman Rockwell painting. Too often film companies sweep through communities like the blitz. They figure, "We've got what we want, let's move on." It's a boomtown mentality.'

After years of suffering at the hands of acting pedants such as Streisand and Hoffman, Redford now took the chance to do to others as he would rather have been done by himself. On set he was poised and calm and easy going, always ready to discuss points of interpretation but willing to allow freedom of expression as well. As a result, *Ordinary People* rapidly developed into a mutual admiration society. 'I had a hunch – bordering on arrogance – that I could communicate with actors,' said Redford. 'After all, I'm one myself. But I knew I didn't have any formal training, any vocabulary. If the trust opened up between me and the actors, it would be okay.'

His hunch was correct and all three principals paid fulsome tributes to his understanding of their problems. Mary Tyler Moore appreciated the way in which he helped her to flesh out her character. In the book, Beth is rather enigmatic but Redford worked with Moore to make her more three-dimensional. She also felt that he drew things out, things she never imagined she'd be able to give. 'He has a wonderful sense of humour and is dear and I love him madly,' she commented with true showbiz hyperbole. 'What he does especially well is shoot lots of takes – what we've rehearsed – and then come in and say, "Okay, now throw out everything we've discussed and just do whatever the hell you feel like doing." After getting a scene, he would ask us to do something completely off the wall and it would work. That's how he gets those wonderful mood changes and unexpected line readings and reactions. There's a very loose atmosphere, filled with mutual respect. He really listens to each one of us.'

Timothy Hutton was already in an emotionally charged state owing to his father's death from cancer four months before *Ordinary People* began. Now he had to submerge his grief in the agonies of Conrad Jarrett. Whenever there was a break in filming, Redford was to be seen strolling through Lake Forest's monied streets with Hutton. As they walked, they talked with Redford building up the younger man's understanding of Conrad and his confidence in his ability to capture the right nuances. 'Everything that an actor could want from a director, Redford was. It's the caring and sensitivity that goes into his work. We had some very intense emotional scenes to do, and he was always there, a wonderful orchestrator. He had all these emotions to play with like a symphony. He was the conductor. That's a director. He never wanted to see acting. He'd say, "Tim, you really feel that? I don't think you felt it." He'd be right, I didn't quite feel it – and I would try it again.'

Sutherland was more restrained but equally positive. 'Redford loves actors. He is patient, and generous, and ungodly observant of what you're doing. You can do a scene and he'll tell you what's wrong – your hand should be on your knee, not on the table – things like that. And he's tactful and almost always correct. He knows what he wants.'

Redford returned the compliments in spades. 'There was an element of trust between all of us which bolstered my confidence. Directing made me realise how poor I am technically as an actor. Donald Sutherland is so able technically, so aware of the lighting and the mechanics. He was wonderful for me, when I was a director. After all these years, I've finally realised how much I really think of actors, what great people they really are. I believe in the actor's rhythms and instincts, his courage. Certain things are coming clear to me. One: it is a completely worthy profession, it can bring people joy; two, it can work on the psyche in a positive way. That's worthy.'

With the visual sense to know what he wanted, but lacking the technical knowledge as to how it might be achieved, Redford resorted to drawing pictures of what he had in his head and giving them to his crew to implement. 'The wonderful surprise I wasn't planning on was to find that the art, which I thought I'd left behind, was brought back in a functional way. I found I was designing shots. Before I knew it, I was developing whole storyboards and as I drew I got more ideas.'

'I resisted the excessive, verbal, film-school attitude – too much analysis, not enough visceral performance,' he said on another occasion. 'I could say, "Light this scene however you have to light it to get this effect." Or, "I don't know what lenses, but this is the look I want," rather than saying, "Put a fifty on it, then switch to a seventy-five, do a wide this, a wide that . . ."' The man most responsible for interpreting these vague instructions was cinematographer, John Bailey. 'We'd spend a lot of time going back and forth, trying to see what the other means,' he recalls. 'Since Redford doesn't know what the rules are – what you can and can't do – he's going to overstep them, and sometimes we'll do something experimentally that really works nicely. There's a real sense of discovery.'

'I had to give one of the best performances of my life,' said Redford in one of his less serious moments. 'I had to walk around the set like I knew what I was doing! If I wasn't certain what to do next, I'd just look very thoughtful and authoritative. In other words, I faked it!' Not entirely true, but not entirely untrue either: whichever way you look at it, Redford was learning on the job.

When post-production on *Ordinary People* was completed, it was clear that he'd learned well but the price of the lesson was high: several months in Los Angeles supervising editor, Jeff Kanew, as he put the pieces together. Not that he was bored, merely appalled by pollution and corporate greed. 'I like working on things like looping; having the privilege of getting something the way you want it is really exciting. It's tough and exhausting and painstaking and all that but I'm fascinated with the entire process. I know it's right when I feel this twinge behind my nose, somewhere behind my sinuses. I mean when you've looked at a scene over and over again, and you still like it. There's a scene with Mary Tyler Moore that has some of the finest, most subtle acting I've ever seen. I never get tired of it. It's like driving up to my place in Utah. There's never any time, when I'm driving up the canyon, that I tire of it. And so I know it's good.'

Perhaps out of respect for the collaboration he needed and received, the actor-turned-director refused to bill *Ordinary People* as 'A Robert Redford Film' in what had recently become the customary manner. 'The only way you could say that is if the person were acting in it alone, had written and directed himself and somehow shot it himself too. Otherwise I think a "so-and-so" film is bullshit, pure ego, agenting.'

When the film opened in September, 1980, the critics were fairly evenly divided between those who thought it was as pretentiously introspective as you would expect from an earnest actor with a limited number of brain cells to rub together and those who commended its taste and integrity and realism. Not for the first time, Richard Schickel lead the pros. 'There are no villains,' he wrote in *Time*, 'only fallible human beings trying to work things out but failing and succeeding in touchingly recognisable ways. That is a rare enough viewpoint to find at the movies now, but coming from a man whose fame might have carried him far from the realm of *Ordinary People*, it seems little short of miraculous.'

The influential Vincent Canby, from the *New York Times*, agreed and praised Redford's way with actors, his discipline and his ability to put his characters on the screen without patronising or satirising them. '*Ordinary People* doesn't look like any director's first movie. With the exception of fleeting flashbacks, which are necessary, I suppose, for exposition, the film's manner is cool, gentle, reserved. It never forces

Directing Donald Sutherland in *Ordinary People*.

the emotions. It watches them erupt and allows us to make of them what we will.'

The *Guardian*'s Derek Malcolm, though resentful of what he calls a 'long-drawn out lesson in analysis which often appears too obvious and schematic', also finds kind words, especially for Mary Tyler Moore. 'Hitherto, merely a very formidable television purveyor of sugar and spice, the actress, for that is what she has undoubtedly become under Redford's skilful prompting, is wholly superb as the dominant mother, claws at the ready beneath the fetching surface and incapable of understanding anyone's neurosis but her own. This is clearly Redford's forte as a director – patience and understanding with his cast. Sutherland too is different and better. He has not, in fact, been so good since he was Fellini's blank-eyed Casanova. Hutton too is remarkable, twisting and turning on the edge of breakdown. It is an excellent first feature because of its care and refusal to indulge its audience with either sentiment or melodrama. And if it ultimately fails as a really first class film, it is only because of a certain literalness of approach, as if liberal and decent feelings were enough. They aren't.'

Predictably the opposition was led by the razor sharp duo from New York, David Denby and Pauline Kael, who set the tone for the Redford witch hunt they've continued throughout the decade. Perhaps because of that city's cool, wisecracking style, they were both particularly irritated with the film's solemnity. Denby felt it suffered from lack of imagination: the Jarretts, with their dull parties and mirthless jokes, their loneliness and their despair, are too boring to be true. Or perhaps too boring to be New Yorkers. 'Sargent and Redford have drained most of the life out of the Jarretts and then said to us, "See how lifeless they are." The Jarretts are a pop-culture myth that people envious of Wasps, or guilty about being Wasps, want to believe in.'

Kael felt she'd been lumbered with an emotional burden from the outset: the stark credits, the pure classical music, the autumn leaves symbolising the onset of winter and death, in this instance the death of the Jarrett marriage. She did praise Redford's way with actors but the rest of it was just too tasteful to ring true. 'The pace is unhurried, and as a director Redford doesn't raise his voice any more than Beth does. Like many other actor-directors, he doesn't reach for anything but acting effects. The cinematographer, John Bailey, lights the images well enough but *Ordinary People* has that respectable, pictorial, dated look that movies get when the director has a proficient team of craftsmen but doesn't really think in visual terms.'

Redford had been knocked by Kael often enough but on this occasion he had no time to brood because the public and the prize givers came out on his side. *Ordinary People* never aspired to *Star Wars*-style millions but it performed steadily at the box-office through the winter of 1981 and accelerated dramatically when the awards season came round in the spring. Where Redford, the actor, had been almost totally ignored (the exception was his Best Actor nomination for *The Sting*), Redford, the director, hit the jackpot to an embarrassing degree. He had accepted the Director's Guild minimum of 105,000 dollars for his first assignment and it was this Guild that named him Best Director in early March, 1981, a vote of confidence that 'thrilled and shocked' him. Whatever he'd said about awards in the past – and he had expressed serious doubts about them when he wasn't winning them – he reneged on now by attending the ceremony. 'This is a very heavyweight crowd,' he told the Guild members in an acceptance speech made from behind a barrage of over eager photographers. 'I am honoured.'

At the Academy Awards the next month, it was the same story, only more so. *Ordinary People* was nominated in five major categories and one minor one. Mary Tyler Moore failed to capitalise as Best Actress, but Alvin Sargent won for the Best Adapted Screenplay and Timothy Hutton beat Judd Hirsch among others for Best Supporting Actor. The film took Best Picture and Redford, impeccable in a dinner jacket and accompanied by Lola wearing a huge and inappropriately folksy shell and bead necklace, was pronounced Best Director.

'I just didn't think I was going to see this,' he said as he received his

Oscar, 'but I am no less grateful. I would like to express my debt to the directors I've worked with in the past, for what I've learned from them, consciously or unconsciously. I couldn't go too much further without expressing what for me is the greatest gratitude, and that keys around the word trust. I really am grateful for the trust I have received from a terrific cast – Mary, Donald, Tim, Judd, Liz – I love them and I appreciate their love too. So thank you all.' Small wonder that when people ask him if he liked his new line of work, he has an unusually succinct reply: 'Directing is sheer delight.'

The Oscar triumphs were the culmination of three years of intense activity. Redford had used his fallow period in the late seventies to come to three vital decisions: he would act again, he would direct and he would develop Sundance. From 1980 onwards, it would no longer be a private paradise financed by a ski resort to which the public could come on a daily, but not an overnight, basis. It would be a centre for the arts and the preservation of the environment and the old American ways. The Sundance Institute and the Institute for Resource Management were born.

Although it has since expanded into other areas, the Sundance Institute started out as a non-profit making organisation dedicated to encouraging 'serious' film makers – directors, actors, producers and, above all, writers. They didn't have to be young but they did have to be American and they did have to be interested in something more substantial than the Hollywood dream factory. The high-roller mentality which believed that a film had more chance of grossing 100 million dollars if it cost thirty million to make had no place in Redford's scheme. Nor did attracting the teen-scream audience. His aim was to make good three- to five-million-dollar narrative films about adult concerns, films such as *Ordinary People* of which he once said, 'I don't know what this picture will say to teenagers, but I hope it has a message for their parents. I hope it tells them loud and clear to listen to what their children have to say.'

From the start, the heart of the Sundance blueprint was a June workshop at which chosen film makers would gather. 'Above all, I didn't want it to be a film school or any kind of festival,' Redford pronounced. 'I never learned anything in school, and I'm not big on festivals because people aren't really exchanging ideas, they're just lecturing each other. I wanted some action, for this to be a work-oriented place.'

Redford had no intention of putting his own money into the project beyond what was needed to set up offices in Sundance and Salt Lake City. Economics aside, he didn't want the Institute to be a Redford benefit. He'd already withdrawn from political and ecological projects when people insisted on making him the focus. He wasn't about to repeat the mistakes of others in his own back yard. His feasibility study began in the autumn of 1978 when he enlisted Sterling Von Wagenen, Lola's cousin, as Sundance's executive director. His qualifications were slight – he'd spent a couple of years organising alternative film festivals in Utah – and it took him until December, 1979, to raise 20,000 dollars, partly through the good offices of Mike Medavoy, executive Vice-President of Orion Features. He used the money to inspect comparable organisations: the American Film Institute in Los Angeles and the Eugene O'Neill Theater Center in Waterford, Connecticut.

By early 1980, the embryo project had attracted powerful friends. On the artistic side, the most important were Brian O'Doherty of the National Endowment for the Arts and Howard Klein of the Rockefeller Foundation. On the financial front, Redford was gratified to find support from such giants as Sony, Exxon and Northwest Energy. He was also confident enough to appoint a board of trustees from those he admired in film making circles. The first name on the list was his friend and Utah neighbour, Sydney Pollack, and he was joined by screen-writer Waldo Salt, an Oscar-winner for *Midnight Cowboy* and *Coming Home*, George White, President of the O'Neill Center, and Frank Daniel, co-chairman of the Film Division of Columbia University.

Once these heavyweight talents started touting for film scripts, they arrived by the ton, creating a huge reading problem for the trustees who had to select half-a-dozen for the first June workshop in 1981. Michelle Satter, Sundance's Director of Feature Film Programmes, remembers it as 'inspired chaos'. After eleven years at the Institute of Contemporary Arts in Boston, she'd come west to co-ordinate a conference for the commissioning and marketing of independent films. Its subject was the exhibition of specialist films in the 1980s and at it she met Redford. When it was over, he asked her to work for him and she agreed, which was how she came to be in on the ground floor.

'Redford started it with the idea of giving back some of what he'd been given,' she told me when we met at her office in Redford's Burbank headquarters. 'Initially we looked for American regional stories which meant we got involved with a lot of earnest, well-intentioned material. Over the years, it proved to be a limiting factor so now we look for compelling original stories of all kinds. Words such as daring, and offbeat, and comedy have come into the selection process. There were two areas in which Redford thought he could help film makers. One was to improve their story-telling skills, the other was to provide them with experience of working with actors. A lot of people were coming in from documentaries which meant they had no experience of actors.'

The writers chosen for the workshop discussed their scripts with professionals like Salt and Pollack, rewriting as necessary to implement their suggestions. If they were interested in directing their own work, they were allocated two or three actors from an ensemble assembled by Redford and his team; if not, a would-be director was appointed. Either way, key sections of the script were filmed and analysed before the month was out. The purpose was not to help get the films made, but to create an understanding of how they might become artistically and commercially viable. At best, this would enable them to be financed through regular channels; at worst, it would give the people involved a chance to learn from their mistakes, and in an environment in which they could feel free to make them.

'Fear is a very big platform for how things work in Hollywood,' Redford explained. 'The stakes are so high, there's so much tension, that it's hard to work, even for me. So what's it like for the young talent coming along? We'd like to provide an umbrella, an alternative to this incredible pressure, but not mollycoddle anyone. I'm not interested in the "independent" film maker who "disdains" Hollywood, but isn't good enough to succeed there. I'm not against Hollywood. I don't want my own studio. I'm just trying to do something else with Sundance. What I'd like to do is to make art the core, and see if business can get around that.'

Judiciously spoken because it was to Hollywood that his fund raisers would have to go, caps in hand, to raise the money needed to develop the Institute. The third annual budget for 1983 was 625,000 dollars, of which 160,000 dollars was spent on the June workshop. This covered air fares, food and cabin rentals for the eighty or so people invited. These comprised twelve writers and directors for seven projects, sixteen actors and eleven technicians, plus forty-odd resource people to advise them. Major stars like Karl Malden and Robert Duvall came and went as their schedules permitted, giving their time for nothing, but the resident actors were paid minimum rates. Redford himself supervised as and when he could, flying in and out in a helicopter between business appointments in Los Angeles.

By 1983, the 'camp-like' pattern for the workshop was established and it still works the same way today. The workshop guests stay in well-appointed rustic cabins dotted around the lower slopes along the winding canyon road and eat at a central cafeteria set up for the duration. Young volunteers, often assisted by Redford's teenage daughter Amy, serve a healthy breakfast of natural cereal and buckwheat cakes between eight and nine a.m. Then the day's programme gets under way, with the members of the individual projects meeting for rehearsal and filming. In the afternoons, the writers may choose to work in their cabins or to enjoy Sundance's fishing, walking and riding. The evenings are given over to joint discussion, often following a screening in the newly-built 150-seat cinema. In the early days, anyone who wanted to drink anything stronger than beer had to give their orders to the driver who made the daily 'decadence run' to Provo, but wine is now available in the Sundance shop.

David Schickele, a director from San Francisco, went through the 1981 workshop, but emerged with mixed feelings. 'They make it clear that an invitation to Sundance carries no promises. Still, it's only human to have your ear to the ground politically. It can't hurt to have Sydney Pollack's attention, right? The quality of the advice you get at Sundance is the best. You get very high there. But when you come down from those mountains, it's like decompression.'

When Redford arrived at that first workshop clutching his new Oscar and his bright hopes, he knew little more than that he wanted to commit himself to something outside his previous experience. 'I'd always missed a sense of community, of a workplace where you could experiment, exchange ideas and get excited without some meter ticking away. Do you know what I've learned from Utah, from living my life as I have? That you only keep things if you're willing to take risks – that you should make the best use you can of places and time, because with a certain success, a certain refinement in your life, you lose the very thing you started with, or you think you stand to lose it because the stakes are so high . . . so you try nothing new.'

The Institute for Resource Management, like the Sundance Institute, was set up in response to the shortcomings Redford saw in himself and in those he associated with. In the middle and late seventies, the newly converted environmentalist had trumpeted his message from assorted roof-tops, earning himself as much opprobrium as praise. 'Your initial impulse, especially when you're young, is emotional,' he admitted in 1980. 'You get emotional when you see them strip-mining land and you remember how beautiful it was or when you see the air grey with fumes. But later you start to see the full picture. People need work, and if they depend on jobs that produce pollution, they can't afford to see the pollution. Finally you have to ask, "What's going to work here?" You can yell and pound your fist, but pretty soon you're a predictable radical and easy to ignore. "There he goes again", that sort of thing. Or you can take a more pragmatic, behind-the-scenes approach.'

As the nihilistic decade drew to a close, he began to find a new direction for his zeal. His original plan had been to set up an Institute for Natural Resources, not to ban all development but to ensure that it was done sensibly. Coal, for example, should be mined, but not in national parks. This was to be achieved by training resource managers in economic development and environmental protection, so that they would make decisions that no one would regret in twenty-five years' time. 'I want teachers from different walks of life, not just some environmental university,' Redford stated categorically. 'I think the only way we're going to move forward is to bring industry and the environmentalists together.'

For this, he decided he needed some governmental affiliation, a possibility under Carter, had his administration not been bogged down in inertia, but not under Reagan who assumed control in 1980 on a big-business boom ticket. Redford responded with some lateral thinking along the lines of how he could usefully bring industry and environmentalists together and came up with the Institute for Resource Management. This organisation was established in 1983 to identify and resolve areas of conflict between opposing vested interests.

Over breakfast at Sundance, IRM chief, Terry Minger, described it as a 'conflict resolving group operating mostly in the Western part of the United States. We try to enter as a relatively neutral party,' he explained. 'If we err, it is on the side of the environment because we have an environmental bias, but we have to be trusted by industry and by the government.'

The IRM's first triumph occurred in the Bering Sea in 1985. Big oil companies had long wanted to drill in the waters off Alaska, the site of what are thought to be America's largest untapped reserves. Environmentalists and native fishermen had long resisted: the waters are among the world's richest salmon grounds and home to dozens of endangered species, among them certain varieties of whales, walrus and seals. The Reagan administration, faced with possible curtailment of Middle East oil supplies owing to mounting pressure in the region, was keen to exploit this valuable resource but attempts to open up the geologically promising Bristol Bay to the drillers ended in court action that could take years to resolve.

It was at this point that the IRM came in with a view to persuading the traditional adversaries to go to the negotiating table. Nineteen oil companies, among them Texaco, Conoco, Standard Oil, Chevron and Phillips, were asked to identify the tracts of continental shelf they most coveted; the inhabitants of coastal villages, fishermen and environmentalists were asked to draw maps of the areas they would most like to protect. Where there was direct conflict, compromises were hammered out. The negotiators met on four occasions, usually for two or three days at a stretch, over ten months. It was necessary to get top level decision-makers to the table and this is where Redford's name came in useful. 'Being personally invited by Robert Redford and knowing that he would be there was, for some people at least, an important factor in getting them there,' said IRM executive, Paul Parker.

The first meeting at Morro Bay, California, included – appropriately enough – an offshore cruise and a shrimp fry on an industry workboat, a vessel notorious for its upsetting effect on inexperienced sailors. 'People need a chance to see how much agreement is possible between seemingly intractable opponents,' said Redford in the *Harvard Business Review*. 'We eliminated the long tables and sterile rooms and mixed people together. The elements helped. We began with an informal get-together on a boat cruise that soon ran into nine-foot seas. People began clutching each other and getting seasick. By the time they returned, they were so grateful, they would have hugged anybody. Through human contact, a barrier had been broken. Thank you for participating in this segment of *The Love Boat*,' he joked, by way of farewell.

'Redford made it clear at that first meeting and all along that, while he is concerned with the environment, he's also concerned with jobs and development,' said Max G. Pitcher, Vice-President of North American exploration for Conoco Inc. 'Redford's influence with the environmentalists was significant. There were some he visited one-on-one and said, "Look, you have the policy makers of a large group of the industry present and this may be your only chance to talk to that group face to face. Therefore don't be intractable."'

The final accord recommended that forty-eight million acres should be leased to the oil companies and 240 million acres set aside for conservation. No government representatives had been present at the talks, but the accord was presented to Interior Secretary Hodel in August, 1984. Both sides agreed that if he adopted the suggestions, they wouldn't contest them in court at a later date. The Bristol Bay area was excluded because it was already under litigation and Exxon and Shell refused to co-operate in the Bering Sea accord, but everyone agreed that a breakthrough had been made and that it was due to the good offices of the IRM. Plans are now afoot to use the same techniques to reach agreement in even more hotly contested waters, especially in California where the coastal residents are incomparably more numerous and vocal than they are in Alaska.

The IRM has also intervened effectively on the North American mainland. In New Mexico and Arizona, there are long-running disputes over water rights between the resident subsistence farmers and the out of state developers who want to use this limited natural resource for tourist-oriented hotels and golf courses. On the Indian reservations, the inhabitants fight the mining companies over extraction rights and the environmentalists over conservation. On the border between Alaska and the North West Territories, Americans, Canadians and Eskimos conflict over oil drilling, wildlife refuges and the annual migration of the caribou. As the IRM has just six permanent staff at Sundance, they can't do the research themselves but their growing reputation combined with Redford's name make it easy for them to enlist help from scientists and universities. 'It's all due to Bob,' says Terry Minger. 'The IRM is his creation, his original idea. It works because of him.'

14

Business As Usual

During his second long absence from movie making, Robert Redford divided his time between making sure everything was working out at Sundance, and doing a bit of unaccustomed Third World travel, a move brought on by his ever-increasing inability to mingle invisibly with his compatriots. He has always said that he felt like a panther in lion's clothing but when he tried to make himself into a dark-haired person on a ski trip to Sun Valley, the brown wig slipped off the red-blond mane when he was half-way down the slope.

The incident put him off disguises so when his next holiday came round in the winter of 1982, he took up the Himalayan challenge that had haunted him ever since Sir Edmund Hillary beat him to the top of Everest in 1953. Accompanied by a small group of friends who were sworn to secrecy to protect his privacy, he spent sixteen days in Nepal hiking to the Everest base camp at 18,000 feet. As is usual trekking practice, the party's baggage was carried by a team of Sherpas. 'That was really strong stuff,' he commented. 'It was such a pleasure to be with people you could feel were happy, and it wasn't tied to any degree of achievement as we know it.'

But, much as he might deride achievement on occasion, he still couldn't get it out of his system. After *Ordinary People*, he really had no occasion to act again. He could have made a handsome living or a subsistence one out of Sundance; he could have made the kind of pictures he liked as a director or a producer; he could have hired the finest artists to teach him to paint; he could have gone anywhere in the world and done whatever he pleased. He was, in other words, his own man in every sense but one: he still needed to act. It wasn't even as if the forty-five-year-old Redford had any illusions left about the ability of movies to change the world. 'I did believe early on that *The Candidate* might have some impact politically,' he told David Ansen of *Newsweek*. 'What I've come to realise is that it's not so. But it won't stop me. Because I can't help it. This country is just too interesting. And I consider myself a real part of it. And it drives me crazy. And it interests me no end.'

By the mid-eighties, it seemed as if acting was an addiction: he could give it up for three years, but not forever. And there were other contradictions in the stop-go career that never quite stopped. Redford has said that his acting price is negotiable downwards if the part is right, but the fact remains that it never has been negotiated downwards and, as the years passed, it looked less and less likely that it ever would be. His chosen trio for the mid-eighties were *The Natural*, *Out of Africa* and *Legal Eagles*, respectively a lousy adaptation of a book by a celebrated novelist; a colonial epic in which he played one of the screen's least likely Englishmen; and a lightweight comedy. Popular big budget successes they certainly were but as artistic achievements they were non-starters.

Village Voice's Andrew Sarris never wrote a truer word than when he described *The Natural* as 'a futile effort to make cinematic ice cream out of literary vinegar'. By changing Bernard Malamud's flawed, but despairing, first novel into a romantic frolic with an upbeat ending, the film makers committed a mortal sin to which Redford should never have lent his name. Those originally to blame were Roger Towne and Phil Dusenberry, screenwriters with hip reputations based, it would seem, on talents other than reading and writing. However, Redford was no stranger to tailoring scripts to suit his purpose and he certainly had the clout to do so here as the twenty million dollar budget was raised on his name alone. As the director was Barry Levinson, now an Oscar winner for *Rain Man* but then making only his second film after the much more intimate and personal *Diner*, it was also his place to do so.

That he didn't suggests that he saw himself more as Tri Star's Roy Hobbs, an incorruptible all-American hero, than as Malamud's Roy Hobbs, a man doomed by his human failings. When Hobbs first appears in 1924, he is a nineteen-year-old baseball genius armed with Wonderboy, the bat he carved himself out of the wood of a tree struck by lightning after his father's death. His simple dream is to be the best and he pursues it, bat in hand, from his mid-western farm to Chicago where he will try out for the Cubs.

En route the train stops at a small prairie town where everyone is in a carnival mood and Hobbs is enticed into a duel with The Whammer, a character based on Babe Ruth, one of baseball's ruling kings. The man who discovered Roy makes a bet with Max Mercy, a leading sports columnist, that his protégé can strike out The Whammer in three pitches. He does, but the achievement attracts the attention of a twenties siren who baffles him with Homer and Sir Lancelot before taking him to a hotel room and shooting him in the stomach. Hobbs is in Chicago all right, but much closer to death than glory.

Baseball player extraordinaire in *The Natural* (1984).

Cut forward fifteen years to 1939 when he reappears for the none too skilled New York Knights. Neither the book nor the film makes any attempt to explain why his come-back has been so long delayed, concentrating instead on his meteoric career as the oldest rookie in the major leagues. With the help of Wonderboy, the Knights rise up off the floor and Hobbs is duly rewarded with a choice of ladies, Iris Gaines, his childhood sweetheart, and Memo Paris, the club manager's wanton niece. Up to this point, it is the story according to Malamud but here the lines diverge. Where literature decreed that Hobbs should again succumb to temptation by accepting a bribe, Hollywood decided that he should not repeat his mistakes. Not only should he be a Persil-White Knight, he should put aside the platinum-haired temptress in favour of the corn dolly with whom he grew up. And so, in due course, the film draws to a positively sickening conclusion.

The Natural appealed to Redford on several levels. As an ex-baseball scholar whose father and grandfather had been obsessed with the game, he felt that it was in his blood. Then again *Downhill Racer* was one of his favourites among his films, so he was enthusiastic about playing another winner who was also a loser. He first tangled with Roy Hobbs in the mid-seventies when he was at the right age to play him. 'Because of all the tradition associated with baseball, I felt the way to do a baseball story was the way Malamud had gone about it – in an allegorical, mythological way.'

However, the rights to the novel weren't available at the time and it wasn't until 1982, when Barry Levinson visited Sundance to discuss possible projects with the actor, that the subject came up again. 'I really thought I'd moved past *The Natural*,' Redford explained, 'but I got excited about doing it with Barry. I felt it should have the same intimate, personal feeling I had seen in *Diner* mixed with the more bizarre and eccentric elements of the story.'

By this time, the revamped ending was already set. Roger Towne justified his decision by saying: 'In the book Roy Hobbs doesn't learn anything from his experience. Malamud wanted to say something about exploitation, and he wanted to show that our idols had feet of clay. I felt you could say those things without crushing an audience at the end. I guess when he wrote the book, Malamud didn't believe that people could change. I just don't think that idea was in keeping with the sensibility of anyone involved in this movie.'

Levinson, over eager perhaps to get his big break in Hollywood, agreed. 'When I read the script, the ending seemed right. At least it seemed right for now. Maybe in the fifties, which was the beginning of disillusionment, it wasn't.' What Redford thought went unrecorded but Levinson, armed with his commitment to play Roy Hobbs, was able to approach Gary Hendler, the head of the newly formed Tri Star studio, with some confidence. As Hendler was Redford's ex-lawyer and Tri Star, handsomely funded by Columbia Pictures, CBS and Home Box Office, was looking to launch itself with a prestige project, his agreement was a formality. The twenty-million-dollar movie was on its way and a top class cast was signed to prove it. Robert Duvall played the cynical sports journalist, with Glenn Close as the virtuous maid and Kim Basinger as the seductress. Further down the line there were parts for such hardy veterans as Wilford Brimley and Richard Farnsworth, with cameos for Joe Don Baker as The Whammer and Barbara Hershey as the murderous fan.

Most of the shooting took place in the late summer and early autumn of 1983 in Buffalo in upstate New York. Not only had the rather run-down city kept much of its thirties architecture intact, but it had one of America's few remaining period stadiums, the 40,000-seat War Memorial Stadium, the home of the minor league Buffalo Bisons. The baseball bats and the balls were made specially for the film: thirties bats were larger than those used nowadays and the balls had black and red stitching instead of the red used today.

To add authenticity to the games, Levinson held try-outs in New York, complete with in-field drills, out-field drills and pitching drills, with a view to recruiting baseball players who could act, and actors who could play baseball convincingly. Redford spent two months preparing his own swing with semi-professional players half his age. 'The first time he came up to the plate, a lot of us had our fingers crossed,' said executive producer Mark Johnson, 'but he took seventy pitches, lined a lot of them into the out-field and hit several 300 feet into the right-field stands. Suddenly everyone breathed a sigh of relief, thinking, "Hey, this guy is good."' Maybe, but these magic moments were not captured on film. Instead Redford swings and misses or swings and hits, then the film cuts to the ball in the air or to another player rounding first base. Crowd scenes with up to 10,000 extras in period costume presented a further challenge to a director who had rarely had to control more than ten people at a time in *Diner*.

Neither *The Natural* nor Buffalo saw the best of Robert Redford. While the cast and crew stayed downtown in the Hilton, the star lived alone in a house on a lake an hour's drive away. During filming, he ignored autograph hunters, ducked photographers and refused to acknowledge the crowds of cheering extras. Whenever a shot finished, he strode sullenly back to his thirty-foot trailer under the stands, looking neither right nor left. Locals compared him very unfavourably with other actors who had worked in Buffalo, most notably James Caan in *Hide in Plain Sight* and Burt Reynolds in *Best Friends*.

'You're besieged,' Redford said in mitigation. 'Every time you leave your trailer, you're hit on by people wanting autographs and flashing bulbs in your face. You have to concentrate on what you're going to do out there. And you can hear, every now and then, "Oh, you're stuck up", because you weren't able to look at them, weren't able to sign their baseball, whatever. If you were me for a month, you might change it to two weeks.'

At one point, Redford left town to attend the funeral of Sidney Wells, his daughter Shauna's boyfriend of three years' standing. The couple were close to announcing their engagement when he was brutally murdered and Redford rushed to his daughter's side to share her grief and protect her from the press. As soon as shooting on *The Natural* ended, he and Shauna accepted an invitation from Richard Leakey, the celebrated palaeanthropologist, to visit his dig on the shores of Lake Turkana in northern Kenya. During the three-week trip, they explored the site where he made his most recent discoveries about early man and Redford dug up some 1.7 million-year-old fossils.

The Natural is filmed with one prime purpose in mind: making Robert Redford look thirty – or nineteen – instead of forty-six. 'He's photographed looking like a wary, modest god,' wrote Pauline Kael who, as usual, wasn't fooled, 'with enough back lighting and soft focus to make him incandescent even when he isn't doing a thing. The movie is a fantasy and Barry Levinson must have wanted the picturesque, prose-poetry-style that the cinematographer, Caleb Deschanel, supplies, but Redford is its principal beneficiary. Though part of the point of the movie is that the rookie hero is older than his team-mates, we never see a well-lighted handsome young face; the other Knights are photographed as if they were made of putty.'

Deschanel, who went on to open his own account as a director with *Crusoe*, was proud of his cinematography but doubted that Levinson, whose other films he much admired, was the right man for this job. 'I felt the film had the potential to be a lot better than it was,' he told me on location on his own film in the Seychelles. 'The book is a real tough book but the movie got softened in the course of making it. I'm not sure why. It's probably a combination of a lot of different factors. The movie had so many different influences.'

He was however a Redford fan, having discovered that the rumours about his liking for being filmed exclusively from one side were false. 'The first thing I did, that I always like to do, is break the rule right from the beginning. Once you do that and you're successful at it you can do everything you want. Redford has as much power on the movie as anyone but he's also a very intelligent person. He knows a lot about movie making so it's not like discussing it with someone who doesn't know what they're talking about. I enjoyed working with him.'

It is hardly surprising that Redford, presented with Deschanel's flattering images of youthful vigour at dailies night after night, had no complaints. He also built up a good working relationship with Levinson, staying on when filming was completed to work with him in the editing-room and on the dubbing stage. Always aware that he might be accused of pushing his Oscar down the less experienced man's throat, he was careful to defer to Levinson whenever their opinions diverged. 'In this business, with egos being the way they are, it was a pleasure to work with Barry,' he commented. 'He was always open to suggestions, and yet he wasn't afraid to say if he disagreed. He didn't look at me as this kind of monstrous thing. It was just two people talking.'

The Natural may have been harmonious in the making, but any illusions as to the reception the bastard child could expect from the critics ended abruptly when it opened in early May, 1984. Malamud had never been consulted and he didn't comment now, but others were less restrained. Vincent Canby made the reasonable assumption that those who wished to adapt an established literary work would also wish to preserve and illuminate it.

'Instead,' he wrote in the *New York Times*, 'Roger Towne and Phil Dusenberry who wrote the screenplay and Barry Levinson, the director, seem to have taken it upon themselves to straighten out Mr. Malamud's fable, to correct the flaws he overlooked. They supply explanations that the novel resolutely avoided, reshape characters for dramatic conveni- ence and, strangest of all, they transform something dark and open- ended – truly fabulous – into something eccentrically sentimental. All this might be justified if the film then succeeded on its own as something else. However, this *Natural* may well baffle people who come upon the remains of its story for the first time and wonder what Mr. Malamud was up to.'

Although the other actors came in for a certain amount of praise, Redford didn't fit most people's image of Roy Hobbs. 'He is too cool, poised and complacently good-looking to suggest Malamud's callow, woman-hungry rookie,' wrote Andrew Sarris, accurately summing up the consensus. 'Somehow you can never feel the hay sticking out from behind Redford's ears. Once a very appealing realistic actor with excellent timing, he walks through *The Natural* with a very sluggish and stand-offish attitude towards the other players. Not that he has anything to worry about in a script that allows the character he plays to come out on top in every situation without working up a sweat.'

The same could not be said of *Out of Africa* in which Redford succumbed to the worst piece of casting in his career. The Honourable Denys Finch Hatton was six feet four inches tall, a bald old Etonian and the younger son of an earl. Elspeth Huxley recalls him quoting Latin and Greek poets in the original and flying from Nairobi to London for an opera and back again the next day. In Kenya, he was a mythic being, an athlete and an aviator, a First World War hero who became a legendary white hunter. Though capable of great wit and charm, he was an elusive character who prized independence above the security of marriage. In other words, it is hard to think of anyone with less in common with a smallish tow-headed middle-class Californian family man.

Redford was drawn three ways to *Out of Africa*: he identified with the loner aspects in Denys Finch Hatton whom he described as, 'a man who does not engage, but he doesn't do it out of fear, he does it out of real choice'; he was persuaded to lend his name by Sydney Pollack, who produced and directed the film; and he was paid 6.5 million dollars and given top billing for a role he completed in three trips to Kenya over eight weeks. As Meryl Streep was paid a reported four million dollars less for working non-stop for five months, Redford was quids in.

Out of Africa is Karen Blixen's account of the seventeen years she spent in the Ngong Hills outside Nairobi trying to grow coffee where coffee couldn't be grown. Born into the wealthy Danish middle classes, she was spurned by the man she loved, Baron Hans von Blixen-Finecke, and settled instead for his twin brother, Bror. He was a merry rake with a capacity for going through a lot of money fast and, in 1913, he was quick to invest Karen's fortune unwisely in cheap, bad Kenyan land.

Once his wife was installed with 1,200 Kikuyu and Somali servants and field hands, he became a white hunter, an occupation that gave him plenty of opportunities for womanising. As their marriage pact had never been based on fidelity, Karen was pleased enough with her side of the bargain, at least until she found she had syphilis. An almighty snob, she exulted in being called Baroness and happily despised Kenya's British settlers, a fairly rough bunch in the country's early days as a crown colony.

For much of her time in Africa she was deeply in love with Denys Finch Hatton who used her farm as a base between safaris. Blix, as the Baron was known, accepted the situation without rancour, even to the point of introducing Denys as 'my wife's lover and my best friend', despite the fact that some of Karen's friends believed the relationship to be platonic. When Blix wanted to marry again, the couple divorced but Denys, a determined bachelor, proved remarkably evasive when Karen tried to make him tie the knot. When he was killed while flying his own plane and the farm went bankrupt, Karen returned to Denmark to write under the pen name, Isak Dinesen.

Several distinguished directors, among them Orson Welles and David Lean, had looked longingly at what Huxley refers to as Blixen's 'poetic distillation of her African experience' without coming up with a

Safari-bound with Meryl Streep in *Out of Africa* (1985).

way of structuring it into a film. In the early seventies, Nic Roeg considered making it with Julie Christie as Karen and Ryan O'Neal as Blix. The successful attempt came about when Columbia asked Kurt Luedtke, a former newspaperman who had written the script for the Sydney Pollack film, *Absence of Malice*, to prepare a first draft. His task was made easier by the publication of Judith Thurman's prize winning biography of Karen Blixen in 1982. In due course, Luedtke showed his work to Pollack. 'If someone had asked me whether I wanted to do *Out of Africa* at that point, I would have said no,' Pollack recalls, 'but as I read, I got hooked.'

Luedtke was perceptive enough to doubt Redford's suitability to play Finch Hatton, but Pollack was not to be deterred. If he, an Indiana Jew who had never set foot in Africa, was going on this great adventure, he would only do so with his friend batting on his side. Once the thirty-million-dollar budget was approved by Universal, he and Redford spent a lot of the summer of 1984 discussing the evolution of Denys Finch Hatton for the wide screen. Although Blixen's book concentrates on her response to Africa and its people rather than her love for Finch Hatton (who is barely mentioned), the film was designated a doomed romance, full of melting moments to bring the mega stars picturesquely together under wide African skies. Whether or not Denys and Karen were lovers in real life, they certainly would be now. 'Bob was very realistic about it being Meryl's movie,' said Pollack. 'There was no bull about beefing up his part. He's an admirer of hers, he likes to do love stories and he loved this one.'

Redford was preoccupied with how long he should wait to connect with Streep. Most of his Pollack films had long periods of romantic anticipation, brief stylised connections and a melancholy dissolution, and this one proved to be no exception: more than an hour passes before Redford and Streep fall in love. 'I always ask him, "How long am I going to wait before we get together this time?" ' Redford joked. ' "And what am I going to get? Ten seconds before things start falling apart?" '

Then there was the tricky question of accent. Streep who, as all the world knows, believes herself to be the mistress of every foreign tongue, addressed the Danish vowels with her customary enthusiasm. 'I had a faahrm in Aahhfrikar,' she intoned as the film opened and she was still at it two and a half hours later. Redford too took voice coaching and, after a week, everyone agreed that his old Etonian tones showed great promise. Pollack, however, had second thoughts. 'The movie audience knows every pore of Redford's face,' he explained. 'If he shows up and says "Hello, old boy!" the audience will crack up. So we settled on something slightly more cultivated than American speech, but not exactly British either.' This was probably realistic: if he insisted on having Redford, he could never have Finch Hatton, so he might as well have as much of the Redford the world knows and loves as possible.

Redford, of course, was ready with a properly earnest rationale. 'It's harder and harder these days to find an intelligent piece of material that has integrity and quality and doesn't have all the obvious escape hatches: violence, sex. I liked it because it was about dignity and intelligence in human beings, in relationships. It was about the difficulty of relationships and independence; in other words, the contest between independence and dependence, and adventure and security. Even though the part was an Englishman, I was attracted to it. But you know it was a very tricky part, the toughest part I've ever played because it was the most purely symbolic: there was nothing to it. You look at it carefully; just being there is kind of what's called on.'

And being there was what he was. Though both Redford and Streep had allegedly jumped at the chance of working together, their initial meeting was described as 'unpromisingly polite, reserved and formal'. So it remained up until the first day of shooting when Michael Kitchen, cast as Finch Hatton's safari partner, Berkeley Cole, broke the ice by explaining how he'd smuggled a package of 150 pairs of fifteen-dollar latex ears into Kenya to avoid its complex customs regulations. The ears were fitted daily to the extras playing the tribesmen as modern Kenyans no longer pierce and stretch their lobes as they did in 1914. 'Ears?' said Redford. 'I thought you were bringing in the football.' The next day he turned up with a football. When he started kicking it around between takes, Streep hitched up her period clothes and joined in. The show was on the road.

But it was never easy. At this time, Kenya was new to film making and neither the government nor the gods were particularly helpful. For the first time in three years the rains didn't fail. Nor did they stop when they should have done, which meant that the five-month schedule contained more wet days than dry. The government refused permission for the unit trucks to move at night which posed enormous logistical problems in a country where many of the roads are graded tracks that flood whenever it's wet.

Nor was the film ideologically welcome to the Kenyans, mostly because Karen Blixen and Denys Finch Hatton were openly racist by today's standards. Letters appeared in the local papers and the situation was exacerbated when it was revealed that the film company was paying black extras a fifth of what they paid white ones. Supply and demand was the reason given, and it is, of course, true that there are more available black Kenyans than white ones. When 500 young white males were required to form an army, the producers started recruiting tourists, Peace Corps volunteers and expatriate teenagers, then turned to the offices in Nairobi to make up the shortfall, paying approximately thirty dollars a day.

Pollack is a nervous film maker, and never more so than when stranded on the Dark Continent. 'I had gathered from Bob that Sydney likes to work under that kind of pressure,' Streep commented, 'the kind that would kill a normal person. He directed during the day and did his producing chores at night. On his days off, he looked miserable. But I had faith in him. The director who tells you everything is fine is the one you're not happy being in the hands of. Sydney worried so much that I knew he'd tie up the loose ends.'

Pollack's worries included a full menagerie of trained lions imported from California and a number of other animals, welcome and unwelcome. 'Dealing with lions, giraffes and buffaloes is worse than having a bunch of kids in your picture. When we were down in the Masai Mara under canvas, as they say, one of the soundmen zipped himself into his tent with a puff-adder, which is the deadliest snake in the world. Another night we were awakened by the sound of two hippos beating the shit out of each other. Every day, every hour, I asked myself, "What am I doing here?"'

Like Redford, Pollack is a blue-jeans man in all but the smartest hotels, but his are always impeccably pressed and his approach to his job is equally punctilious. 'Neat?' Redford jokes. 'He'll almost break into a cold sweat about things not being in order, and I suspect that's not going to diminish as he gets older. We've worked together so much that there is a tremendous rapport but I do have to stop myself saying things that might strike other actors as disrespectful. Things like, "God, you're not going to put the camera there? What a dumb shot!"'

Another bone of contention was the 60,000-dollar Gipsy Moth, made in 1929 and shipped out from Britain to double as the plane which killed Denys Finch Hatton. Its owner, Cliff Lovell, who stood in for the star in the flying sequences, claimed that there were also times when it looked like killing Robert Redford, so rash was he at its controls. 'He could easily have written off my plane,' he commented with the pent-up irritation of a man worrying more about his possession than its pilot. 'He nearly ran it into some tree stumps and he came close to hitting the film crew. At one point, the director screamed, "Stop that plane." Redford rather fancies himself as a pilot, but I broke into a sweat every time he climbed into the cockpit.'

When *Out of Africa* opened in America in Christmas week, 1985, it was inevitable that the jackals would gather around Redford. Pauline Kael starts her condemnation quietly: '*Out of Africa* dribbles on, adult, diligently cryptic, unsatisfying', but gathers venom as she goes. By the time she gets to Redford, she has worked up a fine head of steam. 'He is as American as ever, and his fluffy hair is a golden dream. He speaks his lines crisply, but he seems adrift, lost in another movie, and Pollack treats him with unseemly reverence. His role is a series of grand entrances and lingering exits. Pollack must be trying to set up a glorious doomed romance in an exotic setting, but when Streep and Redford are on safari, drinking wine out of crystal glasses and dancing on the earth between two camp fires, or when they're in the wilds and he's shampooing her hair, or even when they head for a jungle tent and everything is primed for passion, they seem too absorbed in themselves to notice each other.'

David Denby, having accurately identified the sardonic banter between Streep and Klaus Maria Brandauer who plays Blix as the most memorable thing in the movie, goes on to condemn Redford as the least. 'He is so far out of his league that at first one feels sorry for him. But only at first. Whether he can't do it or won't do it, we're disgusted with him by the end. Having lost the instincts that steered him through the wonderful soft-shoe performances in *The Candidate* and *The Way We Were*, he's simply not putting out for the camera. The jaunty lines sound absurd in his mouth and he doesn't provide the physical dash that would make up for the flat line readings. Streep's great love for him, and his resistance to committing himself to her, make no sense at all. Here is this laid-back American unaccountably overvaluing his freedom and holding himself aloof from a woman patently too good for him. Some romance!'

Andrew Sarris also regretted the lack of chemistry between the stars, but exonerated Redford up to a point by describing him as 'the fall-guy for the inescapable crass vulgarity of the whole project'. Vincent Canby subscribed to the platonic nature of the Blixen–Finch Hatton connection and made the assumption that, in Karen's mind, it was none the less real for that. The problem for him was that the film's Finch Hatton was quite unworthy of her passion, real or imagined. 'The character of Denys, as written by Mr. Luedtke and played in a laid-back contemporary American manner by Mr. Redford is a total cipher, and a charmless one at that. It's not Mr. Redford's fault. There's no role for him to act,' he wrote in the *New York Times*.

The public were not deterred by such cruel shafts. Nor were the Oscar-makers who loaded *Out of Africa* with plaudits including Best Film and the Best Actress award for Meryl Streep when the ceremonies came round in April, 1986. Redford wasn't nominated, but he was used to that. He did, however, look for a change of pace for his next movie. In tune with the policy of working with newer directors which he'd implemented first with Barry Levinson, he contacted Ivan Reitman through their mutual agent, Michael S. Ovitz, in August, 1984 to see if there were anything they could do together.

There was, Reitman, a man who had made millions out of blatantly juvenile comedies such as *Animal House* and *Ghostbusters*, had a screenplay in his closet that had fallen on hard times. *Legal Eagles* had

been written two years earlier by Jim Cash and Jack Epps Jr., current Hollywood favourites thanks to *Top Gun*, as a buddy-buddy vehicle for Dustin Hoffman and Bill Murray, Reitman's discovery and regular star. Both men had withdrawn. Was Redford interested in replacing one of them?

With a lot of reservations, the answer was yes. At first glance, it is hard to see what the mountain man and the ebullient Canadian, an immigrant from Czechoslovakia during early childhood, had in common. What Reitman has called his 'schlockmeister' image developed out of his emotional accord with a generation of *National Lampoon* and *Saturday Night Live* buffs. He co-produced the highly successful *Animal House* in 1978, then directed and produced *Meatballs* and *Stripes*, establishing the careers of John Belushi and Bill Murray in the process. Then came *Ghostbusters*, a record-breaking comedy with a gross of 31 million dollars. Whether they take place in the fraternity house or the holiday camp, the army or the high-rise haunted streets of New York, these films depend on boisterous, silly, post-adolescent high jinks. In Reitman's world, the heroes are extrovert, jokey and male, and the women are invisible except as objects of unfulfilled lust.

When Redford first read *Legal Eagles*, he cringed. He may have been looking to present himself in a more youthful light-hearted manner after the tragic intensities of Roy Hobbs and Denys Finch Hatton but this was ridiculous – literally. He demanded – and got – five rewrites. When the cameras rolled, it was on a romantic comedy with a decidedly forties flavour. The inspiration came from *Adam's Rib*, released in 1949 with Spencer Tracy and Katharine Hepburn as opposing lawyers who become friends. By the autumn of 1985, *Legal Eagles'* assets included two leading ladies played by top line eighties actresses, Debra Winger and Daryl Hannah, a supporting cast headed by Brian Dennehy and Terence Stamp and a handsome thirty-eight-million-dollar budget, a substantial proportion of it slated to go Redford's way.

'There was only one reason for doing *Legal Eagles*,' he told *Première*'s Michelle Halberstadt, 'and that was it'd been so long since I'd done something light, and after *Out of Africa*, which was a very heavy piece, I just wanted to have fun, do something comic. I had no interest in it other than that.'

His role is Assistant District Attorney Tom Logan, a high-powered Manhattan lawyer. He is tipped to reach the very top until he is fired for spending the night with glamorous Chelsea Dearden (Hannah), a vacant performance artist accused of theft and murder. At the outset, Laura Kelly (Winger), one of the city's most dynamic, if least well-

A stolen moment of passion for Denys Finch Hatton (Redford) and Karen Blixen (Streep).

dressed, defence attorneys, is his natural enemy but soon they join forces to represent Ms. Dearden. The plot, which involves explosions and gun battles as well as some sharp courtroom exchanges, is pure baloney. The success of *Legal Eagles* lies in its funny lines, many of them spoken with perfect timing by the adept Ms. Winger, and the relationship between its stars. Winger is the pulled-together member of the duo, with Redford as the klutz, a perspective culled, according to Reitman, from the actor's self-image.

'Because Bob rarely does interviews, I had very little sense of who he is. He is known as a fine, upstanding man who has a strong social conscience, which is great for playing the part of an assistant district attorney, but I was wondering where the comedy would come from. In time, he started telling me stories about himself – about his sense of humour, about his now and then bemusement, about his clumsiness.' These revelations led to the evolution of Tom Logan, a man who locks himself out of his car and drops a bag of groceries so that his girlfriend and his daughter can exchange lovingly indulgent glances. Like Redford, an insomniac, Logan whiles his nights away tap dancing in the bathroom.

The New York scenes weren't helped by Redford mania which made it almost impossible to film with any degree of calm, until Reitman hit upon the idea of setting up shots in one place and shooting them in another. He used a Redford look-alike for this, displaying him prominently in the street and allowing the crowds to gather. Meanwhile the real one was getting on with the job unobtrusively a few blocks away.

Debra Winger may well be the best actress of her generation, but she is also one of the most difficult, and she fought steadily, if unavailingly, with Reitman through a shooting schedule that stretched from ten weeks to four months. 'I had never really done a full-out comedy,' she explained, 'and what appealed to me originally about *Legal Eagles* is hardly seen on-screen. I never planned to be in a pyrotechnic movie. It was intended to be a movie like *Adam's Rib*, a sophisticated romantic comedy about relationships. Imagine my dismay to find myself jumping in the East River while I'm thinking about *Adam's Rib*. I had a lot of disagreements with Ivan as the film changed character. But he's a very strong personality, and he made the film he wanted to make.'

Later she added, 'I don't regret doing it, but I don't think it stands on its own against good films. It was fat – almost forty million dollars – and, politically, I'm opposed to that kind of money unless it's an epic. I took my salary and left.'

However, she and Robert Redford became close friends, so close indeed that the newspapers reported a romance between them. 'Everyone was waiting for total disaster, but we got along great. We're so different. I think he was intrigued, and I liked the fact that he was older

Legal Eagles (1986): Robert Redford and Debra Winger argue the case.

and set in his ways so I could rouse him up a little bit. I called him the Unnatural, which got him upset, although the people who work for him call him God. When we were shooting, there were times he was a bit diplomatic for my taste, but he was definitely a gentleman. He was as disgruntled about the way it went as I was, but he never said anything. At the end of shooting we both said we'd still like to do a comedy together!'

Those who noted that romance was in the air were right: the problem was they got the wrong man. Redford had introduced Winger to Timothy Hutton, a friend of his after their association on *Ordinary People*, and it was to the home in the Malibu Hills which she shared with him that the actress returned after shooting on stage nineteen at Universal Studios. Although Redford announced publicly just before Christmas, 1985 that his marriage to Lola had ended amicably, there is nothing to suggest that it was because of Ms. Winger, then at the height of her passion for Hutton. The couple married in March, 1986, in a Jewish ceremony among the redwoods and cypress groves of Big Sur, the start of a short, stormy liaison that ended two years later.

Legal Eagles opened in October, 1986 to generally appreciative reviews and a poor public response. Too expensive by far, it made forty-seven million dollars at the box-office which was not enough to save Universal's Frank Price, the studio boss responsible for giving it the go-ahead. Film critics tend to be of an age to mourn the fact that Hollywood doesn't make this kind of movie any more and to give praise where praise is due for trying to do so now. The shortcomings in character and plot were duly noted, as was the fact that Debra Winger had most of the best lines. There was a generally lukewarm response to Redford in his klutz mode, almost as if the critics didn't quite know how to interpret his change of status.

'Mr. Redford is no amateur when it comes to comedy, but Mr. Reitman and his writers push him to uncomfortable lengths in *Legal Eagles*,' wrote Vincent Canby. 'The star is very game, but not altogether persuasive, as the sort of fellow who tap dances in the bathroom when he can't sleep. Whether the fault is in the material or the performance is impossible to tell, but when he's supposed to be spontaneous, he behaves very much like a cinema icon, showing us that he is, after all, human.'

The *Independent*'s Mark Lawson assessed the film as 'conventional, warm and puppyish', before coming to the following conclusion. 'Redford is in irritatingly good shape for a man of fifty but there is a sense that certain lines in the script ("That look in your eyes – pure blue steel") are doing what the camera used to do unaided and, for twenty years, his development as an actor has been on hold; he cannot, surely, embody Young America for ever.' Perhaps the actor agreed because his next project tackled America at its very oldest.

15

Extraordinary People

'Going to Sante Fe is like going to Greece. It's not that special compared to other areas. The piñon pines are no different than piñon pines elsewhere. But there has been culture there longer than in most places, and you feel it.' Robert Redford said these words to Michael Rogers of *Rolling Stone* in 1979, and they have proved prophetic. Over the past ten years, his spiritual orientation has moved southwards, away from the culture of his own forebears and towards that of the Latin Americans and the native American Indians who jointly populated New Mexico. It is almost as if he found a place which responded to his much trumpeted, dark, Irish passion, suppressed for so long under the golden cool of Wasp America. Better still it was safe: geographically and emotionally on the fringes of the United States but within the boundaries. The golden loner and self-styled patriot could still eat Oreos here.

Recently the man who would acquire mountains sealed his bargain with New Mexico by buying land outside Sante Fe. The 220-acre plot lies high on a bluff off a main road rising from the desert floor to the edge of the Sangre de Cristo range. It is bisected by a stream and Redford plans to build a simple adobe house on it. He will surely have no problems with his solar heating in a territory continuously grilled by sun, shining out of clear, deep, blue skies.

Even by Sundance standards, this isn't getting away from it all: New Mexico enjoyed artistic associations long before D. H. Lawrence passed this way, and today every shop in Santa Fe's over-restored plaza sells native art, native jewellery or native crafts to tourist hordes. Redford's silver Porsche Carrera mingles on an equal-cost basis with Mercedes and Range Rovers in the picturesque low-rise adobe streets. This is a place where rich people play at subsistence ranching, and poor men live precariously through survival farming. Merely being here doesn't put Redford on the side of the angels.

207

The new home will be a memento of the kind only a multi-millionaire could afford of *The Milagro Beanfield War*, one of the most difficult, star-crossed and underrated films of Redford's career. Given the startling success of *Ordinary People*, his second film as a director was always going to pose extraordinary problems. Even on the simplest psychological level, there would be people who thought that winning an Oscar at the first attempt was having life too easy, especially for a man already more than blessed by the Gods. 'I think I'm a bit of a target,' Redford told me in Santa Fe as the razzmatazz for the *Milagro* première drew to a close. 'That's just the way it is. There's nothing I can do about that. There may be too great a level of expectation, too much attention, a certain amount of cynicism. Not anything I wouldn't expect.'

By this time, he was well past hope and into the realms of pure survival. He'd personally been involved in the filming of *The Milagro Beanfield War* for over seven years, and the project itself had been up and running for twelve. It began with a novel by John Nichols, an east-coast intellectual whose political views were transformed by the Vietnam War. Before it, he believed in the American's inalienable right to make money; after it, he believed that American imperialist aggression was at least as much to blame for World War II, Korea and Vietnam as anyone else's aggression.

In 1969, he moved to Taos, New Mexico to embrace the uncluttered desert life. As American involvement in the south-east Asian conflict ran down under Richard Nixon, he turned his attention to Latin American issues and found them, in microcosm, right on his doorstep. On the one hand, there were Hispanic farmers trying to till the arid soil; on the other, the developers, backed by investors with financial muscle and political contacts in the state capital. The key to the success of both these enterprises lay in water rights that had been disputed since capitalist eyes first fell on the area in the thirties. In the post-war climate of expanded tourism, what once belonged to the New Mexicans had been stripped away, legally and illegally. Peasant farmers were asked to sell the one asset they couldn't do without – land; if they refused, boundaries were redrawn and they found themselves left high and dry anyway.

John Nichols wrote his book, quickly, between November, 1972 and February, 1973, then spent a further eight months polishing it for publication in 1974. Milagro is Taos, a valley with wide skies, a ski resort, a number of museums and a solid tourist presence about sixty miles north of Santa Fe. The Beanfield is a symbolic patch, cut off from water which runs along its boundary by the rights and wrongs of commercial conquest. It belongs to Joe Mondragon, a fiery odd-job man who can't afford to feed his family. One day, he lets in the forbidden water and plants his beans. The War is of his making, but only in the sense that he starts it. Keeping it going involves everyone in the community: the Ladd Devine consortium, with its plans for a water-absorbing golf course, takes on the villagers, led by feisty garage owner, Ruby Archuleta. The war is impeded by the doubters, those who see conflict with big business as likely to harm Milagro's fragile infrastructure to their personal disadvantage, and the liberals who prefer to sit on the fence. Observing the central conflict is a Greek chorus of ancients, men steeped in the myth and magic of the region stemming from a time long before the Anglos arrived.

The Milagro Beanfield War sold slowly, and mostly on campuses, where its polemic as well as its humour was appreciated and applauded. The film option was bought by Tomorrow Entertainment who hired a scriptwriter called Tracy Keenan Wynn to turn the 630-page novel into a 120-page screenplay. He was the first of many to discover that Nichols was not a great polisher: *Milagro* has more than 200 characters and a meandering plot line that defies structure. Wynn delivered his first attempt on October 1, 1975 and his second, written from the point of view of Joe Mondragon, a year later. By writing it as one man's war, it was hoped to attract a major star but short, dark gentlemen with no Hispanic connections like Dustin Hoffman, Al Pacino and Charles Bronson turned it down. The consensus was 'who cares about down-trodden Mexican-Americans anyway?'

The answer was Moctesuma Esparza, a civil rights activist and documentary film maker from Los Angeles, who snapped up the option when Tomorrow Entertainment finally threw in the towel in December, 1979. He had a grant from the National Endowment of the Humanities to make a number of films featuring chicano culture and he took the obvious first step of approaching Nichols to write his own screenplay. A month later, Tomorrow called Esparza to say CBS Theatrical Films was ready to go with *Milagro* but the producer declined. 'They had had their shot. They were good fellows, but I had my own vision.' It was one he shared with Nichols: together they would create a small ensemble film, a worthy educational piece suitable for showing on public television, but all that changed dramatically when he received a call from Robert Redford in the spring of 1980.

As *Ordinary People* hadn't been released at the time, Redford had to show it to Esparza in order to convince him that he was competent to direct his film. 'I was bowled over,' the producer recalls, 'so I said to Bob, "Whaddya want?"' Redford wanted the same as Esparza: a low-budget independent film with Hispanic actors. 'My overriding interest was that I thought it was a wonderful piece about culture, and the eccentricities of culture, and the possible wipe out of that culture by development,' he commented. 'But it is really about the people; it's the people that interest me always. I would never make a movie for a cause alone; I don't think that works. If you have a message to deliver, then you better damn well couch it in entertainment, in good quality entertainment.'

He has also said that he understands Hispanic culture because he'd grown up in Santa Monica, then the home of a number of Mexican-Americans. As he would have been under ten at the time, this is dubious vanity with considerable benefit from hindsight. It is much easier to accept his liking for *Milagro*'s David and Goliath theme, its humour, compassion and mysticism. Once Redford was in, the project took on green-light status because he had the clout to make it happen. But not fast.

Of Nichols' action-oriented comedy slapstick script, he said, 'Okay, what we have here is totally uncontrolled energy basically going nowhere. Now let's see if we can't start turning it into a film.' So the author was sent back to his portable manual typewriter at the end of his rutted drive in Taos town. In the summer, he writes in the garden shed; in winter, at the kitchen table. Three of each would pass – and four more drafts – before everyone accepted that he would never get it right on his own. 'If the film stumbles,' he told me just before *Milagro*'s première, 'it may be because Redford tried to bite off more than he can chew. It is an enormous thing to attempt to have fifty speaking parts in a two hour film. It means you give short shrift to some of the characters. It would have made it an awful lot easier to write it from a single point of view.

'*Ordinary People* was a real powerful film,' he went on, 'particularly for a middle-class, white, Anglo-Saxon Protestant, uptight, puritanical human being like me. I always had a problem with communication so I was really excited by it, but that doesn't mean someone can do a 180 degree turnaround into a totally different area. That's what interested Redford. Could he pull it off? If I were him, I don't know if this is what I'd choose for my second directorial project. It's almost like part of the exhilaration for him is daring himself to fall flat on his face. I've got nothing but admiration for his *chutzpah*.'

In 1985, David S. Ward, winner of an Oscar for his work on *The Sting*, was called in to rethink the screenplay. Having read the novel, he didn't see how it could be made into a film, but allowed Redford to persuade him to try. Although it took him three drafts and further polishing from Nichols, Redford was confident enough to go ahead with casting after the first. Over a nine-month period, Esparza interviewed 2,000 Hispanic actors and videotaped 150 of them for Redford to look at. The net was widely cast all over Latin America: the Brazilian Sonia Braga, known in America after *The Kiss of The Spiderwoman*, was first choice for Ruby Archuleta but there was something of a war over Joe

Mondragon. Should it be the New Yorker Chick Vennera or the Hollywood comic Cheech Marin? Esparza went for Cheech but Redford wanted the younger, leaner Chick and in due course he was hired.

On the Anglo front, the names were better known but the parts were much smaller, with people working for far less than their normal rates for the privilege of being in a Robert Redford film. One who received the call was Melanie Griffith. 'He asked me to test for Flossie Devine, the wife of the big landowner,' she explained with some indignation. 'He said he thought I was too young but I should do the test. He wouldn't be there but I should send it to him. I told him, "no way". Later I was in New York doing pick-ups on *Something Wild* and he called me. "I'm in the Rockefeller Center," he said. "Can I come and see you?" I said, "Yeah."'

The next week she read for him – and with him – in Los Angeles and the part was hers. What's more, he had a new fan. 'Beside the fact he's such a good actor, he's so handsome,' she told me breathlessly. 'It's like you're going "Oh, my gosh, is it really Robert Redford?" He's even more handsome in the flesh but he's such a normal man, not like a movie star. He doesn't have an attitude and think he's great. He's very smart, really creative and he doesn't go for all the Hollywood bullshit which is nice.'

Griffith was joined by Christopher Walken as Kyril Montana, the agent whose mission it is to end the beanfield war as quickly and quietly as possible, and John Heard as Charlie Bloom, the liberal drop-out lawyer whose reluctant duty it is to prolong it. There was also a scene-stealing part as the indestructible ancient, Amarante Cordova, for a seventy-four-year-old Mexican, Carlos Riquelme, who had never worked north of the Rio Grande before. Ruben Blades, a Panamanian salsa singer/songwriter, approached Redford direct to good effect. 'We didn't talk about the movie at all. We talked about the environment, politics, painting. Almost in passing, I asked him, "You gonna do this movie?"' Redford said he was and cast Blades as the ambivalent Sheriff Bernabe Montoya.

These and many other people gathered in Santa Fe in early August, 1986, for *Milagro*'s much delayed start. With a ten-million-dollar budget and a ten-week shooting schedule, the film was not exactly fat: it would need all the luck that was going to come in under the wire and it never looked like getting it. The location scouts had selected Truchas, a forty-five-minute drive into the Sangre de Cristo mountains from the production office in Santa Fe, as the site of the beanfield but the numerous plaza scenes were due to be shot in the closer and more substantial town of Chimayo. At the last minute, its residents turned greedy and demanded more money than Redford was prepared to pay.

When he refused, they told him to get lost, and he did, but time too was lost while the plaza was built in Truchas.

'I totally admired their decision,' Redford said later. 'They didn't want a film company there. I wouldn't want a film company in my community. I thought that's their decision. Instead we went to the place I'd wanted to go in the first place. Chimayo was down in the valley. When they didn't want us, we went up high to 9,000 feet where you could see the mountains. Truchas was different, strange things could happen there. It was where I wanted to be.'

The delay and the change of venue turned out to be crucial because the credibility of the flooding of the beanfield depended on its lying in land parched by months of summer sun. However, winters come early at 9,000 feet and seventy per cent of the film had to be shot out of doors, making it hard to provide sufficient cover indoors to keep the crew working if the weather turned nasty. And, from the start, it did. 'We had the coldest day, the most rain in a month and the earliest snowfall in the history of New Mexico,' said Blades succinctly. 'We had all this rain when it wasn't supposed to rain. I mean we're talking about water rights – and then this rain comes pouring from the skies! It was like "What's your problem?" ' As filming dragged on into November, the rain turned to unseasonal snow which first coated the beanfield, then turned it into soup.

Poised for 'Action' on *The Milagro Beanfield War* (1988).

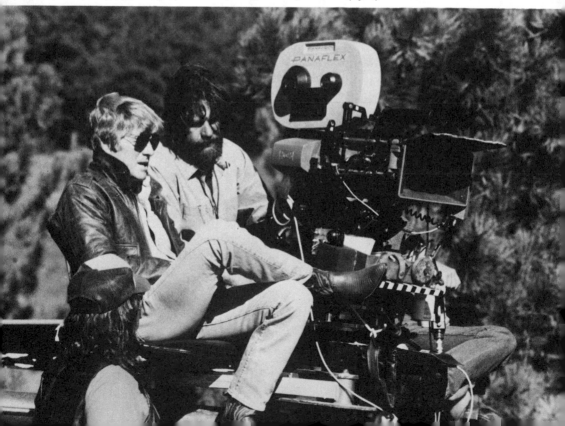

Redford coped with these and other problems with his customary panache. David Ward was summoned to the set and kept busy with constant rewrites for seven weeks. 'It was as hectic a shoot as I've ever been on,' he recalls. 'We were scrambling all the time and sometimes you have to be adaptable about when you can see Bob. There were times when I didn't get to sit down with him till after midnight.'

As with *Ordinary People*, Redford was still concentrating on the actors and drawing pictures for the crew. While they translated them into reality, the man who hated to rehearse, himself, would go through the scene in private with his cast. 'The actors deserve that. Acting is a very important part of the process, and I think it gets continually shoved aside or diminished, particularly in the *auteurist* time we live in. For an actor to do his or her best work, he or she should be comfortable; and to do that, I think you need to spend time with him or her in an intimate atmosphere. I try not to play out the roles myself but it's very hard not to. In life, that's how I explain myself, with my children, my wife, my friends. When I tell a story, I act out the parts of the story. But as a director, I have to be careful I don't intimidate people or get them angry or bummed out or whatever.'

By their own accounts, the actors responded to this treatment with affection and respect. 'He's very open-hearted,' said Melanie Griffith. 'I didn't feel nervous because he's an actor himself so he understands. He taught me a lot, little tiny things that make a scene seem real. And he knew exactly what he wanted. There was no getting to the set and going "dum de dum de dum, I can't figure this scene out", which I've had directors do. He'll shoot until he gets what he wants but he knows when he's got it.' Chick Vennera added, 'He was easy, one of the easiest, because he cut through all the stuff. He allows you to go ahead and start feeling your freedom and, as an actor, he understands the problems. John Schlesinger was like that.'

Sonia Braga, whose name was romantically linked with Redford when the completed film was shown at the 1988 Cannes Film Festival after journalists noted that they had adjoining suites at the Hotel du Cap in Antibes, says that he was a gentleman from their very first meeting. 'I liked him, the way he thinks, when we met, but I was in love with the character, he was in love with the character. That was the connection. He doesn't see actors as men and women, but as human beings, so the pleasure of working with him is the same for a man or a woman. Sure he can be sensitive when he wants something from you but the miracle in *Milagro* is that he's talking about something he really cares about.'

By the time the production was snowed out in late November, it was clear that the film couldn't be completed in time for its planned release a year later. Cast and crew would have to gather again in Truchas in August, 1987 to shoot matching footage. Both the budget, which went up by four to five million dollars, and forward planning went out of the window. Although some of this was due to bad luck, Redford has said that his very presence was partly to blame. 'I am a liability,' he told me. 'It's hard for me to go anywhere. There are always tourists round the set taking photographs of me. All this attention on me as an actor makes it doubly difficult for the other actors.

'Then the media ask, "Will it be as good as *Ordinary People*? Can you top *Ordinary People*? Are you worried about topping *Ordinary People*?" I'd tell them, "I'm not thinking about it. You are. *Ordinary People* is gone, past. I never think about the past." But when people ask constantly, I have to deal with it and it becomes a pressure. Plus people are looking at me more negatively this time, they're looking for me to take a fall, and that adds to pressure. I have to work to keep the blinders on. Even getting to and from the set was difficult. I'd hoped it would be quieter.'

While waiting for conditions in Truchas to match the existing footage, Redford was editing *The Milagro Beanfield War* in Los Angeles. On occasion, he'd fly to Utah in the evening and return the next morning just to spend the night out of town. 'The L.A. I knew as a kid has gone,' he told Mike Barnicle in *Esquire*. 'It's much bigger today, much dirtier, much more sprawling, much more developed. It is like a big two-year lease. Everything is two years. Marriages, friendships, neighbourhoods, people, studio heads. Restaurants where you can get a quarter-pounder on a patent leather bun and only pay forty-eight dollars for it because the place is in. For two years, you're hot, it's hot, and then it's gone. L.A. isn't even the west any more. In the west, the real west, you can feel the level of cynicism being reduced from what it is back east. People have positive energy in the west. L.A. is where people end up when they have no place else to go.'

In the end, the extended period of mountain-deprivation depressed him so much that he decided to build his own 150-seat cinema and extend the existing editing facilities at Sundance. By February, 1987, the work was completed and the director moved in: for the rest of the ski season, he was on the slopes in the morning and at work on the film in the afternoon. When Sydney Pollack came to visit, he said, 'Hell, I want to edit my films here', and he will probably be the first of many of Redford's associates to make what could be the next great escape from the tyranny of Hollywood.

There were further delays while a Spanish language version of *The Milagro Beanfield War* was prepared, a marketing device that had been successfully pioneered on *La Bamba* the year before. When the film was finally unveiled in late March, 1988 in New York and Los Angeles, the reviews and the attendance figures reflected what Redford must have always suspected, but has never admitted: even civilised non-Hispanic

Americans don't want to know about the plight of New Mexican peasants.

Certainly the *New York Times*'s Vincent Canby didn't. 'For reasons not entirely clear the decent, picturesque chicanos of the Milagro Valley have been denied the right to irrigate their farms with water now being channelled to a huge development called the Miracle Valley Recreation Area. Instead of farms, the valley will soon be dotted with condominiums, golf-courses, tennis courts and swimming pools,' he begins.

Later, he gets into his stride. 'If *The Milagro Beanfield War* were more sharply focused, it might have had some of the primitive appeal of an old cattlemen-versus-the-railroad western. However, the movie can't quite bring itself to be so crude and, in avoiding clichés, it avoids telling any particular story whatsoever. The screenplay is jammed with underdeveloped, would-be colourful characters, including a philosophical chicano angel, who faces a succession of fearful confrontations with the law that come to nothing. The narrative is a veritable fiesta of anticlimaxes, from the time the sun sets at the beginning of the film until it sets, yet again, behind the closing credits. The film is very big on sunsets and sunrises. It also has a touristy appreciation for all manner of things folkloric. What it doesn't have is dramatic coherence or backbone. Even the villains are spineless.'

He concluded that 'this is not Mr. Redford's finest hour', an insult his victim is only too ready to trade. The review, he insists, is not Mr. Canby's finest hour either. 'I can tell you right off that he missed the point,' Redford explained to me. 'He refers to Chicanos but they are immigrants from Mexico. The people in the film are New Mexican, not Spanish, not Indian, not Mexican, but a composite of those cultures. This is a person who not only lacked knowledge about this area but sounds predisposed to want a certain kind of film, and not accept the film he's given. That happens a lot. Obviously he didn't see the film because he was looking for something else.

'That's an extension of Hollywood's attitude that no one would want to see a movie about a bunch of poor Mexicans,' he continued, widening his attack to include other critics. 'You'd have to be pretty jaded or warped to take that attitude as a reviewer, but some reviewers are pretty irresponsible, or bitter and unhappy in their own personal lives, and that reflects in their reviews. Even so I imagine you'd get blasted out of your chair if you had the attitude that no one wants to see a movie about a bunch of Mexicans running around the mountains. It may be what a lot of the public will feel but I think that can be overcome if a film has entertainment value, if it touches your heart, if it makes you laugh. I don't know that reviews count that much. I make the film I want to make the best way I can. I assume the studio will do its job and get it to the people. Then I let the people decide.'

Robert Redford

And they did. After a limited fifteen-week release in 159 cinemas, *The Milagro Beanfield War* had taken a meagre thirteen million dollars at the American box-office. The response was much warmer in cinemas in Continental Europe, at Cannes where the film was shown out of competition and at London previews. Can it be that Americans see New Mexico as a foreign country with which they have no conceivable concern, whereas we see it as another region of the United States, intrinsically as interesting as any other, perhaps even more so thanks to being less exposed? If the answer is yes, it will come as no consolation to Robert Redford as he follows his lonely crusade to explain his countrymen to one another.

'My film tries to do two things on a political level. It tries to make us aware of another culture and of our own history. Gabriel Garcia Marquez and Isaac Bashevis Singer totally accept the bizarre and the mystical in their own cultures in their writing but in America we don't. We think it's strange to talk of saints and angels and voices. I tried to present it with total acceptance in *Milagro*, but I'm not of that culture which makes it difficult. My own culture says, "What is Redford doing here?" It's crossed my mind how people from other countries will accept it, but that's about all.'

The message, it seems, is for American minds only but, as Mr. Redford should know, self-styled prophets are rarely welcome in their own countries: on this front, he can expect to be a lone Wasp voice crying into the wilderness for a good while yet.

16

A Kingdom In The Snow

As the *Milagro* festivities fade away and Redford retreats to Sundance to take stock of his future, he has the right to be well pleased with what he sees. The short drive up Provo Canyon to the resort is as winding and unspoiled as any conservationist could wish for. The buildings scattered across the hillside blend in with the environment so that the visitor has no impression of modern development. However, the calm is somewhat deceptive because the Sundance Institute is in the midst of whirlwind expansion. The initial 625,000-dollar annual budget had risen to 1.8 million dollars in 1987; by 1990, it will be over two million dollars. After the long decade of planning, Redford is on a rollercoaster high as he fills in the ticks on the checklist of his ambitions.

The new cinema and the editing rooms, built like everything else out of local stone and rough wooden planks, stand unobtrusively behind the existing restaurants. Further up the hill, the Sundance Amphitheater, used for children's productions during the summer months, is due both for rebuilding – at a cost of 1.3 million dollars – and reprogramming under the supervision of Maurice Sendak. In recent years, it has also been used for open-air concerts featuring 'Great Movie Music' played by the Utah Symphony Orchestra. The preservation of old film scores is another facet of the business: Redford has described the composers as 'the unsung heroes of the film making process' and plans are afoot to treat their work accordingly. Other additions are dance and video, making an agenda that will give Sundance credibility in all branches of the performing arts.

In the midst of all this activity, it is ironic that the film side of The Sundance Institute should be struggling to find a viable identity. In its first seven years of operation, it has put its creative muscle behind a number of worthy projects of which the best known are *El Norte*, *The Ballad of Gregorio Cortez*, *Promised Land* and *A Trip to Bountiful*. It also produced Eugene Corr's *Desert Bloom* in partnership with Columbia, an experiment that is unlikely to be repeated because of the potential conflict of interest between commerce and art. 'We realised that we weren't equipped to produce,' said Michelle Satter, Sundance's Director of Feature Film Programmes. 'As a producer, you could be in a position where you had to fire the director and we would never want to fire a director we'd developed. We believe we function best as a research organisation with a strong educational bias.'

All the films that have come out of Sundance conform to Redford's original concept in that they are small, liberal and American, but their reception has sown seeds of doubt. One problem is that earnestness habitually stands in the way of entertainment, a factor which severely limits audiences. Another is that major recognition has been conspicuously absent, the sole exception being Geraldine Page's Oscar nomination for *A Trip to Bountiful*. This means that the films are neither financial nor artistic successes which suggests that the Sundance policy needs radical rethinking. Satter agrees that the Institute has outgrown its roots and looks rather enviously across the Atlantic at radical film makers like Stephen Frears and David Leland.

Citing *My Beautiful Laundrette, Sammy and Rosie Get Laid* and *Wish You Were Here*, she explained why she admired the British approach. 'There is a lot more energy there. It is difficult to make left-wing, independent films in the United States and I don't think film makers with real talent are working in that area. American independent film is not in a very healthy state in terms of the issues it explores. We would like Sundance to balance reactionary elements in Hollywood and most of our scripts reflect some kind of liberal viewpoint but good Americana is hard to find. Nowadays we're looking for something unique in the writing rather than a sweet little story.'

As Redford is the only constant on the eight-person selection committee, he must take ultimate responsibility for the direction the Institute takes. Although he consults frequently with staff who say they feel free to argue with him, he is in a position to call the shots whenever he wishes. 'He likes to know what you're thinking, he likes to review ideas, but there are a lot of areas in which his word is final,' says Satter. 'He is a man of great passion and he responds to passion in other people. He wants to be open to their ideas, but he does have very strong opinions. One of his talents is being able to watch a short documentary and spot the director's potential as a feature-film maker. I've always admired his ability to make that connection.'

In an attempt to broaden the Institute's base, Redford introduced a writers' week in 1986. When Satter and her team of readers have sifted through 800 to 900 scripts and Redford and his committee have made their final choice, the lucky writers are invited to Sundance in January. This gives them time to revise their work along lines suggested by the

Institute's advisers before they return for the June laboratory. The theory is that making the screenplays viable before involving actors and directors will result in better quality footage when the cameras turn, and ultimately in a higher number of films finding financial backing in Los Angeles.

This is clearly sensible but the 1988 list of writers indicates that Sundance is replacing its original idealistic approach with a rather more commercial one. Instead of choosing first timers, the committee went for proven track records, a policy which enabled Maurice Sendak to direct his first feature, *Very Far Away*, and Bob Comfort, an experienced television writer, to switch to the wide-screen with *Dog Fight*. Mark Romanek, whose début film, *Static*, was full of wit and innovation, was another to benefit with *Crash*, an adaptation of a novel by J. G. Ballard. Arguably, this change of heart will make Sundance less experimental, not so much a place for encouraging raw recruits as a feather-bed for establishment figures wishing to build on existing achievements. Can it be that the competitive Redford has tired of backing unknowns with the lack of glittering prizes which this entails?

Another addition to the Redford file is the United States Film Festival, held each January in the neighbouring ski resort of Park City. Despite a suspicion of festivals that once bordered on dislike, he took over the ailing event in the mid-eighties and it is now presented by the Sundance Institute in its own image and likeness. In other words, all the films in the competitive drama and documentary sections are American, with the rest of the world banished to special seasons outside the mainstream action. In 1988, Redford drew the line at including *The Milagro Beanfield War* in the programme on the grounds that it would be 'self-serving' but the festival, which he opened in person, did number two Sundance projects, *Promised Land* and *Rachel River*, in a line-up of twelve.

One of very few to dent Redford's ingrained parochialism in recent years is the Nobel Prize-winning Colombian, Gabriel Garcia Marquez. In 1987, the actor arranged for the novelist to visit America, then terrorised him by driving him round Los Angeles at '150 miles an hour'. Or so Marquez has claimed. In 1988, the Cuban-based author returned the compliment by arranging for Redford to give a series of lectures at his film school in Havana. 'He is an extraordinary actor,' he commented, 'with a genuine concern for social and cultural problems. I see him as a man who is really trying to use cinema as a new art form.'

Currently the two men are discussing a film of a Marquez book but, despite his increasing absorption in Spanish-speaking America, Redford doesn't feel that he is ready to direct so alien a subject himself. 'I would like my culture to be able to accept his culture, but I think it would be wise to have his work made by someone who understands it instinctively. *Milagro* is set in my own country but Marquez's country is too far removed.'

The Institute of Resource Management is also looking beyond the borders of the United States, but rather more dramatically so, as the target for collaboration is the Soviet Union. The IRM's latest concern is global warming, a subject on every American's lips because it allegedly caused the broiling summer of 1988. Terry Minger, who runs the Institute for Redford from its Sundance base, predicts that overall temperatures will rise by between three and five degrees centigrade by 2050, with changing weather patterns and ice-melt resulting in higher ocean levels.

The greenhouse effect, as it is popularly known, is caused by the destruction of the ozone layer. This is partly the result of natural phenomena, primarily methane gas emitted by cattle and termites. Other destructive factors – automobiles, aerosol sprays, coal, oil and gas-burning plants in factories and homes – are integral to modern life. Forestation, especially in tropical areas, should be a balancing factor but the systematic clearing of trees to make way for roads and cities has further increased the termite population.

Minger admits that reversing these trends is far beyond the wit – or the wishes – of man: control is the only solution. The Soviets come into the picture because global warming is an acceptable issue in a country where almost every environmental topic is out of bounds. They don't want to discuss acid rain or water pollution or the squandering of natural resources, all areas in which they have too much explaining to do, but over-warming allows them to point the finger at the West on the grounds that it must bear the brunt of the responsibility for the destructive emissions. 'It is politically advantageous for them,' Minger explains, 'and we need their co-operation to deal with it.'

Redford planned to set the ball in motion when he was invited to introduce a season of his films in Moscow in May 1988, an occasion which gave him an opportunity to meet Gorbachev. 'I'm being brought over as a film person,' he told me shortly before he left, 'but I hope to discuss the greenhouse effect as well. Gorbachev has done some interesting things, or rather he's trying to do some interesting things.'

Minger, who accompanied Redford on the trip to fill him in on the details, saw the meeting as the start of a joint American–Soviet venture that would lead to regular exchanges in both countries. America's National Center for Atmospheric Research in Boulder, Colorado, a private institution that already receives input from scientists from a number of countries including Britain, would welcome Soviet involvement in its programme to control global warming. Minger sees the collaboration as a way of building on the recent United Nations agreement on the subject signed by the West and the Eastern bloc but not, as yet, by all the Third World countries. 'Our object is to involve the world community. We can't stop deforestation and pollution but the challenge is to come up with adaptations. If the oceans rise, one would be the ability to grow foods in salt water.'

On the resort front, too, Sundance is expanding, albeit on a relatively modest scale. The object is to increase revenue to partially support the two Institutes but not at the expense of peace and quiet. Until the early eighties, visitors had to stay down in Provo. Then came the Sundance Mountain Inns – one-of-a-kind private homes with three to six bed-rooms and two to five bathrooms, making a total of 100 beds. When their owners are away, these are rented out complete with services like shopping, making breakfast, lighting fires and baby-sitting provided by innkeepers, for the most part enthusiastic teetotal students from Brigham Young University.

In 1987, Redford decided to supplement the accommodation with thirty-seven cottages, some of them studios and some of them one- or two-bedroom cabins. Set in aspen woods with views of Mount Timpa-nogos, they are made from handsome cedar planks with the high-pitched ceilings and the slabbed stone fireplaces which characterise the whole of Sundance. Redford concerned himself with every detail of their design, inside and out, then employed architects and engineers to turn his ideas into reality.

'Bob wanted cosy, small, well-used spaces,' Brent Beck explained. 'He said that small spaces could be wonderful if they were used as they are in Europe. Europeans understand space. Americans waste it. Bob is not ostentatious in anything he does, not in his clothes or his cars or anything he buys. When the cottages were going up, he said, "lower this, widen that, I want more light". Later he had carpet samples, couch samples, furniture samples and light fittings brought in and he chose everything himself. He said, "I want down comforters, this quality of linen and pillows, this brand of soap and shampoo." What he didn't like, he changed. Every detail you see is him.'

The details in my studio included oatmeal carpeting, a sofa-bed with apple-green and russet linen set among tall cedar roof-supports to give a four-poster effect, wrought iron broncho-shaped bedside lights, wooden furniture with brass handles, rattan chairs, Neutrogena toiletries, decaffeinated coffee and a dried flower arrangement. The amenities included a hot tub, a television and a range of high-quality kitchen equipment. The use of vertical space was impressive, the view magni-ficent and everything sparkled with cleanliness. The effect was sup-remely comfortable and peaceful, even solitary, and quite unlike any of dozens of ski resorts I've visited. If Redford hadn't chosen to be an actor, a patron of the arts, a film theorist, a director or a businessman, he could certainly have made a handsome living as an interior designer.

'Bob's got values,' says Beck by way of explanation. 'The cottages cost the same per square foot as ones in Deer Valley or Beaver Creek that sell for 500,000 dollars. He pre-sold the studios for 79,000 dollars and the two-bedroom cabins for 250,000 dollars all freehold and completely furnished. He isn't here to rip people off. Same with the restaurants and the store. There is a mark-up and that's it. He is a very conscientious human being and all his employees have the same idea of what service should be as he does. His view is no different from the lift operator's.'

The lucky buyers of these windfall dwellings include David Puttnam and other Redford friends. All but three of the cottages – Puttnam's is one of the exceptions – go into a rental pool for visitors to use, but anonymity is strict. You have no way of knowing if you are sleeping in Tom Brockaw's bed or not. A second area has been marked out as suitable for a further thirty-seven cottages, subject to approval from Redford and the County, but Brent Beck is not over optimistic.

'It was a real struggle for Bob to get himself mentally to the point of building the first lot. This is a very private area and every tree that goes means something to him. It took a lot of people to persuade him. Now he sees it was a wise choice but he won't even talk about building any more until the existing cottages are full all the year round with a six-month advance-notice period. We can't compete as a ski resort with the big boys but we do have heart and soul. Bob doesn't ask film people to come here, he doesn't want it to be known as a place stars come, and just because they're in the same business, it doesn't mean they are his friends. They come because of what Sundance doesn't have, no loud music, no discos, no resort facilities. These people are at parties and dinners every night in L.A. When they're here, they just want to curl up in front of the fire with a good book.'

Over the past three years, the skiing has been improved by the addition of a new triple chairlift and the purchase of two 100,000-dollar grooming machines, but the size of the car park has actually been reduced to make way for the cinema and editing rooms. Once 450 cars are in place, the gates slam shut and the latecomers must go elsewhere. Up on the mountain, Bearclaw's Cabin offers panoramic views, a Snow Kitchen which prepares hamburgers and hot dogs, a range of soft drinks and a lot of Jeremiah Johnson memorabilia. No lavatory though: skiers must head for the woods, just as the cast and crew did on the film. 'We are decidedly different from all the other ski areas,' says Redford, 'and committed to staying that way. I don't want Sundance to be big. We have all the things a resort has, on a much smaller scale. I like to have big skiing and a small parking lot.'

In changed marital circumstances and with increasing commitments to the Institutes more than balancing out the acting jobs he vetoes, Redford is now to be found in Sundance more often than not. When he separated from Lola officially in 1985, she went on living in the Fifth Avenue apartment and he moved into another luxury penthouse close by. He numbers former New York Mayor John Lindsay and Dick Cavett among his closer friends in the city, at least to the extent that he is prepared to dodge through the kitchens of restaurants to dine with them. However the older he gets the less he is prepared to expose himself to his oppressively adoring fans. Such is his aversion to unscheduled company that he buys two seats on the plane when travelling coast to coast so that no stranger gets to sit next to him.

He feels sufficiently at ease in the mountains to brave the stares in Keith's Lunch, a modest Provo haunt that regularly serves him beer and chicken-fried steak. But even in Sundance, he is not always as alone as he would wish: people have even been known to trek through the wilderness to watch him eating breakfast on his front porch, an intrusion that infuriates him. 'I've always believed that I owe the public a performance, and that's it. I have no obligation to share my private life. One of the things I miss most from my youth is watching people in cafés and bars. I would sketch them, talk to them, take notes, but I can't do that any more. As much as you try to be a regular guy, you can't. That's gone, and you have to find some replacement for it. And that gets harder and harder.'

Gone too is family life as he once knew it. Bob and Lola were so successful in their plan for bringing up their children as ordinary people that none of them have shown any wish to follow in the footsteps of their famous father. Shauna, the eldest, is exceptionally beautiful and apparently perfectly content to be as good a wife as her mother was. Jamie, with the neatly cut hair and neatly pressed clothes which characterise today's wealthy young Americans, is professionally and gainfully employed in Chicago. Only the teenage Amy, a student who spends much of her time with her mother in Manhattan, displays any of her father's liking for a more casual approach to life.

Redford has claimed that it was his children, in their younger days, that kept him away from drugs, gambling and any tendency he might have had to be a playboy. Nor would they allow him to be pompous: whenever he tried to impose his will on theirs, they would chant, 'R.R. Superstar, who the hell do you think you are?' Redford allows self-mockery to go some stages further by having lavatory paper with images of himself on every square of tissue in his bathrooms and a poem written some years ago by Jamie on his wall. It reads:

> 'I call my dad Redford the Runner.
> There are other things he thinks funnier.
> But every day he goes to the trouble
> To keep his body from turning to rubble.'

'My kids are my best friends,' he comments. 'Basically they know what a clod I am. They know the person who is shy and awkward in social situations. They know the person who bumps into things, who opens the refrigerator door and says, "Where is the juice?" and everyone starts laughing because they know it's right in front of me on the second shelf.'

This evident rapport with his own children spills over into his relationships with other young people. The rule, according to actor Gavan O'Herlihy, who was called on to play tennis daily with Redford for six weeks when he was preparing *All The President's Men*, is to laugh and joke with him as if he were an equal. Michael Hoffman, a young director who worked at Sundance on his feature, *Promised Land*, agrees. He remembers Redford turning up of an evening, six-pack in hand, to chat and play table-tennis in his cabin.

'He likes the boys, he likes to sit down and have a beer and discuss whatever he's reading or American Indians or the time he saw a ghost. He's a real raconteur, very funny and very charming. I was intimidated at the thought of meeting him – everyone who goes to the June lab is – but he was sitting on the lawn when I arrived and he took some sort of interest in me from that moment. Right from the beginning, I teased him back. I was very cocky with him which is not my instinct usually, but I guess it helped. He gets very tired of having people agreeing with him.'

Hoffman also reports that Redford's zest f   ⸗ung up practical jokes is untouched by time. When he attended the June workshop, Karl Malden, then fronting a famous series of American Express commercials, was one of the resident advisers. When a visitor left his credit card in the Tree Room Restaurant, Redford enlisted Malden's assistance, then had the card owner tracked down. 'Mr. Redford wants to see you in his office,' the astonished man was told. 'He thought he'd been visited by God,' says Hoffman. 'Redford put his arm round him and led him up this little path. Then Karl Malden steps out from behind the bush waving the card and saying, "Don't leave home without it", just as he does in the ad. Everyone cracked up and they spent the rest of the afternoon together. Redford has a terrific sense of humour.'

On the work front, however, he is much more awe-inspiring, especially when the acolyte's finished film is screened. 'I was terrified when he first saw *Promised Land* because he's not someone who's prone to praise on the whole. I don't really smoke but I went through a whole pack in an hour and a half. I hoped he'd say something like, "Well, it's not a disaster. There's probably something we can save." I could hardly believe it when he turned to me and said, "I love this. I'm so proud to be part of it."'

Though Hoffman's experiences of working with Redford were excellent on a personal level, there were certain professional drawbacks. Because the film could never have been made without him, the young director asked him by way of thanks if he would be a non-active executive producer, and Redford graciously agreed. 'In retrospect, having his name on it had some detrimental effects,' Hoffman recalls. 'It created a lot of expectation for a very little story and it meant that it wasn't a film a critic could discover. Bob had been there first! It certainly has its flaws, but once Bob had said he liked it, no one who'd helped me make it would ever criticise it. His word was gospel. No one would tell me what they really thought!'

Redford's easy manner with men of all ages doesn't carry over into his relations with women. Lola may have curbed his baser instincts by locking him into too early a marriage but her unswerving devotion has allowed him to see women as the lesser sex morally as well as physically. 'I find vulnerability very attractive and, of course, no threat,' he says, with commendable honesty but little appreciation of the progress women have made in the last twenty years.

There is a degree of vindication in the fact that he usually sees women at their worst: either drooling stupidly over him or acting aggressively to prove they're not chasing him. On one occasion, Craig Bedami, the owner of Park City ski resort, left two lift passes with his assistant for Redford to pick up. 'Whatever you do, don't make a scene or any kind of fuss,' he told her. When Redford arrived accompanied by Paul Newman, the girl obediently handed over the passes, then fell off her stool in a dead faint and had to be taken to hospital. Faced with behaviour like that, it is hardly surprising that the actor feels a degree of contempt for the 'weaker' sex.

Neither Bob nor Lola has spoken in public of the reasons for their estrangement, but there are signs that an old-fashioned marriage has become a thoroughly modern separation. According to Brent Beck, all five Redfords still gather at Sundance for Christmas, a season of goodwill that begins with an open-air cantata performed by the Salt Lake Vocal and Chamber Ensemble on the Sunday before the feast day. 'Everyone who works here or is staying here is invited, usually about 350 people. It's Bob's gift to his guests. He hosts it and welcomes them, then leads the candlelit procession. It is a contemplative occasion, not an excuse for going out and getting drunk.'

The most likely explanation for the Redfords living apart after nearly thirty years together is that Lola grew out of her subservient role. Having committed herself to marriage and motherhood as an unfledged and not very well-educated nineteen-year-old, she gradually found an identity through her work for Consumer Action Now. When she first lobbied for customers' rights in the corridors of Washington in the mid-seventies, she never traded on being Mrs. Robert Redford. Ten years later, she decided to catch up on her studies by taking a degree course in social psychology at the University of Vermont. By her mid-forties, with her children increasingly less dependent on her, she was ready to go it alone.

Certainly the split was no part of Redford's grand plan. 'Of course I like women,' he says, 'but I'm not interested in loveless sex or sexless love. I don't see the point of leading a double life and cheating.' And he never has led one: everyone is agreed on that. Now that he is potentially a free man, he is a target for limitless speculation. Debra Winger, his co-star in *Legal Eagles*, is often cited, but psychology is against an affair between them. Winger is hard-drinking and outspoken in a way which Redford, prim, tight-lipped and self-disciplined, would find deeply embarrassing. It is hard to imagine his risking his privacy with a woman who comes out with such quotations as, 'the sexiest thing in the world is to be totally naked with your wedding ring on'.

Sonia Braga, dubbed 'the thrill from Brazil', is another matter. As a Latin American, she would be doubly attractive to Redford: she comes from the culture which currently interests him the most, and she would understand, though not necessarily subscribe to, the idea that behind every successful man there is a loyal and loving woman. True to her origins, she has a passionate nature but evidence as to her involvement with Redford rests mostly on the fact that she hung out with the film unit for weeks after her part in *The Milagro Beanfield War* was completed.

One of the perils of Redford's position is that women who don't know him invariably want to. These include Princess Diana who selected him and Clint Eastwood as the Americans she would most like to meet over dinner at the White House in the autumn of 1985. Redford managed to duck the invitation but he was not so lucky when the supplicant was French model Nathalie Naud. She struck up a friendship with Bernie Pollack, the costume designer on *The Milagro Beanfield War*.

He asked Redford to meet her and the actor agreed to be photographed with her in an apartment in Los Angeles, the first fan shots he'd permitted in twenty years. The duplicitous Naud tried to turn the thirty-minute meeting into a major affair by claiming publicly that Redford had bombarded her with flowers and love letters and suggestions that they should live together. 'Bob is everything that I have always wanted in a man, mature, intelligent and objective about life,' she wrote. 'He appeared with a gleaming smile, jeans and a T-shirt. He looked like a student. A strange electric shock ran up my spine.' Furious at having been conned, Redford responded with a fierce salvo from a

With Sonia Braga, the lady they call 'the thrill from Brazil'.

battery of international lawyers but it is small wonder that he is deeply suspicious of strange women.

Professionally too his relations with them are restricted by his unstated, but self-evident, preference for working with men. He has never been directed by a woman, and probably never would be. Nor do they feature as producers or in key positions other than as actresses in Redford films. The scriptwriters and directors invited to Sundance are primarily men, as are the advisers who come to help them. On the critical front, Redford reserves his most unkind words for Pauline Kael, his adversary in a feud that has lasted nearly twenty years. Kael's admiration for Redford lasted only until he became famous when it was replaced by persistent sniping. The actor's patience ran out entirely when she accused him of giving the Indian the finger at the end of *Jeremiah Johnson* when he felt he was saluting a noble adversary. Relations have been cool ever since.

'Pauline Kael has such a loathing of self that she takes it out on everyone else,' he told *Première*'s Michele Halberstadt. 'If you don't make the movie she wants to see, she criticises that rather than the movie you made, and it becomes very personal. And what you finally end up seeing is a woman baring her own self-loathing to the public at large.'

But will Ms. Kael ever have another Redford performance to savage or has he done with acting for ever? At the time of writing, there are no clues but the answer is probably not. He may be torn between the need for adulation and the limitations acting places on his freedom, but it is hard to imagine his quitting altogether. For one thing, the success of Sundance depends on his high profile leadership: raising money is a lot easier if potential sponsors don't have to ask, 'Bob who?' For another, he is too young to retire.

Perhaps there are clues to his future in his attitude to Paul Newman, one of very few men with the power to make him jealous. 'If you're lucky, you'll have a few friends who will tell you, "Hey, that's bullshit,"' he told Mike Barnicle in *Esquire*. 'You need that. Especially in this business. If I had to, I'd probably say that Newman is my best friend. He's the greatest. Not much I wouldn't do for him. A couple of weeks ago, we went out to have dinner with him in Connecticut, and we're driving home and I'm thinking to myself: "God, here's old Paul. What is he? Sixty, sixty-one? I don't know. He looks great, feels great, has a lot of money, gives to great causes, he's in love with his wife, he races his cars when he wants to, makes a movie when he wants to, he's incredibly happy and still has that face that looks the way it did when he was twenty." God, by the time we got home, I wanted to shoot myself. I'd love to make one more movie with him. Just one more. The two of us.'

All things being equal, he probably will. He will also direct and lecture and take up causes. He will not run for President, or so he currently swears. Instead he will sit on his mountain, a middle-aged man, claims Newman, who has stated publicly that he could never get close to him, even as his best friend. Strangers lower their voices reverentially when they come into the Redford presence and raise them in slight adrenalin-fuelled hysteria when they leave it. 'I respect the fact that it's hard for new people to be totally comfortable or totally natural,' he says of this awkward reaction. 'Believe it or not, I'm basically a shyer person than people realise and that's probably why I chose acting as a profession – to get over my shyness or to keep out of jail, either one.'

He may joke about it but it is hard to escape the conclusion that the mature Redford is a loner trapped in an elaborate gilded cage of his own devising. The key is his inability to pull down his own emotional barriers even for those who know him best, the bars are the fact that he doesn't want to. 'Plastic surgery can do anything with the human nose – except keep it out of other people's business,' he comments bitterly. It is a slick superficial remark, but it sums up his attitude to the rest of the world rather well: with Robert Redford, it's always, 'Don't call me, I'll call you' – and, business aside, it's not often that he picks up the phone.

Filmography

1962

WAR HUNT

Cast Private Raymond Endore: John Saxon; Private Ray Loomis: Robert Redford; Captain Wallace Pratt: Charles Aidman; Sergeant Von Horn: Sydney Pollack; Private Crotty: Gavin MacLeod; Charlie: Tommy Matsuda; Corporal Showalter: Tom Skerritt; Private Fresno: Tony Ray.

A T-D Enterprise Production for United Artists. Producer: Terry Sanders; Director: Denis Sanders; Screenplay: Stanford Whitmore; Cinematographer: Ted McCord; Art Director: Edgar Lansbury; Sound: Roy Meadows; Assistant Director: Jack Bohier; Editor: John Hoffman. Running time: 81 minutes.

1965

SITUATION HOPELESS – BUT NOT SERIOUS

Cast Herr Frick: Alec Guinness; Lucky: Michael Connors; Hank: Robert Redford; Edeltraud: Anita Hoefer; Lissie: Mady Rahl; Herr Neusel: Paul Dahlke; Quartermaster Sergeant: Frank Wolff; Sergeant: John Briley; Wanda: Elisabeth Von Molo; Senta: Carola Regnier.

A Paramount Pictures Release. Producer/Director: Gottfried Reinhardt; Screenplay: Silvia Reinhardt, based on *The Hiding Place*, a novel by Robert Shaw and adapted by Jan Lustig; Cinematographer: Kurt Hasse; Art Director: Rolf Zehetbauer; Costumes: Ilse Dubois; Music: Harold Byrns; Assistant Producer: Jose de Villaverde; Assistant Director: Henry Sokal; Editor: Walter Boos. Running time: 97 minutes.

INSIDE DAISY CLOVER

Cast Daisy: Natalie Wood; Raymond Swan: Christopher Plummer; Wade Lewis: Robert Redford; Walter Baines: Roddy McDowall; The Dealer: Ruth Gordon; Melora Swan: Katharine Bard; Gloria Goslett: Betty Harford; Harry Goslett: John Hale; Dancer: Paul Hartman; Cop: Harold Gould; Old

Lady: Ottola Nesmith; Cynara: Edna Holland; Milton Hopwood: Peter Helm.

A Park Place Production for Warner Brothers. Producer: Alan J. Pakula; Director: Robert Mulligan; Screenplay: Gavin Lambert based on his own novel; Cinematographer: Charles Lang; Costumes: William Thomas; Music: André Previn; Assistant Director: Joseph E. Kenny; Editor: Aaron Stell. Running time: 128 minutes.

1966

THE CHASE

Cast Calder: Marlon Brando; Anna: Jane Fonda; Bubber: Robert Redford; Val Rogers: E. G. Marshall; Ruby Calder: Angie Dickinson; Emily Stewart: Janice Rule; Mrs. Reeves: Miriam Hopkins; Mary Fuller: Martha Hyer; Damon Fuller: Richard Bradford; Edwin Stewart: Robert Duvall; Jason 'Jake' Rogers: James Fox; Elizabeth Rogers: Diana Hyland; Briggs: Henry Hull; Mrs. Briggs: Jocelyn Brando; Verna Dee: Katherine Walsh; Cutie: Lori Martin; Paul: Marc Seaton; Seymour: Paul Williams; Lem: Clifton James; Mr. Reeves: Malcolm Atterbury; Mrs. Henderson: Nydia Westman; Lester Johnson: Joel Fluellen; Archie: Steve Ihnat; Moore: Maurice Manson; Sol: Bruce Cabot; Slim: Steve Whittaker; Sam: Ken Renard; Mrs. Sifftifieus: Pamela Curran.

A Horizon Picture for Columbia Pictures. Producer: Sam Spiegel; Director: Arthur Penn; Screenplay: Lillian Hellman, based on the novel and play by Horton Foote; Cinematographer: Joseph La Shelle; Art Director: Robert Luthardt; Music: John Barry; Assistant Director: Russell Saunders; Editor: Gene Milford. Running time: 135 minutes.

THIS PROPERTY IS CONDEMNED

Cast Alva Starr: Natalie Wood; Owen Legate: Robert Redford; J. J. Nichols: Charles Bronson; Hazel Starr: Kate Reid; Willie Starr: Mary Badham; Knopke: Alan Baxter; Sidney: Robert Blake; Jimmy Bell: Ray Hemphill; Charlie Steinkamp: Brett Pearson; Lindsay Tate: Bruce Watson; Tom: Jon Provost; Hank: Quentin Sondergaard; Johnson: John Harding; Salesman: Dabney Coleman.

A Seven Arts–Ray Stark Production for Paramount Pictures. Producer: John Houseman; Director: Sydney Pollack; Screenplay: Francis Ford Coppola, Fred Coe, Edith Sommer, suggested by a one-act play by Tennessee Williams; Cinematographer: James Wong Howe; Art Directors: Hal Pereira, Stephen Grimes, Phil Jeffries; Music: Kenyon Hopkins; Assistant Director: Eddie Saeta; Editor: Adrienne Fazan. Running time: 110 minutes.

1967

BAREFOOT IN THE PARK

Cast Paul Bratter: Robert Redford; Corie Bratter: Jane Fonda; Victor Velasco: Charles Boyer; Mrs. Banks: Mildred Natwick; Frank: Ted Hartley; Aunt Harriet: Mabel Albertson; Restaurant Proprietor: Fritz Feld; Telephone Man: Herbert Edelman; Delivery Man: James Stone.

A Paramount Pictures Release. Producer: Hal B. Wallis; Associate Producers: Neil Simon, Paul Nathan; Director: Gene Saks; Screenplay: Neil Simon, based on his own play; Cinematographer: Joseph La Shelle; Costumes: Edith Heath; Editor: William A. Lyon. Running time: 106 minutes.

1969

BUTCH CASSIDY AND THE SUNDANCE KID

Cast Butch Cassidy: Paul Newman; The Sundance Kid: Robert Redford; Etta Place: Katharine Ross; Percy Garris: Strother Martin; Sheriff Bledsoe: Jeff Corey; Woodcock: George Furth; Agnes: Cloris Leachman; Harvey Logan: Ted Cassidy; Marshal: Kenneth Mars; Bike Salesman: Henry Jones; Macon: Donnelly Rhodes; Large Woman: Jody Gilbert; News Carver: Timothy Scott; Fireman: Don Keefer; Flat Nose Curry: Charles Dierkop; Bank Manager: Francisco Cordova; Photographer: Nelson Olmstead; Card Players: Paul Bryar, Sam Elliott; Bank Teller: Charles Akins; Tiffany's Salesman: Eric Sinclair.

A Campanile Production for Twentieth Century-Fox. Executive Producer: Paul Monash; Producer: John Foreman; Director: George Roy Hill; Screenplay: William Goldman; Assistant Director: Steven Bernhardt; Cinematographer: Conrad Hall; Art Directors: Jack Martin Smith, Philip Jeffries; Costumes: Edith Head; Music composed and conducted by Burt Bacharach; Editors: John C. Howard, Richard C. Meyer. Running time: 110 minutes.

DOWNHILL RACER

Cast David Chappellet: Robert Redford; Eugene Claire: Gene Hackman; Carole Stahl: Camilla Sparv; Machet: Karl Michael Vogler; Tommy: Joe Jay Albert; Mayo: Dabney Coleman; Stiles: Tom J. Kirk; D. K. Bryan: Timothy Kirk; Jimmy Creech: Jim McMullan; Tony Kipsmith: Oren Stevens; Bruce Devore: Rip McManus; Rob Engel: Jerry Dexter; David's Father: Walter Stroud; Lena: Carole Carle; Gabriel: Robin Hutton-Potts; Meier: Heini Schuler; Haas: Eddie Waldburger; Istel: Marco Walli.

A Wildwood International Production for Paramount Pictures. Producer: Richard Gregson; Director: Michael Ritchie; Screenplay: James Salter, based on *The Downhill Racers*, a novel by Oakley Hall; Cinematographer: Brian Probyn; Art Director: Ian Whittaker; Make Up: William J. Lodge; Assistant

Director: Kip Gowans; Production Manager: Walter Coblenz. Running time: 101 minutes.

TELL THEM WILLIE BOY IS HERE

Cast Cooper: Robert Redford; Lola: Katharine Ross; Willie Boy: Robert Blake; Liz: Susan Clark; Calvert: Barry Sullivan; Hacker: John Vernon; Benby: Charles Aidman; Wilson: Charles McGraw; Finney: Shelly Novak; Newcombe: Robert Lipton.

A Jennings Lang Presentation for Universal Pictures. Producer: Philip A. Waxman; Director: Abraham Polonsky; Screenplay: Abraham Polonsky, based on *Willie Boy – A Desert Manhunt*, a novel by Harry Lawton; Cinematographer: Conrad Hall; Art Directors: Alexander Golitzen, Henry Bumstead; Costumes: Edith Head; Music: Dave Grusin; Assistant Director: Joseph Kenny; Editor: Melvin Shapiro. Running time: 98 minutes.

1970

LITTLE FAUSS AND BIG HALSY

Cast Big Halsy: Robert Redford; Little Fauss: Michael J. Pollard; Rita Nebraska: Lauren Hutton; Seally Fauss: Noah Beery; Mom Fauss: Lucille Benson; Moneth: Linda Gaye Scott; Photographer: Ray Ballard; Marcy: Shara St. John; Rick Nifty: Ben Archibek.

A Paramount Pictures Release. Producer: Albert J. Ruddy; Director: Sidney J. Furie; Screenplay: Charles Eastman; Cinematographer: Ralph Woolsey; Art Director: Larry Paull; Production Manager/Assistant Director: Terry Morse; Editor: Argyle Nelson, Jr. Running time: 99 minutes.

1972

THE HOT ROCK

Cast Dortmunder: Robert Redford; Kelp: George Segal; Murch: Ron Liebman; Alan Greenberg: Paul Sand; Abe Greenberg: Zero Mostel; Dr. Amusa: Moses Gunn; Lieutenant Hoover: William Redfield; Sis: Topo Swope; Ma Murch: Charlotte Rae; Happy Hippy: Seth Allen; Warden: Graham P. Jarvis; Roll, the Bartender: Harry Bellaver; Dr. Strauss: Lee Wallace; Albert: Robert Weil; Miasmo: Lynne Gordon; Bird Lady: Grania O'Malley; Cop at Police Station: Robert Levine; Otto: Fred Cook.

A Twentieth Century-Fox Release. Producers: Hal Lander, Bobby Roberts; Director: Peter Yates; Screenplay: William Goldman, based on the novel by Donald E. Westlake; Cinematographer: Ed Brown; Production Designer: John Robert Lloyd; Art Director: Bob Wrightman; Costumes: Ruth Morley; Music: Quincy Jones; Assistant Director: Ted Zachary; Editors: Frank P. Keller, Fred W. Berger. Running time: 101 minutes.

THE CANDIDATE

Cast Bill McKay: Robert Redford; Lucas: Peter Boyle; John J. McKay: Melvyn Douglas; Jarmon: Don Porter; Nancy: Karen Carlson; Jenkin: Quinn Redeker; Henderson: Morgan Upton; Corliss: Michael Lerner; Starkey: Kenneth Tobey.

A Wildwood–Ritchie Production for Warner Brothers. Producer: Walter Coblenz; Director: Michael Ritchie; Screenplay: Jeremy Larner; Director of Photography: John Korty; Cinematographer: V. J. Kemper; Production Designer: Gene Callahan; Costumes: Patricia Norris; Assistant Director: Michael Daves; Editors: Richard A. Harris, Robert Estrin. Running time: 110 minutes.

JEREMIAH JOHNSON

Cast Jeremiah Johnson: Robert Redford; Bear Claw: Will Geer; Del Gue: Stefan Gierasch; Crazy Woman: Allyn Ann McLerie; Robidoux: Charles Tyner; Swan: Delle Bolton; Caleb: Josh Albee; Reverend: Paul Benedict; Qualen: Matt Clark; Lebeaux: Richard Angarola; Lieutenant Mulvey: Jack Colvin.

A Warner Brothers Release. Producer: Joe Wizan; Director: Sydney Pollack; Screenplay: John Milius, Edward Anhalt, based on *Mountain Man*, a novel by Vardis Fisher, and *Crow Killer*, a story by Raymond W. Thorp and Robert Bunker; Cinematographer: Duke Callaghan; Art Director: Ted Hanworth; Music: John Rubenstein, Tim McIntire; Assistant Director: Mike Moder; Editor: Thomas Stanford. Running time: 110 minutes.

1973

THE WAY WE WERE

Cast Katie Morosky: Barbra Streisand; Hubbell Gardiner: Robert Redford; J.J.: Bradford Dillman; Carol Ann: Lois Chiles; George Bissinger: Patrick O'Neal; Paula Reisner: Viveca Lindfors; Rhea Edwards: Allyn Ann McLerie; Vicki Bissinger: Diana Ewing; Pony Dunbar: Sally Kirkland; Peggy Vanderbilt: Marcia Mae Jones; Brooks Carpenter: Murray Hamilton; Bill Verso: Herb Edelman; Actor: Don Keefer; El Morocco Captain: George Gaynes; Army Corporal: Eric Boles; Army Captain: Roy Jensen; Frankie McVeigh: James Woods; Jenny: Connie Forslund; Dr. Short: Robert Gerringer; Judianne: Susie Blakely; Rally speaker: Brendan Kelly.

A Rastar Productions Presentation for Columbia Pictures. Producer: Ray Stark; Director: Sydney Pollack; Screenplay: Arthur Laurents, based on his own novel; Cinematographer: Harry Standing, Jr.; Production Designer: Stephen Grimes; Costumes: Dorothy Jeakins, Moss Mabry; Music: Marvin Hamlisch; Lyrics: Marily & Alan Bergman; Assistant Director: Howard Koch, Jr.; Editor: Margaret Booth. Running time: 118 minutes.

THE STING

Cast Harry Gondorff: Paul Newman; Johnny Hooker: Robert Redford; Doyle Lonnegan: Robert Shaw; Lieutenant William Snyder: Charles Durning; J. J. Singleton: Ray Walston; Crystal: Sally Kirkland; Billie: Eileen Brennan; Luther Coleman: James Earl Jones; Erie Kid: Jack Kehoe; Eddie Niles: John Heffernan; Agent Polk: Dana Elcar; Loretta: Dimitra Arliss; Benny Garfield: Avon Long; Kid Twist: Harold Gould.

A Bill/Phillips Production for Universal Pictures. Executive Producers: Richard A. Zanuck, David Brown; Producers: Tony Bill, Michael & Julia Phillips; Director: George Roy Hill; Screenplay: David S. Ward; Cinematographer: Robert Surtees; Art Director: Henry Bumstead; Costumes: Edith Head; Music adapted by Marvin Hamlisch; Assistant Director: Ray Gosnell; Editor: William Reynolds. Running time: 129 minutes.

1974

THE GREAT GATSBY

Cast Jay Gatsby: Robert Redford; Daisy Buchanan: Mia Farrow; Tom Buchanan: Bruce Dern; Myrtle Wilson: Karen Black; Nick Carraway: Sam Waterston; George Wilson: Scott Wilson; Jordan Baker: Lois Chiles; Meyer Wolfsheim: Howard da Silva; Klipspringer: Edward Herrmann; Mr. Gatz: Robert Blossom; Wilson's Friend: Elliott Sullivan; Dog Vendor: Arthur Hughes; Catherine: Kathryn Leigh Scott; Mrs. McKee: Beth Porter; Mr. McKee: Paul Tamarin; Pamela Buchanan: Patsy Kensit; Pamela's Nurse: Majorie Wildes; Gatsby's Bodyguard: John Devlin; Reporter: Jerry Mayer; Miss Baedeker: Regina Baff.

A Paramount Pictures Release. Producer: David Merrick; Director: Jack Clayton; Screenplay: Francis Ford Coppola, based on the novel by F. Scott Fitzgerald; Associate Producer: Hank Moonjean; Cinematographer: Douglas Slocombe; Production Designer: John Box; Art Directors: Eugene Rudolf, Robert Laing; Costumes: Theoni V. Aldredge; Music Supervisor: Nelson Riddle; Choreographer: Tony Stevens; Assistant Directors: David Tringham, Alex Hapsas; Editor: Tom Priestley. Running time: 146 minutes.

1975

THE GREAT WALDO PEPPER

Cast Waldo Pepper: Robert Redford; Axel Olsson: Bo Svenson; Ernst Kessler: Bo Brundin; Mary Beth: Susan Sarandon; Newt: Geoffrey Lewis; Ezra Stiles: Edward Herrmann; Patsy: Kelly Jean Peters; Maude: Margot Kidder; Dillhoefer: Philip Bruns; Werfel: Roderick Cook.

A Jennings Lang Presentation for Universal Pictures. Producer/Director: George Roy Hill; Screenplay: William Goldman, based on a story by George

Roy Hill. Associate Producer: Robert L. Crawford; Director of Photography: Robert Surtees; Art Director: Henry Bumstead; Set Decorator: James Payne; Costumes: Edith Head; Make-Up: Gary Liddiard; Sound: Bob Miller, Ronald Pierce; Music: Henry Mancini; Air Sequences Supervisor: Frank Tallman; Assistant Directors: Ray Gosnell, Jerry Ballew; Editor: William Reynolds; Sound Effects Editor: Peter Berkos. Running time: 107 minutes.

THREE DAYS OF THE CONDOR

Cast Turner: Robert Redford; Kathy: Faye Dunaway; Higgins: Cliff Robertson; Joubert: Max Von Sydow; Mr. Wabash: John Houseman; Atwood: Addison Powell; Barber: Walter McGinn; Janice: Tina Chen; Wick: Michael Kane; Mitchell: Jess Osuna; Thomas: Dino Narizzano; Newberry: Robert Phalen; Heidegger: Lee Steele; Hutton: Garrison Phillips; Jimmy: Frank Savino; Dr. Lappe: Don McHenry; Fowler: Michael Miller; Mrs. Russell: Helen Stenborg; Martin: Patrick Gorman; Jennings: Hansford Rowe, Jr.; Mae Barber: Carlin Glynn; Mailman: Hank Garrett; Messenger: Arthur French; TV Reporter: John Connell; Ordinance Man: Ed Crowley.

A Wildwood Enterprise Co-Production for Paramount Pictures. Producer: Stanley Schneider; Director: Sydney Pollack; Screenplay: Lorenzo Semple, Jr. & David Rayfiel, based on *Six Days of the Condor*, a novel by James Grady; Director of Photography: Owen Roizman; Production Designer: Stephen Grimes; Art Director: Gene Rudolf; Set Decorator: George De Titta; Music: Dave Grusin; Assistant Directors: Pete Scoppa, Mike Haley, Ralph Singleton, Kim Kurumada; Special Effects: Augie Lohman; Supervising Editor: Frederic Steinkamp; Editor: Don Guidice. Running time: 117 minutes.

1976

ALL THE PRESIDENT'S MEN

Cast Carl Bernstein: Dustin Hoffman; Bob Woodward: Robert Redford; Harry Rosenfeld: Jack Warden; Howard Simon: Martin Balsam; Deep Throat: Hal Holbrook; Ben Bradlee: Jason Robards; Bookkeeper: Jane Alexander; Debbie Sloan: Meredith Baxter; Hugh Sloan: Stephen Collins; Dardis: Ned Beatty; Sally Aiken: Penny Fuller; Foreign Editor: John McMartin; Bachinski: David Arkin; Donald Segretti: Robert Walden; Frank Wills: Frank Wills (guard at Watergate building); Barker: Henry Calvert; Martinez: Dominic Chianese; Arguing Attorney: Bryan E. Clark; Markham: Nicholas Coster; Kay Eddy: Lindsay Ann Crouse; Miss Milland: Valerie Curtin; Gonzales: Nate Esformes; Sturgis: Ron Hale; McCord: Richard Herd; Judge: Frank Latimore; National Editor: Paul Lambert; Carolyn Abbott: Allyn Ann McLerie; Baldwin: Gene Lindsey; George: George Pentecost; Sharon Lyons: Penny Peyser; Al Lewis: Joshua Shelley; Ray Steuben: Ralph Williams.

A Wildwood Enterprise Production of a Robert Redford–Alan J. Pakula Film for Warner Brothers. Producer: Walter Coblenz; Director: Alan J. Pakula;

Screenplay: William Goldman, based on the book by Carl Bernstein & Bob Woodward; Director of Photography: Gordon Willis; Camera Operator: Ralph Gerling; Production Designer: George Jenkins; Set Decorator: George Gaines; Supervising Sound Editor: Milton C. Burrow; Music Editor: Nicholas C. Washington; Associate Producers: Michael Britton, Jon Boorstin; Assistant Editors: Bill Green, Art Levinson. Running time: 138 minutes.

1977

A BRIDGE TOO FAR

Cast Lieutenant General Frederick 'Boy' Browning: Dirk Bogarde; Staff Sergeant Eddie Dobun: James Caan; Lieutenant Colonel 'Joe' Vandeleur: Michael Caine; Major General Robert Urquart: Sean Connery; Lieutenant General Brian Horrocks: Edward Fox; Colonel Bobby Stout: Elliott Gould; Major General Stanislaw Sosabowski: Gene Hackman; Lieutenant Colonel John Frost: Anthony Hopkins; General Ludwig: Hardy Kruger; Dr. Spaander: Laurence Olivier; Brigadier General James M. Gavin: Ryan O'Neal; Major Julian Cook: Robert Redford; Lieutenant General Wilhelm Bittrich: Maximilian Schell.

A United Artists Release. Producers: Joseph E. Levine, Richard P. Levine; Director: Richard Attenborough; Co-Producer: Michael Stanley-Evans; Screenplay: William Goldman, based on the book by Cornelius Ryan; Director of Photography: Geoffrey Unsworth; Camera Operator: Peter MacDonald; Production Designer: Terry Marsh; Art Directors: Roy Stannard, Stuart Craig; Composer/Conductor: John Addison; Sound: Simon Kaye; Associate Producer: John Palmer; Assistant Director: David Tomblin; Editor: Anthony Gibbs. Running time: 175 minutes.

1979

THE ELECTRIC HORSEMAN

Cast Sonny Steele: Robert Redford; Hallie Martin: Jane Fonda; Charlotta: Valerie Perrine; Wendell: Willie Nelson; Hunt Sears: John Saxon; Fitzgerald: Nicholas Coster; Farmer: Wilford Brimley; Leroy: Timothy Scott; Gus: Will Hare; Danny: Allan Arbus; Toland: Basil Hoffman; Bernie: Frank Speiser; Bud Broderick: Quinn Redeker; Tommy: James Kline; Dennis: James Novak; Lucinda: Sarah Harris; Louise: Tasha Zemrus.

A Columbia Pictures & Universal Pictures Release. Producer: Ray Stark; Director: Sydney Pollack; Screenplay: Robert Garland, based on a screen story by Robert Garland and Paul Geer and on a story by Shelly Burton; Director of Photography: Owen Roizman; Production Designer: Stephen Grimes; Art Director: J. Dennis Washington; Set Director: Mary Swanson; Music: Dave Grusin; Songs sung by Willie Nelson; Associate Producer: Ronald L. Schwary; Assistant Director: M. Michael Moore; Costume

Designer: Bernie Pollack; Editor: Sheldon Kahn. Running time: 121 minutes.

1980

BRUBAKER

Cast Brubaker: Robert Redford; Dickie Coombes: Yaphet Kotto; Lillian: Jane Alexander; Deach: Murray Hamilton; Larry Lee Bullen: David Keith; Walter: Morgan Freeman; Huey Rauch: Tim McIntire; Abraham: Richard Ward; Purcell: Matt Clark; Rory Poke: Albert Salmi; C. P. Woodward: M. Emmet Walsh; Carol: Linda Haynes; Willets: Ronald C. Frazier; Caldwell: Everett McGill; Duane Spivey: David D. Harris; Birdwell: Joe Spinell; Pinky: James Keane; Zaranska: Joe Van Ness; Wendel: Val Avery; Glenn Elwood: Konrad Sheehan; Leon Edwards: Nathan George; Jerome Boyd: Don Blakely; Warden Renfro: Lee Richardson; Senator Hite: John Mc-Martin; Doctor Gregory: Roy Pool.

A Twentieth Century-Fox Release. Executive Producer: Ted Mann; Producer: Ron Silverman; Director: Stuart Rosenberg; Screenplay: W. D. Richter, based on a story by W. D. Richter & Arthur Ross; Director of Photography: Bruno Nuytten; Art Director: J. Michael Riva; Set Director: John Franco; Costumes: Tom Bronson, Bernie Pollack; Music: Lalo Schifrin; Associate Producer: Gordon Webb; Assistant Director: Jon C. Anderson; Technical Adviser: Thomas O. Murton; Editor: Robert Brown. Running time: 132 minutes.

ORDINARY PEOPLE

Cast Calvin Jarrett: Donald Sutherland; Beth Jarrett: Mary Tyler Moore; Conrad Jarrett: Timothy Hutton; Berger: Judd Hirsch; Swimming Coach: M. Emmet Walsh; Jeannine: Elizabeth McGovern; Karen: Dinah Manoff; Lazenby: Frederic Lehne; Ray: James B. Sikking; Sloan: Basil Hoffman; Ward: Quinn Redeker; Audrey: Mariclare Costello; Ruth: Elizabeth Hubbard; Grandmother: Meg Mundy; Stillman: Adam Baldwin; Grandfather: Richard Whiting; Buck Jarrett: Scott Doebler; Van Buren: Carl DiTommasso; Truan: Tim Clarke; Genthe: Ken Dishner; Gail: Lisa Smyth; Mitzi: Ann Eggert; Bryce: Randall Robbins; John: John Stimpson.

A Paramount Pictures Release. Producer: Ronald L. Schwary; Director: Robert Redford; Screenplay: Alvin Sargent, based on the novel by Judith Guest; Director of Photography: John Bailey; Camera Operator: James Glennon; Art Directors: Phillip Bennett, J. Michael Riva; Set Decorators: Jerry Wunderlich, William Fosser; Costume Designer: Bernie Pollack; Make-Up: Gary Liddiard; Music adapted by Marvin Hamlisch; Assistant Director: Steven H. Perry; Editor: Jeff Kanew. Running time: 124 minutes.

1984

THE NATURAL

Cast Roy Hobbs: Robert Redford; Max Mercy: Robert Duvall; Iris Gaines: Glenn Close; Memo Paris: Kim Basinger; Pop Fisher: Wilford Brimley; Harriet Bird: Barbara Hershey; The Judge: Robert Prosky; Red Blow: Richard Farnsworth; The Whammer: Joe Don Baker; Sam Simpson: John Finnegan; Ed Hobbs: Alan Fudge; Young Roy: Paul Sullivan, Jr.; Young Iris: Rachel Hall; Ted Hobbs: Robert Rich III.

A Columbia Pictures Release. Executive Producers: Roger Towne, Philip M. Breen; Producer: Mark Johnson; Director: Barry Levinson; Screenplay: Roger Towne & Phil Dusenberry, based on the novel by Bernard Malamud; Director of Photography: Caleb Deschanel; Camera Operator: Craig Denault; Production Designers: Angelo Graham, Mel Bourne; Art Directors: James J. Murikami, Speed Hopkins; Associate Producer: Robert F. Colesberry; Assistant Directors: Chris Soldo, Patrick Crowley; Music: Randy Newman; Editor: Stu Linder. Running time: 122 minutes. 137 minutes original running time.

1985

OUT OF AFRICA

Cast Karen Blixen: Meryl Streep; Denys Finch Hatton: Robert Redford; Bror/Hans von Blixen-Finecke(l): Klaus Maria Brandauer; Berkeley Cole: Michael Kitchen; Farah: Malick Bowens; Kamante: Joseph Thiaka; Kinanjui: Stephen Kinyanjui; Lord Delamere: Michael Gough; Felicity: Suzanna Hamilton; Lady Belfield: Rachel Kempson; Lord Belfield: Graham Crowden; Sir Joseph: Leslie Phillips; Belknap: Shane Rimmer; Juma: Mike Bugara; Kanuthia: Job Seda; Ismail: Mohammed Umar; Doctor: Donal McCann; Banker: Kenneth Mason.

Mirage production for Universal Pictures. Executive Producer: Kim Jorgensen; Director/Producer: Sydney Pollack; Co-Producer: Terence Clegg; Screenplay: Kurt Luedtke, based on *Out of Africa* and other writings by Isak Dinesen, *Isak Dinesen: The Life of a Storyteller* by Judith Thurman and *Silence Will Speak* by Errol Trzebinski; Director of Photography: David Watkin; Camera Operator: Freddie Cooper; Production Designer: Stephen Grimes; Associate Producers: Judith Thurman, Anna Cataldi; First Assistant Director: David Tomblin; Original Music composed and conducted by John Barry; Editors: Frederic Steinkamp, William Steinkamp, Pembroke Herring, Sheldon Kahn. Running time: 162 minutes.

1986

LEGAL EAGLES

Cast Tom Logan: Robert Redford; Laura Kelly: Debra Winger; Chelsea Deardon: Daryl Hannah; Cavanaugh: Brian Dennehy; Victor Taft: Terence Stamp; Bower: Steven Hill; Blanchard: David Clennon; Forrester: John McMartin; Jennifer Logan: Jennie Dundas; Judge Dawkins: Roscoe Lee Browne; Carol Freeman: Christine Baranski; Barbara: Sara Botsford; Marchek: David Hart; Sebastian Deardon: James Hurdle; Hit Man: Gary Klar; Clerk: Christian Clemenson; Doreen: Lynn Hamilton.

A Universal Picture. Executive Producers: Joe Medjuck, Michael Gross; Producer/Director: Ivan Reitman; Screenplay: Jim Cash & Jack Epps, Jr. from a story by Ivan Reitman, Jim Cash & Jack Epps, Jr.; Director of Photography: Laszlo Kovacs; Camera Operator: Ray de la Motte; Art Director: Ron Hobbs; Associate Producers: Sheldon Kahn, Arnold Glimcher; Music: Elmer Bernstein; 'Love Touch' performed by Rod Stewart; Editors: Sheldon Kahn, Pembroke Herring, William Gordean. Running time: 116 minutes.

1988

THE MILAGRO BEANFIELD WAR

Cast Sheriff Bernabe Montoya: Ruben Blades; Ladd Devine: Richard Bradford; Ruby Archuleta: Sonia Braga; Nancy Mondragon: Julie Carmen: Horsethief Shorty: James Gammon; Flossie Devine: Melanie Griffith; Charlie Bloom: John Heard; Amarante Cordova: Carlos Riquelme; Herbie Platt: Daniel Stern; Joe Mondragon: Chick Vennera; Kyril Montana: Christopher Walken; Mayor Sammy Cantu: Freddy Fender; Nick Rael: Tony Genaro; Emerson Capps: Jerry Hardin; Jerry G: Ronald G. Joseph; Carl: Mario Arrambide; Coyote Angel: Robert Carricart.

A Universal Picture. Executive Producer: Gary J. Hendler; Producers: Robert Redford, Moctesuma Esparza; Screenplay: David Ward & John Nichols, based on the novel by John Nichols; Director of Photography: Robbie Greenberg; Camera Operator: John Toll; Art Director: Joe Aubel; Co-Producer: Charles Mulvehill; Music: Dave Grusin; Editors: Dede Allen, Jim Miller; Associate Editors: Eric Beason, Nancy Frazen. Running time: 115 minutes.

Bibliography

Sources of reviews are mentioned in the text.

Agan, Patrick. *Hoffman vs. Hoffman – The Actor and The Man*. New English Library, 1987.

Ansen, David (with Katrine Ames). Robert Redford: 'An American All-Star'. *Newsweek*, May 28, 1984.

Applebome, Peter. 'Robert Redford Takes To The Beanfield.' *New York Times*, November 30, 1986.

Barnicle, Mike. 'All Robert Redford Wants to Be is Paul Newman.' *Esquire*, March, 1988.

Barry, Anne. 'Robert Redford is *sooo* handsome and *sooo* happily Married.' *Cosmopolitan*, October, 1970.

Basch, Harry & Slater, Shirley. 'The Reluctant Resort.' *Los Angeles*, November, 1987.

Bauer, Jerry. 'Why I Won't Be A Baddie.' *Sun*, March 16, 1979.

Blundy, David. 'Robert Redford.' *Sunday Times*, April 25, 1976.

Bragg, Melvyn. 'Interview with Robert Redford.' *New Review*, Volume 3, Number 27, June, 1976.

Bygrave, Mike. 'Redford.' *You Magazine*, November, 1985.

Cimons, Marlene. 'A Superstar on the Stump.' *Los Angeles Times*, May 15, 1974.

Cimons, Marlene. 'Mrs. Redford Goes To Washington.' *Los Angeles Times*, October 2, 1974.

Cocks, Jay. 'Ready or Not, Here comes Gatsby.' *Time*, March 18, 1974.

Connelley, Christopher. 'Milagro Muddle.' *Première*, March 1988.

Connew, Paul. 'Rude Redford Slammed.' *News of the World*, December 8, 1985.

Cooper, Jilly. 'Interview with Robert Redford.' *Sunday Times*, March 9, 1980.

Cooper, Jilly. 'The Redford Rating.' *Daily Mail*, March 10, 1980.

Dahlin, Robert. 'Robert Redford.' *Publishers' Weekly*, March 6, 1978.

Davis, Ivor. 'He'd make love like playing tennis – with grace, zest and respect for the rules.' *Daily Express*, September 24, 1974.

Davis, Victor. 'Interview with Robert Redford.' *Daily Express*, February 17, 1983.

Davis, Victor. 'Why Lola walked out on her Superstar.' *Daily Express*, November 28, 1985.

De Dubovay, Diane. 'Interview with Robert Redford.' *Woman's Own*, October 25, 1980.

Denby, David. 'Redford Hunts Streep in *Out of Africa*.' New York, September 16, 1985.

Dern, Hugh. 'Flap Over Redford's Air Antics.' *News of the World*, March 23, 1986.

Dillon, Barry. 'Redford: The Way He Was.' *Sunday Mirror*, July, 1980.

Donnelly, Mark. 'Robert Redford's Sundance.' *Westways*, 1987.

Downing, David. *Robert Redford*. W. H. Allen & Co. Ltd., London, 1982.

Dunbar, Jeremy. 'Rough Ride Filming in Africa.' *Glasgow Herald*, May 27, 1986.

Farber, Stephen. 'An All-Star Team Puts *The Natural* on Film.' *New York Times*, June 5, 1984.

Farber, Stephen. 'Where There's Smoke, There's a Fiery Actress Named Debra Winger.' *New York Times*, July 6, 1986.

Geery, Daniel. 'Redford: A Cry for The Wilderness.' *Los Angeles Herald Examiner*, January 30, 1978.

Gullett, Scott. 'Robert Redford's New Mexican Love Affair.' *New Mexico Monthly*, March, 1988.

Halberstadt, Michele. 'Redford: A Conversation.' *Première*, March, 1988.

Hall, William. 'What A Scorcher!' *Sunday Magazine*, January 26, 1986.

Hawkins, Felicity. 'The Hunter and The Huntress.' *Sunday People*, February 23, 1986.

Hiscock, John. 'Redford: Who does he think he is?' *Sun*, January 23, 1981.

Horowitz, Jay. 'From Slapstick to Yuppie Fantasy.' *New York Times*, June 15, 1986.

Hoy, Aletha. 'Redford Keeps Star Secrets.' *Sunday Mirror*, July 23, 1978.

Huxley, Elspeth. 'Triangle of Love.' *Mail On Sunday*, March 2, 1986.

Jacques, Steve. 'Robert Redford.' *News of the World*, April 11, 1976.

Keogh, Malcolm. 'The Comeback Kid.' *Daily Mirror*, May 26, 1970.

Lenburg, Jeff. *Dustin Hoffman, Hollywood's Anti-Hero*. St. Martin's Press, New York, 1983.

Lewin, David. 'Why Robert Redford Doesn't Want To Be Loved.' *Daily Mail*, October 22, 1984.

Lewin, David. 'Is Rusty Redford Past It?' *Sun*, March 17, 1986.

Lewin, David. 'The Hidden Life of Robert Redford.' *Daily Mail*, February 7–10, 1977.

Lomax, Jack. 'Redford Rules!' *Sunday Magazine*, October 14, 1984.

Lombardi, John. 'In The Rockies.' *New York Times Magazine*, October 20, 1983.

Luckinbill, Laurence. 'Oh, You Sundance Kid.' *Esquire*, October, 1970.

Malcolm, Derek. 'The Kid from Sundance.' *What's On In London*, June 24, 1977.

Malcolm, Derek. 'The Sundance Kids.' *Guardian*, May 3, 1988.

Mann, Roderick. 'Redford, The Star.' *Sunday Express*, December 20, 1970.

Maslin, Janet. 'The Pollack Touch.' *New York Times*, December 15, 1985.

McCooey, Meriel. 'The Great Gatsby' (location report). *Sunday Times Magazine*, October 14, 1973.

McLeod, Pauline. 'My Love For Lola.' *Daily Mirror*, March 11 & 12, 1980.

Morella, Joe & Epstein, *Edward Z. Paul and Joanne*. Delacorte, United States of America.

Pattie, Jane. 'The Electric Horseman' (location report and interview). *Cue*, January 4, 1980.

Pietschmann, Richard John. 'The Sundance Kid's Baby.' *Travel and Leisure*, December 1987.

'Robert Redford: When Things Come Together.' *Time*, December 12, 1969.

Redford, Robert. 'Skiing: More Fun Than Acting.' *Family Weekly*, February 1, 1970.

Rogers, Michael. 'Robert Redford, More Than Just a Pretty Face.' *Rolling Stone*, October 2, 1980.

Sarris, Andrew. *Village Voice*, June 24, 1986.

Saynor, James. 'Parable of the Talons.' *Guardian*, October 23, 1986.

Schickel, Richard. 'Why it isn't easy to be a friend of Robert Redford.' *Life*, March 16, 1970.

Smith, Liz. 'The Great Robert Redford.' Magazine interview, 1975.

Spada, James. *The Films of Robert Redford*. Citadel Press, Secaucus, New Jersey, 1984.

Swenson, Paul (with Barbara Bannon). 'Redford: The Citizen From Sundance.' *Utah Day*, July, 1986.

Tallmer, Jerry. 'This Would Make a Movie.' *New York Post*, July 1, 1972.

Thompson, Douglas. 'The Turbulent Ms. Winger.' *You Magazine*, May 25, 1986.

Tickell, Tom. 'The Turn of the Screw.' *Guardian*, January 7, 1981.

Walker, Alexander. 'Redford – Beware of the Bitch!' *Evening Standard*, 1976.

Walker, Alexander. 'The Sundance Kid has come a long way since that night in a manure heap.' *Evening Standard*, September 27, 1976.

Walker, Alexander. 'Fame is the Drag.' *Evening Standard*, August 12, 1980.

Wallis, Neil. 'The Model Who Tells Lies About Redford.' *Sun*, February 3, 1988.

Weiss, Michael. 'Redford Comes Down From His Mountain.' *Ladies' Home Journal*, 1984.

Willows, Terry. 'Diana's Heart-Throbs.' *Star*, October 15, 1985.

Wood, Michael. 'The Dream of Youth.' *New Society*, November 8, 1984.